POLICE–COMMUNITY RELATIONS IN TIMES OF CRISIS

OF CRISIS

Decay and Reform in the
Post-Ferguson Era

Ross Deuchar, Vaughn J. Crichlow
and Seth W. Fallik

With a Foreword by
Scott H. Decker

BRISTOL
UNIVERSITY
PRESS

First published in Great Britain in 2021 by

Bristol University Press
University of Bristol
1-9 Old Park Hill
Bristol
BS2 8BB
UK
t: +44 (0)117 954 5940
e: bup-info@bristol.ac.uk

Details of international sales and distribution partners are available at
bristoluniversitypress.co.uk

© Bristol University Press 2021

British Library Cataloguing in Publication Data
A catalogue record for this book is available from the British Library

ISBN 978-1-5292-1060-6 hardcover
ISBN 978-1-5292-1061-3 paperback
ISBN 978-1-5292-1063-7 ePub
ISBN 978-1-5292-1062-0 ePdf

The right of Ross Deuchar, Vaughn J. Crichlow and Seth W. Fallik to be identified as
authors of this work has been asserted by them in accordance with the Copyright, Designs
and Patents Act 1988.

Cover design: blu inc, Bristol
Image credit: Michael Joven/EyeEm

Contents

List of Tables and Boxes

Tables

Boxes

Acknowledgments

We would like to offer a heartfelt thanks to all of the law enforcement officers, practitioners, and young men who participated in the research fieldwork and gave up their time to talk openly about the issues that are documented across the pages of this book.

We are deeply grateful to Dr Scott Decker for writing the excellent foreword, and to all of our colleagues and friends within the School of Criminology and Criminal Justice at Florida Atlantic University, who have been a constant source of support, encouragement, and "Family" to us all.

Particular thanks go to the Fulbright Commission for opening up the opportunity for our first author to conduct the research featured in the book, and for the life-changing experience of becoming a Fulbright scholar. Our thanks also go to Dr John Smykla for facilitating the whole process and making this happen.

Finally, a special thanks go to our families for all their love and support – to Karen, Alan, Cindy, Arielle, Caiden, and Kaitlyn.

Foreword

Scott H. Decker

School of Criminology and Criminal Justice, Arizona State University

The rule of law is the foundation of Western democracy. It is built on the mutual obligation between citizens and their government. Citizens agree to abide by the laws of their jurisdiction. Explicit in that agreement is the acknowledgment that they are subject to the laws and enforcement of those laws. In return, they get protection from the government. However, agents of the government must act in accordance with rules (procedural law) that govern their conduct. The principle of mutual obligation implies that formal social control will be delivered within the bounds of legally defined behavior by government agents. When the relationship created by that mutual obligation breaks down, you get "Ferguson."

The decay in relationships between citizens and their government (the most visible and active agents of which are the police) began long ago in the United States. A plausible argument can be made that minorities' first encounters with police in the US took place when the slave patrols enforced the interests of wealthy white landowners without regard to limits or principles of mutual obligation. The history of relationships between communities and individuals of color and the police has been largely a story of negative outcomes that stemmed from police practices that broke the covenant between police and policed.

But why Ferguson? In many regards this suburb of St Louis with just over 20,000 people seems an unlikely "ground zero" in the battle for police accountability. Why not a bigger city? Why not a jurisdiction with more media attention? And yet, Ferguson became a symbol for individuals aggrieved by their treatment by the police. Racial profiling in the execution of traffic laws, stop and talk/frisk, traffic fines, and "failure to appear" charges is widespread in the application of the law to minority citizens in the US. The shooting death of Michael Brown sparked outrage not just for that single event but for the countless events that preceded it in communities across the country, including those in the St Louis area. The disorder and violence that erupted in Ferguson gave a voice to everyone who had a problem with the police. And many people took advantage of that opportunity, generating changes that could not have been imagined at the time. Among others, locally these changes included reform in bail, reform in the collection of fines, a decline in the use of traffic revenues as a primary funding source of communities, and the unthinkable defeat of the long-serving County Prosecutor.

Change in the application of the law can be slow, so slow sometimes as to seem a delay rather than change. What produces such change? What motivates individuals who heretofore had not participated in marches, protests, or movements to become active? Clearly the President's Task Force on 21st Century Policing helped institutionalize and sustain many of the changes that emanated from the Ferguson protests. Perhaps most importantly, many police and political leaders acknowledged the need for change.

Ross Deuchar, Vaughn Crichlow, and Seth Fallik tell the story of how the violation of that mutual obligation led to the events in Ferguson. They tell this story in a compelling way, focusing on broader social processes such as legitimacy, racism, and entrenched practices slow to change. They contrast the well-known "warrior" and "guardian" roles in policing to demonstrate alternative models that communities and law enforcement can choose. It is important that they highlight the implications for public safety that come with each choice, underscoring the key role that communities play in providing safety for themselves as well as the police who work in their communities.

One of the great strengths of this book is that it goes beyond the traditional "police vs. community" dichotomy. The authors sought the insights of individuals who work in youth-serving organizations outside of law enforcement. Indeed, many of these individuals function outside formal social-control agencies. The experiences of practitioners and the youth they serve have long held valuable insights for how to make the system work more effectively while it works more fairly. Finally, Deuchar, Crichlow, and Fallik speak with the young men who are the targets of police initiatives, men rarely seen as partners in efforts to provide safe communities.

"Ferguson" has come to be a divisive name. On the one hand, police talk about a "Ferguson Effect" whereby citizens no longer cooperate with the police and are openly hostile toward law enforcement. The community identify different elements as constituting a "Ferguson Effect," include disengagement by the police and an abandonment of community involvement. There is all too little light and a good deal of heat in discussions about this topic. Those looking for data with which to assess the issue would be wise to read this book closely.

This is an important book because of the topics the authors address and the raw honesty with which they address them. The book treats the rule of law as more than an ideal and examines it "in action." The contrast between the ideals and the practice of law are stark, but by illuminating them this work illustrates their importance, and most vitally, lays bare the path ahead. That path does not appear to be an easy one, but if one is to be honest, it never has been.

PART I

Introduction

1

Policing, Communities, and the "Legitimacy Crisis": Context and Empirical Approaches

In this opening chapter, we set the scene for the book by referencing the contextual backdrop of increased accountability and change in American policing, the challenges around police–community relations, and the political and public concern about gang-related criminality as a related symptom of these issues across the United States (US). We introduce the research methods underpinning the empirical work and conclude by providing an overview of each of the subsequent chapters.

Cops in crisis? Ferguson, police legitimacy, and de-policing

> Maybe something in policing has changed. In today's YouTube world, are officers reluctant to get out of their cars and do the work that controls violent crime? ... I spoke to officers privately in one big city precinct who described being surrounded by young people with mobile phone cameras held high, taunting them the moment they get out of their cars. They told me, "We feel like we're under siege and we don't feel much like getting out of our cars" ... I do have a strong sense that some part of the explanation is a chill wind blowing through American law enforcement over the last year. And that wind is surely changing behavior. (James B. Comey, Director of the FBI, 2015, cited in Morgan & Pally, 2016, p 7)

The words of James B. Comey are one example of the numerous discussions and debates that have emerged within American law enforcement contexts in recent years. Moreover, Mr. Comey raised several themes emerging in recent discussions on policing, police–community relations, and youth violence that will be introduced in this chapter and explored further in subsequent chapters of this book. It is suggested that police officers are now "under siege," have become afraid of getting out of their cars, have regularly become the stars of "viral videos," and that a "chill wind is blowing through American law enforcement." Another observation that Comey made at the time is that gang-related violence, predominantly among young men who belong to racial minority groups, has continued to escalate within disadvantaged communities.

As we enter the third decade of the 21st century, it is clearly a challenging time for American law enforcement (Katz & Maguire, 2020), as officers find themselves in the "social media era of policing." Officers' actions are frequently captured on video and quickly uploaded to websites, live-streamed, and viewed by millions. Publicly available digital recordings of deadly use-of-force incidents have led to intense instances of civil unrest and an "unprecedented level of scrutiny" (Shjarback et al, 2017, p 49). Citizen journalism within the context of social media forums, combined with the politicization of policing by mass media, has placed officers under a growing spotlight and accelerated a focus on social accountability in law enforcement contexts around the world (Bonner, 2009; Bonilla & Rosa 2015, Loader & Sparks, 2016). In short, the public's consciousness about issues concerning officer prejudice, discrimination, and brutality has become heightened within the context of increased news and social media consumption and in an age of digital activism (Perry, 2009; Bonilla & Rosa, 2015; Intravia et al, 2018; see also Deuchar et al, 2019). Furthermore, Maguire et al (2017) suggest that police agencies are facing a "major legitimacy crisis" fueled by a growing "anti-police sentiment" (p 739). This has been characterized by declining public trust in several international contexts, and perhaps most prominently within the US (Lee & McGovern 2013; Todak, 2017).

Several high-profile events in the US involving deadly citizen encounters with police have exacerbated the legitimacy crisis. The death of an unarmed Black male in Ferguson, Missouri, was arguably the defining event in this discourse. Two days before the 49th anniversary of the historic public uprisings in Watts, Los Angeles, on August 9, 2014, Darren Wilson – a White police officer – shot and killed an unarmed Black teenager named Michael Brown in Ferguson, Missouri (Auston, 2017). In addition to being unarmed during the incident, a Department of Justice (DOJ) investigation found that several bystanders observed Mr Brown with his hands up, facing away from Officer Wilson, and cooperating with his commands when shots were fired (Deuchar et al, 2018a). The physical evidence of the incident, however, would later be found to dispute some of the bystanders' claims; on reviewing the evidence, a grand jury would ultimately decide not to indict Officer Wilson for any wrongdoing (DOJ, 2015; White & Malm, 2020), an outcome that many members of the public ultimately viewed as unjust and as another example of a system that is remorselessly punitive against African Americans. The events following the shooting set off a "nationwide firestorm" (Auston, 2017, p 12) as protests by local residents emerged and updates, images, and videos of the militarized response by the police and the ensuing confrontations with protestors were disseminated and quickly turned viral on social media (Bonilla & Rosa, 2015). These collective events helped to launch what some have described as a "new civil rights movement" in the US (Maguire et al, 2017, p 740) as the Black Lives Matter (BLM) movement became galvanized.[1]

As a direct consequence of the events in Ferguson, the accelerated influence of BLM, and the subsequent emergence of the President's Task Force on 21st Century Policing (2015) that recommended addressing lingering and ongoing issues of injustice and racism within law enforcement contexts, some have suggested that widespread anti-police sentiment has emerged within the US (Maguire et al, 2017). According to recent discussions, the increased scrutiny of law enforcement has resulted in the emergence of a "Ferguson Effect." In contrast to the more ambiguous language used by Mr Comey to describe the "chill wind blowing through American law enforcement" (Morgan & Pally, 2016, p 8), political commentators such as Heather MacDonald have claimed that officers are conscious of the negative publicity surrounding their profession and have become less willing to do their job as a way of avoiding the likelihood of being accused of racial profiling or excessive force (Wolfe & Nix, 2016). She and others have claimed that there is now a "war on cops," that officers around the country are facing increasing levels of hostility, and that bystanders often stick cellphones in officers' faces and "refuse to comply with orders" (MacDonald, 2016a, 2016b). In addition, claims have been made that crime rates have increased dramatically across the US and that the Ferguson Effect is directly responsible for this (see Maguire et al, 2017 and Chapter 3 for a review).

To highlight the historical context of the Ferguson Effect, we must understand the well-documented history of brutality and discriminatory practices by law enforcement and its ongoing impact on legitimacy perceptions today. In Tyler's (2006) seminal work on why people obey the law, he states that procedural justice is closely linked to State legitimacy and that the State suffers when law enforcement is perceived to be unjust. The legitimacy of the State is best sustained when decision-making, on the part of law enforcement, is perceived to be fair. Racial differences are another facet of the discussion of perceptions toward police. Racial and ethnic minorities tend to be more aware of disparate law enforcement outcomes in their evaluation of police, with Black and Hispanic citizens often experiencing more punitive consequences (Gau et al, 2012), whereas White citizens are often less likely to see prejudice as an important issue (Rice & Parkin, 2010). This may explain, in part, why outrage stemming from Ferguson led to public demonstrations by the BLM movement while evidence suggests that White citizens' confidence in police has been somewhat unaffected by these events (Deuchar et al, 2018a; see also Chapter 2).

The decreased level of police legitimacy emerging in racial and ethnic minority communities as a consequence of Ferguson and other high-profile lethal force incidents has clearly prompted social media platforms like Twitter to become powerful sites for drawing public attention to episodes of police brutality (Bonilla & Rosa, 2015; Owen, 2017; see also Chapter 2). As Bonilla and Rosa reported, Michael Brown was allegedly shot while holding his hands up, and the hashtag #HandsUpDontShoot subsequently became a tool for contesting the systematic profiling and victim blaming suffered by "racialized bodies" of Twitter (Bonilla & Rosa, 2015 p 9).

A raft of evidence (Maguire et al, 2016; MacDonald, 2016a; Morgan & Pally, 2016; Nix & Wolfe, 2016) suggests that the continual negative publicity that has emerged across the US since the Ferguson incident has become associated not only with reduced State legitimacy but also with reduced levels of officer self-legitimacy. This has been linked to an apparent withdrawal by officers from their law enforcement duties (described as "de-policing"), and includes the tendency to hesitate during potentially violent situations for fear of being the next star of a viral video, getting sued, or losing their jobs (for reviews, see MacDonald, 2016a; Morgan & Pally, 2016; Pyrooz et al, 2016b; Wolfe & Nix, 2016; Maguire et al, 2017; Shjarback et al, 2017; Wallace et al, 2018; and Chapter 3). In a more general sense, some believe that the negative portrayal of policing in the media is overshadowing relationships between members of the public and law enforcement officers in minority communities, thus further aggravating police–community tensions (Goldsmith, 2015; Shjarback et al, 2017). A suggested increase in violent crime across the US (MacDonald, 2016b), particularly in minority communities (Shjarback et al, 2017) and among gang members (Morgan & Pally, 2016), has also been linked to de-policing behavior (see subsequent chapters for further, in-depth discussion on the Ferguson Effect, police legitimacy, and the potential emergence of de-policing).

Gangs, violence, and political and public concern about criminality

Public concern regarding a reported increase in youth violence, in some urban contexts, is part of wider discussion on contemporary challenges in policing, police–community relations, and public safety. Across the US, a vibrant debate has emerged among journalists, scholars, politicians, and others concerning national levels of criminality and whether crime rates are dramatically increasing as claimed by some observers (Maguire et al, 2017). Some sources (James, 2018; Statista, 2019; World Population Review, 2019) seem to suggest that, while national levels of violent crime have been falling for decades in the US, there have been reported increases across the country since 2014 (with some exceptions in small-to-medium-sized cities). Still, it is important to recognize the limitations associated with these reported statistics and the issue of unreported crimes.

Data on gang-related violent crime, as a potential symptom and artifact of the current police legitimacy crisis, are very limited, and the Federal Bureau of Investigation's (FBI) homicide reports within its annual Uniform Crime Report are currently the only national and annual report on gang homicides. Since 2000, these data indicate that gang-related murders accounted for a relatively stable percentage of between five and seven percent of all homicides for which supplementary data has been reported to the FBI (see, for instance, data on "gangland killings" in FBI, 2017). However, it is recognized that gang crime is most likely underestimated, given that the National Youth Gang Survey (National Gang Center, 2012) estimates that 13 percent of all homicides committed between 2007 and 2012 in the US were related to gang violence. Wider evidence also suggests that the gang-related homicide rate alone exceeds the total homicide rate in nearly every European Union country, and in New York City police reported that 50 percent of all shootings in 2017 involved a gang member as either perpetrator or victim (Pyrooz & Densley, 2018a). The discrepancy between the FBI and other relevant intelligence sources reflects how data on murders are compiled by the former; moreover, the FBI's estimates are based on data reported by law enforcement agencies, and most police departments either underreport gang killings or do not report them at all.

In recent years, the apparent underreporting of gang-related crime data by law enforcement has become starkly juxtaposed with the political claims surrounding the phenomenon. Political rhetoric from the White House has increasingly become emotionally charged with respect to gangs, with former President Donald Trump using their activity to justify "everything from the building of a wall along the US–Mexico border ... to negatively portraying Latino immigrants more generally" (Rodgers, 2019). Trump has frequently talked about dangerous gang members from MS-13 (a transnational street gang formed in the 1980s in Los Angeles by Salvadoran immigrants) "infesting" the United States (Pyrooz & Densley, 2018a), and used the suggested threat posed by MS-13 to justify his increased use of immigration enforcement (Blake, 2017; see further discussion in Chapter 5).

Despite the recognized presence of a racially stigmatizing rhetoric, the fact remains that American gang members account for an uneven share of crime and violence (Pyrooz & Densley, 2018a). Much research has demonstrated that gang members are more likely to engage in violence and experience violent victimization than non-gang youth, as well as to display disproportionate rates of involvement in numerous other criminal acts, and that neighborhoods with high levels of gang membership tend to have elevated rates of gun violence (Curry et al, 2002; Melde et al 2009b; Decker & Pyrooz, 2010; Melde & Esbensen, 2011; Decker et al, 2013; Huebner et al, 2016; Pyrooz et al, 2016a). Decker et al (2013) draw attention to the national figures from large American cities that indicate that, while gang members comprise less than one percent of the general population, over 20 percent of the homicides in these locations tend to be gang-related. According to Melde & Esbensen (2011), "no social group is more criminogenic than the youth gang" and there is evidently "something unique" about gang membership that "increases youths' participation in serious and violent crime" (p 513 and p 514, respectively).

In this book, we focus our attention on fieldwork conducted in one Southern American state with a recognized and increasingly prevalent gang problem. Violent crime incidents in the neighborhoods where our fieldwork was conducted are known to be disproportionately high compared with the rest of the state because of gang "turf" wars and drug operations in these cities. In the last five years, it has been reported that gang- and drug-related incidents increased by 21.9 percent in one city where observations and interviews were conducted, while declining by 15.4 percent in the surrounding communities. Likewise, in the same period, violent crime in two of the cities studied was exponentially greater than the national average and has been for the last half decade. Further exacerbating the problem in these areas is the fact that more than 20 percent of violent crime between 2010 and 2014 was perpetrated with a firearm. With few physical barriers within the county, violent crime events are also becoming more prevalent in neighboring jurisdictions.[2]

It is important to recognize that there is no agreed-upon definition of a gang; the term has been debated for almost a century since Thrasher's (1927) earliest "synthetic definition" was put forward following his seminal field research (Pyrooz & Densley, 2018b, p 234). From a study of 1,313 gangs in Chicago, Thrasher argued that a gang was an "interstitial group originally formed spontaneously, and then integrated through conflict." He highlighted that gang members most commonly engaged in the following types of behavior: "Meeting face to face, milling, movement through time and space as a unit, conflict and planning" (Thrasher, 1927, p 57). Thrasher's insights reflected the later focus on differential association put forward by Sutherland (1947). This suggests that criminal activity becomes more likely if individuals are exposed to other influences that pass on ideas about lawbreaking (Newburn, 2016) – a theory that has continued to be influential in gang research over the last 70 years (Deuchar, 2013; and see also Chapters 6 and 7 of this book for further discussion on gang research).

Of course, the authors recognize that any increases or disproportionately high prevalence of violent crime in the contemporary era can potentially be explained by individual and macro-level factors as opposed to gang issues (Decker, 2007; Papachristos, 2009). However, as Densley and Pyrooz expressed, such recognition and potential wider explanations do not negate the fact that "violence drives police strategies" (Densley & Pyrooz, 2020, p 14; see also Deuchar, 2013). Law enforcement agencies traditionally focus their attention and resources on "the most dangerous people, places and things" as the factors that tend to drive violence (Abt, 2019, p 3). Thus, American communities experiencing high levels of violence, often involving groups of young men and the use of firearms, most commonly become selected as "hot spots" for both proactive and reactive policing tactics (see Chapters 4 and 5 for further discussion).

Fieldwork was conducted predominantly in racial and ethnic minority neighborhoods, and the authors were mindful of the evidence-base that suggests that young Black and Hispanic men are twice as likely as Whites to self-report gang membership in adolescence and three to four times more likely in young adulthood (Pyrooz, 2014; Pyrooz & Densley, 2018a). As we refer to above, we were also conscious that "violence drives police strategies" (Densley & Pyrooz, 2020, p. 14), and were interested in exploring relationships between officers and young men who reside in gang-affected neighborhoods that may have changed or evolved during the "post-Ferguson" era.

Focus for the book, research methods, and chapter summaries

Backdrop, aims, and purpose

The allegations associated with the Ferguson Effect (as touched on earlier and expanded upon in subsequent chapters), combined with the continued associations between gang members and violent criminality, suggests that the policing of racial minorities in gang-affected neighborhoods may be particularly affected by reduced levels of officer proactivity. However, evidence around the "war on cops" and de-policing rhetoric is contested, and some believe that it is generally unclear whether these issues represent myth or reality (Maguire et al, 2017). For instance, systematic research has challenged whether any type of increased levels of violent or wider crime can truly be directly associated with a Ferguson Effect (Pyrooz et al, 2016b). In addition, some have suggested that there may be benefits to de-policing (should it emerge), particularly in minority communities, since it may alleviate the negative effects of aggressive approaches to order maintenance and reduce antagonistic police–citizen interactions (Shjarback et al, 2017). Furthermore, it may be that the emergence of recommendations from the President's Taskforce on 21st Century Policing (2015) has created momentum within some police departments for officers to work more closely with disadvantaged communities (including gang-involved young men) to identify problems together and collaborate on meaningful solutions (Deuchar et al, 2018a).

In essence, the authors recognized that there has been a paucity of qualitative research that explores the ways in which the policing of racial minority communities most impacted by gang-related crime in the US may have changed or evolved in the "post-Ferguson" era. Moreover, there is a need for a focused discussion on the potential existence of a Ferguson Effect, its impact (if any) on officers, young people, and communities, and the possible relationship between community-oriented police engagement strategies, perceptions of police legitimacy, and gang-related crime reduction. Drawing on our fieldwork sites, this book therefore aims to address these themes and priorities.

Through a multi-perspective, in-depth qualitative research approach, we explore and examine the policing of young men located in communities that are clearly impacted by gang-related crime in a Southern American state and during a time of apparent disarray and crisis in American law enforcement. We zero in on how the policing of gangs, violence, and relationships between officers and racial minority men may have changed or evolved in these neighborhoods in the post-Ferguson era. We explore and examine the potential existence of a Ferguson Effect and its impact on officers, young men, and communities. Our research also explores public perceptions of policing, police–community relations, and gang-related crime, and addresses the merits of community-oriented approaches. Accordingly, the book's overall purpose is to disseminate new empirical insights, but also to provide an authentic and grounded evidence-base that will help to inform future policing practices that not only promote effective crime prevention but also gain public trust.

Approaches to data collection and analysis

As we have alluded to, our data were collected in a Southern American state in 2017. The research arose within the context of a Fulbright scholarship that had been awarded to the first author. Data from observations and interviews were collected in two counties composed of several towns and cities, hereafter and collectively referred to as Palm State. There are approximately 1.6 million residents in Palm State, where the annual median household income is just below $50,000. Most of the residents in Palm State are registered Democratic voters, and the racial/ethnic composition mirrors national rates according to the USA Census Bureau (2017). Overall, crime rates in Palm State are lower than national averages. However, as touched on earlier, over the last five years gang-related incidents of violent crime have increased considerably within the neighborhoods where the fieldwork was conducted.

During the fieldwork, we adopted an ethnographic approach, which has been defined as a form of social research that emphasizes the importance of "studying firsthand what people do and say in particular contexts" (Hammersley, 2006, p 4). This involved engaging in participant observation of police deployments within Palm State, whereby the first author specifically adopted the participant-as-observer role (Gold, 1958). He communicated the research intentions to operational officers and participated alongside them in their daily professional endeavors. Access to the officers was secured through the use of gatekeepers: contact was initially made with senior officers in the County Sheriff's Office and departmental offices by drawing upon the existing contacts and networks associated with the second and third authors and other academics within their institution (which was also the host site for the first author's Fulbright award). Once trust had been established with these and wider operational officers through engaging in deployments, snowball sampling was then drawn upon, whereby those officers the first author initially worked with provided him additional police contacts to engage with in order to expand his observations and insights.

In total, our first author spent approximately 80 hours in the field engaged in participant observation of police practice across the fieldwork sites. Across the two counties, he often engaged officers who were interested in the detection, prevention, and enforcement of violent crime. Some of this work (around 50 hours' worth) was done in the field with frontline officers, which enabled the observation of everything from proactive street-level dialogue with residents to reactive enforcement strategies such as gang-related drug raids; however, a significant amount of time (approximately 30 hours) was also spent observing intelligence gathering and the organizing and dissemination of information among senior officers and detectives. Insights gained from participant observation of police deployments can be found in later chapters (namely Chapters 3–5). The first author also engaged in an additional 25 hours of participant observation of proactive, community-centered engagement exercises and programs, sometimes attended by officers, other practitioners, and community members. More specific detail on these interventions, programs, and their impact can be found in later chapters (see Chapters 4 and 6).

Follow-up semi-structured interviews were conducted with a cross section of frontline officers, their immediate superiors, and wider groups of officers from the same units and/or departments (n = 20). Interviews broadly explored officer perceptions of police–community relations, gang-related offending patterns, their reactions to media and social media representations of law enforcement, political rhetoric, and contemporary society. We also sought to give voice to officers on police–citizen points of conflict, officers' perceptions of policy changes, and the impact of law enforcement in recent years. This often led to discussions on the use of force, but also on the use of proactive, community-oriented approaches, and officers were frequently asked to contextualize their responses based on their historical and institutional knowledge. Participants were recruited via a snowball sample approach, whereby the observed officers were asked to be interviewed and to refer other officers that may be willing to participate in interviews. Most invited participants were willing. This referral system was continued until data saturation was reached (Strauss & Corbin, 1998). Participants had a range of experience, in terms of their length of service and current police ranks, and further detail on this is provided in Chapter 3, with insights from officer interviews captured in Chapters 3–5.

As a means of widening the lens on the issues we were interested in exploring, our first author conducted an additional 16 semi-structured interviews with practitioners beyond law enforcement in one of the county areas within Palm State: public defense lawyers (n = 5), social workers (n = 2), outreach workers (n = 2), youth coaches (n = 4), a juvenile justice worker, a youth prevention manager, and a religious pastor. Two focus groups were additionally conducted with a total of ten young men between the ages of 12 and 16 who were actively and regularly participating in the activities offered within an after-school youth engagement program in one of our fieldwork sites within the same county. Access to these disparate samples of participants was gained through a combination of the first author's initial contact with interprofessional agency members while engaging with community-oriented programs and wider existing contacts associated with his host academic institution. The purpose of the interviews was to explore and examine the practitioners' perspectives on the current challenges faced by young men in the focused communities and the relationship between some of these issues and gang-related violence and crime. The interviews also enabled consideration of their views and perspectives on law enforcement in the post-Ferguson era and whether or not they believed that policing styles had changed and evolved in relation to racial minority men during recent turbulent times. The focus groups enabled further supplementary insights to be gained into the impact of after-school intervention strategies on youth, and into their perceptions about law enforcement beyond this (for further details, see Chapter 6).

Furthermore, semi-structured interviews were conducted with eight men (who were mostly in their twenties) who were currently incarcerated for gang-related offenses in a county jail during the fieldwork. Additional semi-structured interviews were conducted with four young men who were residing in disadvantaged neighborhoods within the same county. Each of these latter young men were on the periphery of criminality and/or had already had formal contact with the juvenile or formal adult justice system for offending-related behavior, sometimes (but not exclusively) relating to gangs. Access to the former group was established through a formal application process to one of the County Sheriff's offices and the county jail within Palm State, while the latter group was accessed via gatekeepers from either the County Sheriff's Office or the county's juvenile justice department. The collective focus of these interviews was to explore the types of social challenges faced by these young men during their upbringings, and their perceptions about law enforcement and the wider criminal justice system. Additionally, these interviews explored their continued hostile relationships with officers and discriminatory forms of justice (see Chapter 7 for further details).

Interviews from all sites were audio recorded and transcribed for ease of data analysis. As a collaborative academic team, we then combined the research field notes emerging from participant observation and the interview data. The data were coded manually, and a thematic analysis was carried out. All participant details were anonymized, and pseudonyms were created to protect their identities in the subsequent reporting of findings. In addition, all geographical places and names of police departments and units were anonymized using pseudonyms. In addition to the use of the pseudonym Palm State, in the empirical chapters we additionally refer to the fictitious names of Queen County, Coconut County, and Needle City as the main contexts of our fieldwork and the sheriff and departmental offices. Other pseudonyms for neighboring cities, communities, and street names are also referred to in our field notes. As mentioned earlier, more nuanced details about data-gathering approaches and specificities associated with research participants can be found in Parts II and III of the book.

Chapter summaries

Following immediately on from this introductory chapter, Part II of the book provides a finer-grain analysis of police–community relations in a new era of police accountability and change. Chapter 2 begins by discussing the rubric of procedural justice and police legitimacy perceptions. We then explore the historical roots of police–community conflict and the ongoing confidence gap in attitudes toward police, and conclude by discussing the impact of BLM and digital media in general as a tool for collective action and empowerment.

Following on from this, Chapter 3 we go on to report on the rise of a somewhat new phenomenon in policing. In doing so, contemporary policing is framed among developing countermovements that place law enforcement in the middle of oppositional belief systems. Against a backdrop of historical inequalities and a lack of law enforcement accountability, we consider why some have questioned whether the public are engaged in a "war" on police. We explore how public discord has had real consequences and been met with a somewhat galvanized de-policing response from law enforcement. The policing and crime costs of the Ferguson Effect, as this phenomenon is also known, are empirically explored. Though often framed through the words and lens of law enforcement, the semi-structured interviews and participant observation field notes set the stage for non-policing perspectives shared in later chapters.

Turning more specifically to the issue of police–community relations, Chapter 4 draws on the context of gang culture as an illustrative context and begins by discussing the reactive and proactive approaches that have been used to police gang violence and criminality in minority US neighborhoods over the years. In the main body of the chapter, insights from participant observation of police deployments and interventions at our fieldwork sites are shared, complemented by the voices of law enforcement officers captured via semi-structured interviews and informal conversations. We illustrate how an increased conceptual awareness of procedural justice had emerged among these officers. Case studies of proactive, community-centered policing approaches are shared that illustrate the active attempts that officers were making to enhance positive relationships, particularly with young Black men, and to prevent violence in gang-affected neighborhoods. These insights were used to illustrate the ways in which officers are increasingly viewing themselves primarily as "guardians" in their approaches to the policing of gangs and the remaining challenges.

Contrastingly, Chapter 5 explores the "warrior" mindset in policing. This mindset is reflected in the highly controversial militaristic strategies that have characterized contemporary policing in many of America's disadvantaged, crime-prone communities. Residents in these locations are often the subjects of disorder-enforcement, stop-question-and-frisk (SQF), and zero-tolerance crackdowns. The conceptualization of warrior policing underlines the concern that officers who see themselves principally as warriors ignore the inherent consequences of forcible approaches in these communities. In this chapter, we present definitions of the contrasting roles of police as guardians and warriors, followed by a critique of warrior policing and the impact of aggressive, and often reactive, enforcement strategies. We also explore the history of militarism and aggressive enforcement in the US, alongside further insights from interviews with our sample of police officers and from our participant observation during deployments.

In Part III, we turn our attention to practitioner and youth perspectives on policing and police–community relations in the post-Ferguson era. Chapter 6 begins by placing the spotlight on the voices of non-police practitioners who worked closely with racial minority youths in one of the counties. Drawing on data from semi-structured interviews, we outline the insights we gained into the current challenges faced by young racial minority males in local communities, and the relationship between some of these issues and gang-related violence and crime in their neighborhoods. Insights are presented into the type of community-centered interventions in place within the county to prevent violence and to re-engage disadvantaged young men (including those involving law enforcement), alongside practitioners' reflections on their nature and impact. The prominent role or apparent absence of law enforcement in these interventions is considered, drawing on the perspectives of practitioners, and supplementary insights from youth focus groups shed light on justice-involved young men's continued distrust of law enforcement. We draw implications from the statements of practitioners on the challenges stemming from the policing of young men located in gang-affected neighborhoods and how this may have evolved in the post-Ferguson era.

In Chapter 7, we turn the spotlight away from practitioner perspectives and onto the views of those who are often most affected by law enforcement strategies – young men in communities of color, and specifically those with offending histories. The chapter draws upon insights from semi-structured interviews conducted in a county jail and in local neighborhoods with young men with criminal histories or those who were on the periphery of criminality. We explore the collective challenges these young men had encountered, including the impact of adverse childhood experiences, social and economic disadvantage, and (where relevant) the influence of gang culture. We also chronicle the young men's lived experiences with racial discrimination in police interventions and the wider criminal justice system. Among the generally despondent narratives shared, we also draw attention to the cautious optimism expressed by some who had recently participated in police-initiated community-engagement programs. In so doing, we draw some conclusions about the young men's juxtaposed exposure to contrasting guardian and warrior police roles, and the continuing and cumulative disadvantage they experienced via law enforcement and – in some cases – the wider criminal justice system.

Part III of the book draws the discussion and analysis together. In the final chapter (Chapter 8), we summarize findings based on ethnographic research in a Southern American state, and address the implications of navigating a post-Ferguson era largely characterized by divisiveness and acrimony. We note emerging issues regarding the policing of racial and ethnic minorities, and suggest approaches to foster more procedurally just practices and improve police legitimacy perceptions. In addition, we reflect on lessons learned from previous police reform efforts and provide recommendations for police–community reforms in troubled times. The book concludes with an Epilogue in which we address difficult contemporary issues related to racial injustice, social conflict and policing. We acknowledge the harsh reality of more "Fergusons" – police violence and public distrust, along with heightened tensions that stem from governmental responses to a global health crisis. We also reiterate key elements of a roadmap for navigating these challenges, and highlight the need for policing reform, and collaborative approaches for improving the quality of life for all residents.

Contribution to the field

To date, the extant literature on American policing and its impact during the post-Ferguson era has largely been dominated by quantitative methods. Missing from these studies are the words and perspectives of officers, offenders, young people, the practitioners who work with offenders, wider groups of young people, and those who serve and represent local communities. We believe it to be essential that the views and attitudes of the aforementioned groups are brought to the forefront of the nation's consciousness. It is also important that real-world insights, featuring observations of police practice in the communities most impacted by gang-related crime, begin to emerge. Accordingly, we believe that the multi-perspective, in-depth, qualitative research approach we have adopted provides an authentic and grounded evidence base that will help to inform future policing practices that not only promote effective crime prevention but also gain public trust.

We believe that this book will primarily appeal to criminal justice scholars, academics and students, and those from related fields such as law, sociology, psychology, political science, public administration, and forensic sciences whose research interests include policing and police–community relations, gang-related crime, criminal justice systems, juvenile justice, race, or ethnicity. However, we also anticipate that our work will be useful to criminal justice professionals, policy makers, and practitioners engaged in outreach and social work services. While the book should be useful to an international audience of readers, it will be of principal interest to American readers due to its specific focus on policing in times of crisis within the US context.

PART II

Police–Community Relations in a New Era of Accountability and Change

High-Profile Shootings, the Media, and Police Legitimacy

As we suggested in the previous chapter, policing in America is facing a crisis of confidence. Unfavorable perceptions toward police are a pervasive challenge for municipal agencies, particularly in communities impacted by high levels of gang-related crime where police departments are understaffed and under-resourced (Mock, 2017b; Police Executive Research Forum, 2019). In an era of 24-hour news cycles, social media activism, and community advocacy, there is growing public outrage due to perceived abuses by the police. Videos on social media depicting police-involved shootings have also led to increased scrutiny, and this has made the work of building community trust even more challenging (Maguire et al, 2017). Moreover, if there is a lack of support for police, residents will be unwilling to cooperate with the police and assist with investigations, and such attitudes can undermine the ability of police officers to do their jobs effectively (Wolfe et al, 2016). In order to understand attitudes toward police in the post-Ferguson era, in this chapter we discuss the rubric of procedural justice and police legitimacy perceptions. We then explore the historical roots of police–community conflict and the ongoing confidence gap in attitudes toward police, and conclude by discussing the impact of BLM and digital media in general as a tool for collective action and empowerment.

Police legitimacy and the confidence gap

Extant research on legitimacy owes much of its framing to Max Weber's work on political legitimacy and the role of legal norms in shaping the relationship between the individual and State. These ideas influenced the contributions of Tom Tyler and others in the field of psychology. These researchers conceptualized legitimacy in terms of subjective beliefs about right and wrong and the appropriate use of governmental power, and this has led to a large body of research on the determinants and consequences of police legitimacy (Tyler, 2006). Therefore, the influence an authority or institution exerts on people is not based on the capacity to use force but rather on the institution's decision-making and whether the rules it enacts are seen as proper and right, and whether, as a result, they ought to be followed. Police legitimacy is part of a process-based model of policing, which suggests that citizens' attitudes toward the process will have a profound influence on their willingness to comply with the law, to accept the decisions of law enforcement, and to help police fight crime.

Police legitimacy also refers to the level of trust in police in the community and whether residents are confident that police have their best interests in mind (Tyler, 2002; Taylor & Lawton, 2012). It also refers to whether police officers are deemed to possess "the moral and not merely legal authority to issue commands, keep the peace, and enforce the law" (Gau et al, 2012, p 334). According to this process-based model, procedural justice is closely linked with police legitimacy. Procedural justice refers to the quality of encounters between police and citizens and whether police are perceived to be treating them respectfully and making quality decisions (Tyler & Wakslak, 2004; Gau, 2011). Studies that pursue this line of inquiry generally demonstrate that legitimacy perceptions are based primarily on concerns about the fairness of processes that police follow when exercising their authority (Sunshine & Tyler, 2003; Reisig et al, 2007; Tyler & Fagan, 2008; Reisig et al, 2011; Reisig et al, 2012). Therefore, if procedural justice perceptions improve, then residents will be more inclined to view the police as legitimate, and this will have a greater impact on attitudes toward future encounters with police than direct negative encounters in the past (Tyler & Huo, 2002; Taylor & Lawton, 2012).

The merits of procedurally just policing were demonstrated recently in a federally funded national study. A $4.75 million US DOJ grant was awarded in 2014 to a research consortium that created the National Initiative for Building Community Trust and Justice. This initiative sought to implement and evaluate trust-building interventions in police departments and communities across the country. The National Initiative comprised a team of academics, law enforcement, faith-based groups, community stakeholders, and civil rights advocates to advance a three-pillar approach – enhancing procedural justice, reducing the impact of implicit bias, and fostering reconciliation. The project was informed by previous knowledge of the successes of community-oriented policing (COP) and the merits of procedurally just approaches.

The National Initiative implemented procedurally just approaches at six pilot sites, many of which were composed of low-income minority neighborhoods. This is an ongoing project that has led to the implementation of training programs for officers to become more equitable and respectful of community members, and strategies for improving police practices and police–community relations. Although gains in community trust have been slow at some of the pilot sites, there have also been notable improvements in attitudes toward the police (La Vigne et al, 2019). Based on these findings, it is suggested that procedurally just approaches would achieve even greater success if combined with structural interventions designed to address social and economic disadvantage, to achieve a more ameliorative impact on police–community relations.

Community-engaged projects, such as the one discussed, reflect the wealth of knowledge emerging from the results of procedurally just interventions, along with decades of empirical research on community policing. It is also noteworthy that American policing has improved over the course of 50 years regarding professional standards for training, recruitment, and technological advancements in crime detection along with a greater awareness of citizens' rights. Yet the problem of public trust persists in many communities, and this is reflected in national surveys on attitudes toward police. According to the Cato institute, 40 percent of African Americans and 59 percent of Hispanics have a favorable view of police, while 68 percent of their White counterparts have a favorable view of law enforcement. African Americans are also far more likely than Whites and Hispanics to believe that police are too quick to use lethal force (Ekins, 2016).

These findings are consistent with survey results from the Pew Research Center that depict a longstanding confidence gap in attitudes toward law enforcement in America, which is largely explained by racial differences in perceptions and experiences (Fingerhut, 2017). This reinforces the notion that residents in predominantly Black communities view police unfavorably due to direct or vicarious experiences of injustice and aggressive law enforcement tactics that include the use of SQF, crackdowns in hot spots, along with a buffet of zero-tolerance approaches to address misdemeanors and minor offenses. It is also suggested that police brutality and the unjust use of lethal force can explain the animosity toward police on the part of young

Black males in particular (Brunson, 2007, and see further discussion on this in Chapters 6–7 of this book).

It is important to consider such attitudes within a historical context given the impact of racial tensions and the notion that much of today's angst stems from unresolved injustice in the past. There is a shameful history that has defined the cognitive landscape of America's urban centers and continues to shape racial distrust and conflict. A case can be made that one of the reasons for the confidence gap in attitudes toward the police is that history has precipitated a sharp contrast in the experience of justice across racial groups that is rooted in the enslavement of Black people in America, the long and arduous journey toward citizenship, and the hope for a more just society.

The roots of racial injustice

Racial animus between police and residents has long been a problem in the US, particularly within the context of predominantly Black urban neighborhoods (Wallace et al, 2018). The roots of this conflict can be traced to the dehumanizing system of chattel slavery. In 1619, slavery began in the US with the arrival of a ship at Jamestown, Virginia, and it continued until the Emancipation Proclamation on January 1, 1863, which was enforced in the courts with the passage of the Thirteenth Amendment in 1865. Slavery was inherently inhumane and brutal. Generations of enslaved people were beaten, humiliated, and denigrated, as women were routinely assaulted, and families lived in constant fear of separation. Former slaveholders and plantation owners might have embraced the truths enshrined in the country's founding documents, but many also held on to a paradox of moral virtue and racial oppression, as they were reluctant to reject the racist culture that drove a system that oppressed formerly enslaved people and deprived them of their rights (Tise, 1987; Schneider & Schneider, 2000).

The Thirteenth Amendment abolished slavery, and soon afterward congress enacted two additional constitutional amendments to protect the rights of the newly freed Black population. The passage of the Fourteenth Amendment in 1868 guaranteed equal protection under the law and citizenship rights to African Americans, while the Fifteenth Amendment of 1870 stated that no one could be denied the right to vote based on race, color, or previous condition of servitude. Given that states often failed to protect the rights of Black people, the responsibility for protecting rights would be shifted to the federal government (Vorenberg, 2004). Yet, despite these progressive changes, the generational impact of slavery and the structural factors that impacted future generations cannot be overstated. A legacy of injustice permeated the social, political, and economic landscape of the country, and criminal justice institutions were no exception.

Southern states used the criminal justice system as a means of social control. "Black codes" were enacted after the Civil War to control African Americans and relegate them to a labor economy based on debt and low wages. This characterized life for people of color during the post-Reconstruction period, and provides context for the drive to imprison unprecedented numbers of Black men, women, and children, who were returned to slavery-like conditions through forced labor and convict-leasing systems that lasted well into the 20th century (Rothenberg, 2013). The oppressive ideology behind de jure segregation helped to sustain Jim Crow laws[1] in the South, and the prison industrial complex which incarcerates more than two million Americans today could be a contemporary manifestation of the same oppressive forces that supported Jim Crow (Alexander, 2010).

The African American experience of law enforcement in the early to mid-20th century was also fraught with challenges. In the decades leading up to the 1950s there were frequent reports of a brutal extrajudicial activity called "lynching," which was often aided and abetted by local police and did great and lasting harm to community perceptions of the criminal justice system. Lynching was more than a hate crime; it was a tool designed to subjugate Blacks by keeping them in constant fear of physical violence. The phenomenon of legally sanctioned racial violence, along with the oppression of Jim Crow laws, stoked the flames that led to a conflagration of civil rights activism and the passage of the Civil Rights Act of 1964. This important legislative achievement was a set of laws that banned discrimination in the workplace, outlawed segregation in public spaces, and banned the unequal application of voting requirements (Waldrep, 2006; Hill, 2016).

While people from a range of ethnic and cultural backgrounds have had negative experiences with law enforcement, there was no group more affected by police brutality in the 1960s than African Americans. During his address at the March on Washington in 1963, Dr Martin Luther King Jr stated that Black people can never be satisfied as long as the Negro was the victim of the unspeakable horrors of police brutality (King & Washington, 2003). During the Civil Rights Era there were numerous boycotts, sit-ins, protests, and other acts of civil disobedience that sparked police violence. Police frequently used their batons, dogs, and even guns to disband large groups of protesters, and there were brutal attacks against Freedom Riders in the South (Williams & Bond, 2013).

There were also high-profile events that sparked outrage and brought the community together. One tragic incident was the murder of Medgar Evers on June 12, 1963. Evers was a 37-year-old civil rights activist who had just arrived home in his suburban neighborhood of Jackson, Mississippi, after a meeting of the National Association for the Advancement of Colored People.[2] Byron De La Beckwith, the prime suspect in the murder case, was a known White supremacist who had been asking around for the location of Evers's home prior to the shooting. Despite the strong evidence against De La Beckwith presented by police and FBI experts, an all-White jury returned a verdict of not guilty and he went free. This miscarriage of justice drew attention to the illegitimacy of the system and caused many to question whether Black men would ever be treated fairly in the courts.

Arguably the most jarring example of racial hatred during this period occurred later that same year. There was a bomb blast at the Sixteenth Street Baptist Church on September 15, 1963 in Birmingham, Alabama, where four girls were killed and fourteen injured, and in the following days there were heated protests and riots, and as a result, two African American boys were killed. In the end, more than 20 people were injured, and Governor George Wallace sent 500 National Guardsmen and 300 state troopers to the city, who were joined by 500 police officers and 150 Sheriffs' deputies. The situation was so violent and disruptive in Birmingham that Dr King held a press conference inviting the US army to come and take charge of the city (Williams & Bond, 2013). All of the suspects in the bombing were Ku Klux Klan members, but witnesses were reluctant to talk. Physical evidence was also lacking, so as a result, the suspects were not indicted. Cases pertaining to the tragedy would eventually be reopened decades later with punitive outcomes coming long after most of the accused had passed away. Regardless of legal outcomes, it is clear that the damage had already been done and many had lost faith in the criminal justice system, and died believing that there would never be justice for the girls or the affected families.

There were other prominent riots during this period. Two examples are the Watts Riots of 1965 and the Detroit Riot of 1967. The Watts Riots occurred in South Los Angeles after Marquette Frye, an African American man, was arrested by a White California patrol officer on a charge of driving while intoxicated. While it is unclear whether the officer used excessive force in his arrest, the resulting riots lasted for six days and resulted in 34 deaths, over 1,000 injuries, and more than $40 million in property damage. The Detroit Riot of 1967 occurred after police raided an illicit after-hours club serving alcohol and arrested all those present, including 82 African Americans. Residents who saw the raid protested, set fires, and vandalized property. The protests spread to other parts of the city and resulted in 43 deaths. Over 7,000 people were arrested and thousands of buildings were burned (Williams & Bond, 2013).

In response to these riots, President Lyndon Johnson launched the Kerner Commission, which comprised social scientists and policy makers, to identify the genesis of the riots and the social unrest. The commission's report identified bad policing practices, a flawed justice system, unscrupulous consumer credit practices, inadequate housing, high unemployment, voter suppression, and other culturally embedded forms of racial discrimination as salient factors that led to anger and violence. It also discussed the negative impact of inadequately trained police officers and military troops on troubled communities. Therefore, structural inequalities were negatively impacting urban ghettos and generating violence.

These findings were controversial from the standpoint of White suburban America, given the implication that "White society" was to blame for many of the disadvantages that plagued urban communities. The commission also warned that the country was so divided that it was poised to fracture into two unequal societies (Kerner, 1988). These concerns are relevant to contemporary perspectives on economic equality and social justice. Throughout the 20th century there were debates about the merits of aggressive law-and-order approaches versus more progressive social support strategies and programs to address problems plaguing minority neighborhoods. This tension continues in contemporary politics as both sides are often locked in an ideological battle in which either side is blamed for problems in urban communities. Ideological beliefs about crime also influence the types of strategies employed by law enforcement. Some police departments embrace a militaristic style that is more conducive to law-and-order-type approaches, and seek to address the crime problem primarily through the use of force. Alternatively, there are "softer" approaches that emphasize the forming of partnerships within communities to involve residents in the co-production of security.

Another example of ideological tensions in policing is the "warrior" versus "guardian" debate, with the former reflecting models of aggressive enforcement and the latter pertaining to models of proactive policing (Stoughton, 2016). It is noteworthy that despite these differences in approaches, to varying degrees, modern police departments have endeavored to incorporate COP into their repertoires. In this regard, America has come a long way from the

1960s. Regardless of the numerous models and versions of community policing and the increasing concern that the meaning of the concept has become practically vague in its implementation, most police leaders would express their enduring support for community policing. Still, commentators continue to question whether widespread support for COP will ultimately have a profound enough effect on citizens to address the crisis of confidence in police from the perspective of citizens.

Ferguson and the Department of Justice Report

While COP initiatives are a major component of the professionalization of policing, and have helped to improve citizens' perceptions of police in the suburbs, the confidence gap in citizens' perceptions persists in less privileged communities. These perceptions are continually fueled by fermenting discord and anger in response to police misconduct. In addition to the frequent reports on the deaths of unarmed Black men at the hands of police, viral videos shared on social media provide confirmation of what many African Americans have believed and experienced for decades. These videos depict the deaths of young men and boys, often under dubious circumstances, and they have become a part of the growing milieu of disaffection toward law enforcement and the lack of trust in the most visible representatives of government on the streets.

Police legitimacy provides an important context for discussions of cases of excessive force. High-profile incidents culminating in the deaths of unarmed Black men such as Eric Garner, Laquan McDonald, Walter Scott, Philando Castille, and Stephon Clark, to name a few, have fueled the increasing public outrage and scrutiny of police and impacted public perceptions of the legitimacy of police. In many ways the problems of the traumatic past are still present. Some of the ensuing investigations pertaining to these incidents revealed that information was intentionally withheld from the public. For example, Laquan McDonald was shot sixteen times by a police officer in 2014 in Chicago, and evidence emerged of a police cover-up. Due to mounting pressure from protestors and activists, the authorities eventually released the dashcam video four hundred days after the incident. Jason Van Dyke, the officer who shot McDonald, was eventually convicted of murder. The police chief resigned, and four officers were fired after it was found that they had signed off on false reports about the incident and provided contradictory accounts of the shooting (Husain, 2019).

In another example, 12-year-old Tamir Rice was shot by Cleveland police, also in 2014. Rice was playing with an air gun at a park on the west side of Cleveland. Someone called the police and mentioned during the call that it was possible that the gun was a fake, but the dispatcher did not relay the caller's doubts to the police. Soon afterward, police pulled up at the scene and drove onto the grass within feet of Rice. According to surveillance footage, Rice was seen reaching toward his waistband and lifting an outer garment. Officer Timothy Loehmann stepped out of the car within seconds and fired two shots, hitting Rice in the stomach. Rice died early the next day and this led to demonstrations in Cleveland and several other cities across the country. The officers faced no criminal charges for the incident, but the city of Cleveland later agreed to pay $6 million to settle a civil rights lawsuit brought by the Rice family. It was also later found that Officer Loehmann had a series of disciplinary incidents on file from a previous department regarding his emotional instability, and this was somehow never revealed during the hiring process.

While these incidents were impactful in shaping public perceptions, the death of Michael Brown in Ferguson and the heated protests that followed are widely regarded as the main catalyst that brought the problems of racial inequality and police–community relations to the forefront of national attention. Ferguson also serves as a historical marker for this era of increased public scrutiny on the conduct of police officers. There have been several high-profile police-involved controversies since then, including the riots in Baltimore, Maryland, which followed the death of Freddie Gray (Cobbina, 2019). However, the events that transpired in the aftermath of Ferguson are worthy of discussion in the context of police legitimacy, the understanding of public perceptions, and the need for significant policing reforms.

As touched on in Chapter 1, the incident that occurred between Michael Brown and Officer Darren Wilson remains unclear (White & Malm, 2020). According to police reports, 18-year-old Brown was walking with a friend, Dorian Johnson, down the middle of Canfield Drive in Ferguson on August 9, 2014. Officer Wilson told authorities he approached the two young men because they were blocking traffic, and authorities said that Brown attacked Wilson in his car and tried to take his gun. Some eyewitnesses said that Wilson was the aggressor and that Brown had his hands up when Wilson began firing, but this version was later disputed. Ultimately, the facts that are not in dispute are that Wilson shot and killed Brown, who was unarmed, and that according to the *St Louis Post-Dispatch*, the entire fatal encounter took less than two minutes (Lopez, 2016).

Protests went on for months. Crowds quickly gathered at the scene of the shooting as Brown's body remained in the street for four hours. Two days after the incident, hundreds of demonstrators were protesting in Ferguson. According to news reports, it took hours for police to process the scene, collect evidence, and move Brown's body, as residents faced off with police and some of the demonstrations turned violent (Lopez, 2016). There were also expressions of anger and frustration that Brown's body was left in the streets so long, and that this reflected the callousness and lack of care taken by the authorities. Furthermore, Ferguson had a long history of distrust between its predominantly White police force and the city's mainly Black population, and this incident was seen by many as another example on a long list of grievances about the harsh and unfair treatment of Black residents by the police (Cobbina, 2019).

Two investigations were launched following the events in Ferguson. One was a criminal investigation led by St Louis County to determine whether Wilson would face charges, and the other was a civil rights investigation led by officials from the US DOJ. The DOJ also commenced a civil rights investigation into the Ferguson Police Department's (FPD) overall track record with racial minorities. The criminal investigation culminated in a grand jury decision not to indict Wilson in November, 2014, and this was met with chaos and more protests. Despite mostly peaceful protests, there were also reports of businesses throughout the city being looted and set on fire, and of police responding by deploying tear gas, as the governor called in the Missouri National Guard. In March 2015, the DOJ's civil rights investigation was concluded, and it announced that they would not bring any federal charges against Wilson. However, the results of their civil rights investigation into the track record of the police department depicted systematic racial discrimination by police and a "pattern and practice" of discrimination in its court system that violated the First, Fourth, and 14th Amendments of the Constitution. The police chief and city manager resigned promptly after the DOJ report was made public (US DOJ, 2015; Hare, 2016).

The DOJ investigation comprised the review of thousands of pages of police records, interviews with city officials and law enforcement personnel, observation of court sessions, and participation in community meetings. It focused on the FPD's use of force, including deadly force, stops, searches, arrests, discriminatory policing, and the treatment of detainees inside the city jail. One of the most striking findings was that the combination of racial bias and Ferguson's focus on generating revenue over public safety had a profound effect on the city's police and court practices. This resulted in patterns of conduct that routinely violated the constitution and federal law and undermined the relationship between the FPD and residents.

Community members were concerned about police stops without reasonable suspicion, arrests without probable cause, infringements on the freedom of expression, and the use of excessive force. Furthermore, the DOJ found that the focus on revenue generation, such as through the issuing of tickets to motorists for moving violations, created an undue burden for the most vulnerable residents. In such a punitive environment, minor offenses can generate crippling debts and result in jail time because of an inability to pay, and this could result in the loss of a driver's license, employment, and housing. The findings also highlighted the disproportionate impact of these policies on African Americans, as well as intentional discrimination and stereotyping by several police officers and court officials. The following is an excerpt from a statement by Attorney General Eric Holder:

> As detailed in our report, this investigation found a community that was deeply polarized, and where deep distrust and hostility often characterized interactions between police and area residents … Our investigation showed that Ferguson police officers routinely violate the Fourth Amendment in stopping people without reasonable suspicion, arresting them without probable cause, and using unreasonable force against them. Now that our investigation has reached its conclusion, it is time for Ferguson's leaders to take immediate, wholesale and structural corrective action. The report we have issued and the steps we have taken are only the beginning of a necessarily resource-intensive and inclusive process to promote reconciliation, to reduce and eliminate bias, and to bridge gaps and build understanding. (US DOJ, 2015)

In 2016, the DOJ pushed for police reform and reached an agreement to overhaul Ferguson's police force and municipal court system. The recommendations that emerged from the agreement reflect the importance of procedurally just approaches and the need to implement strategies for improving police legitimacy perceptions. The recommendations include changing policing and court practices so that they are based on public safety instead of revenue, improving training and oversight, changing practices to reduce bias, and ending the overreliance on arrest warrants as a means of collecting fines. These strategies are part of a court-enforceable remedial process that involves community stakeholders and organizations to provide independent oversight (US DOJ, 2015).

Many of these issues are not unique to Ferguson. Municipal agencies across the country are looking for ways to improve the quality of the services they provide by seeking federal grants for evaluation projects geared toward efficient processes and trust-building strategies. Departments are also encouraged to share knowledge gained from procedurally just approaches instead of waiting for another Ferguson to occur. Indeed, police are facing a challenging proposition when it comes to turning the page on attitudes toward law enforcement, particularly in light of how much time the average person spends online and the influence of social media-inspired outrage.

Social media and collective action

The influence of new communications technologies on collective identity and the formation of social movements has been widely assessed and critiqued. Mass communications have shaped public perceptions since print media gained widespread circulation, and later through the explosive impact of radio, cinema, and television throughout the mid to late 20th century. Notwithstanding the ubiquitous influence of these forms of media, the internet has become a supremely powerful phenomenon. Its influence is evident in business, education, culture, and entertainment, and in its capacity to support networked forms of collective action based on ideals of openness, fluidity, and the co-existence of multiple identities (Della Porta, 2005; Juris, 2008). Moreover, innovations in broadband and cell phone technology, along with changes in behavioral norms, have paved the way for social media to radically increase the bandwidth of globalized interactions.

With rapidly developing technology, the definition of the public sphere was radically transformed, and academic definitions in media research of "the speaker" and "the audience" must now be expanded to include interactive social agents rather than just passive audience members. With the creation of a new interface for public discourse, there has been an emergence of subjective forms of expression that allow for active engagement in a new public sphere (Habermas, 1991). Social media is now indisputably the largest, most diverse and influential public sphere in the history of communications, and it has become both a tool and a catalyst for public outrage. The intensity of social media discourse on racism and police brutality is an important example of how this outrage works.

In the aftermath of deadly encounters with police, public sentiment is amplified by the sharing of video footage on social media. One critique of social media-inspired outrage is that it has done more harm than good, as viral videos often do not provide the context for what actually transpired. Thus, the videos are often biased in their representations of police, and such depictions tend to skew public perceptions negatively. An alternative perspective is that many controversial encounters between police and citizens might never be properly scrutinized were it not for the bystander armed with a cell phone, a Twitter account, and the BLM hashtag. Therefore, social media facilitates important contributions to social justice by providing a platform for marginalized voices. This is supported by findings from a survey by the Pew Research Center which found that Black and Hispanic social media users were more likely than White users to view social media as an effective tool for political engagement (C. Simon, 2018). The belief that their views are not represented by political institutions or the mainstream media could explain why some groups are more inclined to view social media as an effective tool.

The BLM movement reflects these themes. It began in 2013 in response to the trial of George Zimmerman, who was acquitted after shooting and killing 17-year-old Trayvon Martin in Sanford, Florida. Zimmerman, a neighborhood watchman, followed Martin then called 911 to report "a real suspicious guy" in his neighborhood. Much of what happened after Zimmerman spoke to the dispatcher is unclear. However, it is clear that Martin was shot and killed by Zimmerman after a brief physical altercation. In response, the BLM movement was initiated by activists Alicia Garza, Patrisse Cullors, and Opal Tometi who engaged racial minority youths around the country over the circumstances of Martin's death. The popularity of the tag line "Black Lives Matter" increased dramatically with the incidents in Ferguson in 2014, as several BLM activists showed up in Ferguson to organize demonstrations.

According to the social media monitoring company Sysomos, between August 9 and August 25, 2014, the hashtag #Ferguson was used on Twitter 11.6 million times with retweets, and 1.9 million times without retweets (Anderson et al, 2018; Park et al, 2018). The hashtag #BlackLivesMatter was often combined with #Ferguson, as these terms became emblematic of modern racial injustices. According to a Pew study, the BLM hashtag has been used nearly 30 million times on Twitter – an average of 17,003 times per day (Anderson et al, 2018). BLM also reflects a wider trend as there have been other influential social movements since then, such as #LoveWins, #JeSuisCharlie,

#MAGA (Make America Great Again), and #MeToo. This form of expression allows users to give voice to their frustrations and construct collective agency with other users who have also been deeply affected by a specified grievance. Collective agency, also known as collective identity, is an important concept in social movement studies, and has been understood as central to the emergence, trajectories, and impacts of movements, as individuals share cognitive, moral, and emotional connections (Melucci, 1995; 1996; Polletta & Jasper, 2001).

The often heated exchanges on Twitter stemming from these connections reveal the emergence of ideological positions in how different groups, viewing the same media coverage, interpret issues of police brutality and race in strikingly different ways (Carney, 2016). Those who expressed solidarity with law enforcement felt that police were being treated unfairly and that there was a false narrative about what transpired between Michael Brown and Darren Wilson. Thus they used the hashtag #BlueLivesMatter as an oppositional stance to BLM. Others believed that "All Lives Matter" was a less divisive statement that should replace BLM because it promoted a more positive message of racial harmony. These opposing perspectives have been an important feature of the chaotic aftermath of Ferguson, and commentators have acknowledged the constraints of social media, as social movement activity can be co-opted by State agents and politicians for their own political gains. Due to the "noise" on digital platforms there is also the inherent potential for the clear ideology necessary for movements to grow and organize effectively to blur (Carney, 2016). Hence the criticism that BLM has no clear leadership or policy recommendations, despite the notion that the fluidity and versatility of the movement are what makes it unique and powerful (Ransby, 2017).

The divergence of perspectives on BLM demonstrates how social media can facilitate (or frustrate) sense-making, resource mobilization, and coalition building. The irony of this is that social media can provide an impetus to social movements as hashtags start trending and gaining momentum, and it can also damage police–community relations by misrepresenting facts and undermining police legitimacy perceptions (Bonilla & Rosa, 2015; Ransby, 2017). With these issues in mind, it is clear that the confidence crisis regarding policing in the US is fueled by social media. To ameliorate the problem of police–community conflict it would take an equally powerful force to reverse the trend of rising animosity. In addition to the implementation of proven strategies for procedurally just practices, social media can be used for community outreach and as a tool to promote non-classified versions of police strategies with the hope of fostering greater transparency. Systematic changes along these lines, if part of a broader policy plan to address structural inequalities, could help to elicit greater confidence in police. Clearly, the implications of police legitimacy within the context of profound and often daunting technological advancement require police leaders and stakeholders to carefully consider the role of social media in shaping public perceptions. They must also be willing to recalibrate and change with the times.

Chapter summary

In this chapter, we have reviewed the links between procedural justice and police legitimacy within a context of historical racial disadvantage and discrimination in the US. We have documented the shameful history in America's urban centers that continues to shape racial distrust and conflict. We have discussed the racial animus between police and local residents within racial minority communities, tracing the roots of this to the dehumanizing system of chattel slavery, and the continuing illustrations of racial tension between White officers and Black men. High-profile contemporary incidents culminating in the deaths of unarmed Black men have been documented, and the repercussions emerging from the Ferguson shooting were examined. As we have discussed previously, the death of Michael Brown in Ferguson and the heated protests that followed are widely regarded as the main catalyst that brought the problems of racial inequality and police–community relations firmly to the forefront of national attention in recent years. Drawing upon the post-Ferguson activity associated with the BLM movement, we explored and examined the impact of digital media as a tool for collective action and empowerment. As we have argued, it is evident that the confidence crisis regarding policing in America is to some extent fueled by social media in the contemporary era. The daunting technological advancements and increased public consciousness of racially motivated police–community conflict has collectively led to reportedly wide-ranging implications in terms of police legitimacy.

In the next chapter, we begin to explore these implications more fully. We examine the evidence that suggests that the undermining of police legitimacy in the post-Ferguson era and the increased influence of social media has led to an apparent "war on cops" and – in turn – a process of de-policing. We also begin to draw upon our own empirical data to consider how perceptions around these issues impacted on a sample of law enforcement officers who regularly policed racial and ethnic minority communities affected by gang-related crime in one Southern American state.

3

The "Ferguson Effect" and Emergence of "De-policing"

The confidence crisis of law enforcement is steeped in conflict and has caused great harm to the police and public. We are, unfortunately, in a period of continued decline marred by public inquiries into procedural justice and the questioning of law enforcement legitimacy. In this chapter, we report on the rise of a somewhat new phenomenon in policing. In doing so, contemporary policing is framed among developing countermovements that place law enforcement in the middle of oppositional belief systems. Against a backdrop of historical inequalities and a lack of law enforcement accountability, we consider the way some have questioned if the public are engaged in a "war" on police. We explore how public discord has had real consequences and been met with a somewhat galvanized de-policing response from law enforcement. The policing and crime costs of the Ferguson Effect, as this phenomenon is also known, are empirically explored. Though often framed through the words and lens of law enforcement, the semi-structured interviews (of officers listed in Table 3.1) and participant observation field notes set the stage for alternative perspectives shared in later chapters.

The emergence of countermovements

Criticisms of police have occurred during a broader period of social and political unrest in the US. In fact, there has been an emergence of countermovements. The BLM movement, for example, was initially criticized for lacking inclusivity. While few questioned the experiences of Blacks with the police, many other groups have also been subjected to systematic police abuses. In particular, and following the terrorist attacks on September 11, 2001, Muslim, Arab, and Middle Eastern

Table 3.1: Interview participant description – officers

Name	Sex	Race	Service length	Rank	Location
Joshua	Male	White	17	Detective	Coconut County Sheriff's Office
Owen	Male	White	18	Detective	Coconut County Sheriff's Office
Ryan	Male	White	19	Sergeant	Coconut County Sheriff's Office
Calvin	Male	Black	5	Officer	Needle City PD, Queen County
Daniel	Male	White	12	Sergeant	Needle City PD, Queen County
Emily	Female	White	22	Chief	Needle City PD, Queen County
Jennifer	Female	White	4	Officer	Needle City PD, Queen County
Jonathan	Male	Black	10	Officer	Needle City PD, Queen County
Luke	Male	White	30	Outgoing Chief	Needle City PD, Queen County
Andrew	Male	White	26	Detective	Queen County Sheriff's Office
Gabriel	Male	Black	10	Special Agent	Queen County Sheriff's Office
Jacob	Male	White	46	Deputy Chief Sheriff	Queen County Sheriff's Office
Jack	Male	White	15	Detective	Queen County Sheriff's Office
John	Male	White	25	Detective	Queen County Sheriff's Office
Kevin	Male	White	19	Sergeant	Queen County Sheriff's Office
Logan	Male	White	6	Detective	Queen County Sheriff's Office
Michael	Male	White	37	Detective	Queen County Sheriff's Office
Noah	Male	White	31	Sergeant	Queen County Sheriff's Office
Samuel	Male	Black	20	Lieutenant	Queen County Sheriff's Office
Tyler	Male	White	29	Senior Special Agent	Queen County Sheriff's Office

populations in the US experienced additional scrutiny (and at times harassment) from law enforcement (Fallik & Novak, 2013). This led Withrow to state that, "after 9/11 the rules changed and everything we had learned about the social costs and ineffectiveness of racial profiling was largely ignored" (Withrow, 2006, p 244). Concern over terrorism led the US DOJ to pressure state and local law enforcement agencies to enforce immigration laws. To this point, Nguyen stated that the border became, "a critical front in the war on terror" (Nguyen, 2005, p 92). Arizona, in this vein, passed the Support Our Law Enforcement and Safe

Neighborhoods Act of 2010, containing a subsection that compelled law enforcement to question the immigration status of individuals they suspected were in the country illegally. Many felt that the "Show me your papers" provision, as it came to be known, disenfranchised Hispanic and Latino populations, but it was unanimously upheld by the US Supreme Court (Burnett, 2017). Individuals from these groups did not feel as though they were represented or being heard in the BLM movement. As we referred to briefly in the previous chapter, in an effort to be more inclusive, police issues were temporarily reframed under the tagline All Lives Matter. The semantics of "Black" and "All" lives matter were debated on social media platforms, and the phrases were sometimes used interchangeably.[1]

Nevertheless, the All Lives Matter movement was quickly co-opted by the alt-right (AR), who hold extremist beliefs about White supremacy and nationalism. In contemporary society, the AR movement has been inspired by the anonymity of the internet and stoked by identity politics. Relating to the former, socially unacceptable beliefs had few places of respite prior to the age of the internet. Though free speech is protected in the US Constitution, less favorable ideologies were rarely spoken about in public spaces because the holders of these beliefs would be ostracized and shamed. The veil of anonymity offered by the internet has made it easier for many of its users to indulge their worst inclinations, which is compounded by the fact that they are rarely confronted with consequences. Relating to the latter (that is, identity politics), White voters have long been subject to fearmongering with race-baiting and the Southern strategy in the US. The election of President Trump, however, welcomed more fringe, hyperbolic, and tribalistic beliefs into the mainstream. He, for example, proclaimed that illegal immigrants "infest our country," told four non-White congresswomen to "go back home," instituted a travel ban from predominantly Muslim countries, separated families from other countries seeking asylum, and diverted defense funds to build a wall along the southern border (A. Simon, 2018; Oh, 2019). Moreover, this discourse had an indelible effect during President Trump's campaign, as he often disputed established facts and called into question the integrity of his opponents and the news media.[2]

In the age of the internet and identity politics, the AR movement has thrived because many of its followers believe that civil liberties are a zero-sum enterprise, whereby if others receive greater protection under the law, their own standing in society is reduced. This often leads AR sympathizers to espouse racist, misogynistic, anti-Semitic, homophobic, and neo-Nazi ideologies. Hateful philosophies have, unfortunately, been accompanied by a rise in hate crimes since the events in Ferguson, Missouri. In fact, the FBI has reported a rise in victims, offenders, and the number of agencies dealing with hate crimes since 2014. Some have gone as far to blame President Trump's rhetoric for the growth of hate crimes (Hasan, 2019; Kunelman & Galvan, 2019). Counties that hosted Trump campaign rallies, for example, have experienced a 226 percent increase in hate crime incidents (Feiberg et al, 2019; see also Edwards & Rushin, 2018). Additionally, more subtle forms of bigotry have occurred throughout the nation, like the viral videos that have emerged of White people calling the police over innocuous behaviors of Black members of the public (Molina, 2018); upon their arrival, police are then forced to mediate somewhat minor inconveniences among neighbors, something they perceive as being beyond the scope of their duties, especially when based on cultural misunderstandings or minor incivilities and not criminal violations.

As an affront to such bigoted beliefs, many municipalities began removing confederate monuments. The momentum for their removal from public spaces gained traction as more and more of the public came to recognize their existence as constituting continued intimidation of Blacks by a treasonous government.[3] AR protectionists, feeling emboldened by their online presence and the political climate, began appearing in public spaces to defend the existence of confederate monuments. These incidents became catalysts for more formal AR demonstrations, and such events have been met with resistance from communities, BLM counterprotesters, and a new, somewhat militant group called Antifa.[4] In Charlottesville, Virginia, for example, AR supporters gathered at a Robert E. Lee statue for a Unite the Right rally in August of 2017.[5] Many AR demonstrators carried assault-style weapons, wore clothing sympathetic to the Ku Klux Klan/confederacy, and held tiki torches in what can be deemed a mob/vigilante display. Furthermore, Sieg heil salutes[6] and chants of "Jews will not replace us" were prevalent at the Unite the Right rally (Alvarez, 2017). This event turned deadly when a self-identified White supremacist deliberately rammed his car into a crowd of counterprotesters, killing Heather Heyer and injuring 19 others.[7] Though condemning "hatred, bigotry, and violence," President Trump's comments following the Unite the Right rally seemed sympathetic to AR participants, as he asserted that there was "violence on many sides" of the rally and that there were "very fine people on both sides" of the protest (Klein, 2018).

Though generally characterized as politically conservative, the growth of rallies and counterprotests has literally and figuratively placed police in the middle of peaceful and violent demonstrations. On the one hand, they have been tasked with preserving the peace among fundamentally opposed groups. In doing so, they often separate conflicting parties, do their best to mediate situations, and uphold bureaucratic processes through somewhat aggressive zoning tactics. This has created a perceptual deficit that, on the other hand, sees police as protecting bigots, embracing hate speech, and abridging the public's right to assemble through the enforcement of restrictions on public demonstration permits. In both instances, police have been and continue to be at the forefront of the nation's changing discourse and activism. As such, they often bear the brunt of public dissatisfaction, and on occasion that includes violence.

In many ways, therefore, the contemporary state of policing is consistent with what Manning identified as an "impossible mandate," whereby the public places unrealistic expectations on the police, thereby setting themselves up for disappointment (Manning, 1977, p 13). August Vollmer, often considered the forefather of American policing, articulated the issue in 1936, saying,

> One may well wonder how any group of men could perform the tasks required of policemen. The citizen expects police officers to have the wisdom of Solomon, the courage of David, the strength of Samson, the patience of Job, the leadership of Moses, the kindness of the Good Samaritan, the faith of Daniel, the tolerance of the Carpenter of Nazareth, and finally, an intimate knowledge of every branch of the natural, biological, and social sciences. If he had all of these, he might be a good policeman.

An artifact of this condition is that police are often accused of simultaneously policing too little and too much. Where they fall short of the public's expectations, especially in the post-Ferguson era, the public has been somewhat quick to espouse anti-police sentiments.

The "war on police"?

The gulf between citizen expectations and police actions, however, has not gone without repercussion, as several studies find that police experience disrespect, a lack of cooperation, and antagonistic encounters with the public. In Adams (2019), for example, an officer (Henry) was certain that "respect as a whole has went down" and another officer (Timothy) affirmed that "there is a total lack of respect for the police" (p 1756). In our own data, officers (as described in Table 3.1; see Chapter 1 for further detail on our sampling methods) often discussed the public's unwillingness to comply with police orders and an increase in public filming of officer contacts. Detective Owen expressed this sentiment (see also MacDonald, 2016a; Deuchar et al, 2018a; Adams, 2019):

> "I would say post-Ferguson there's more of a challenge. 'Uh, you don't have the right to stop me, I'm filming' ... They're not paying any attention to anything you're saying because they got their phone in your face and they're trying to Facebook Live or Periscope it ... they're not listening. It ultimately creates that lack of cooperation which can eventually lead to an arrest." (Owen, detective, Coconut County Sheriff's Office)

Some officer experiences can be described as simple microaggressions, like being stereotyped by their profession because officers are uncomfortable when they are treated as a category rather than as individuals (Clark, 1965).[8] To this point, Officer Jonathan, who had a decade of law enforcement experience, stressed that "law enforcement, as a whole, is not the same, you know. You're never gonna receive the same level of service, the same level of professionalism."

Law enforcement, therefore, view their interactions with the public and criminal justice system negatively. Regarding the former, Westley revealed that nearly three-fourths of officers felt that the public was against the police, or hates the police, while only 12 percent thought that the public favored the police (Westley, 1970). Similarly, two years into the job, half of the officers in McNamara's study agreed with the statement that "patrolmen almost never receive the cooperation from the public that is needed to handle police work properly" (McNamara, 1967, p 221). More recently, half of surveyed Cincinnati officers reported that citizens disrespected them more often than not (Riley et al, 2006; see also Westley, 1970). In the post-Ferguson era, Morgan and Pally also noted that there appears to be "a decline in community cooperation with the police" (Morgan & Pally, 2016, p 4). In our own sample of officers, Sergeant Ryan insisted,

> "There is a lot of police mistrust, or at least the idea of that went around the country here over the last few years with the Gray case [and] with the Ferguson case. And actually, I wouldn't call it so much mistrust as I would call

it a lack of cooperation. It's the mentality, no one on the street ever wants to be a witness. They could be sitting on their front porches when a shooting happens and yet there are no witnesses." (Ryan, sergeant, Coconut County Sheriff's Office)

Furthermore, anti-police demonstrations by BLM, Antifa, and their sympathizers have not been limited to jurisdictions directly affected by use-of-force incidents. In fact, protests have occurred in locations without overt police–citizen conflicts (Wolfe & Nix, 2016).

In this context, some have questioned if tensions have escalated into an all-out war on police (Nix et al, 2018, p 34; see also MacDonald, 2016b). To this point, Culhane et al (2016) claimed that the public believes that police should have to "pay for" the perceived injustices of other departments, and an officer (Brandon) in Adams (2019) declared that "people want to hurt cops" (p 267 and p 1755, respectively). Likewise, Matt, an officer in a *New York Post* op-ed (Matt, 2014), suggested that the number of officers shot in the line of duty had spiked in the post-Ferguson era. When explored quantitatively, studies propose something other than simple anecdotes. In an analysis of the Officer Down Memorial Page, Maguire et al (2017) found no change in the number of officers murdered in the line of duty pre- and post-Ferguson. In a similar study, White et al (2019) revealed there to have been a 75 percent drop in deaths in the line of duty in the last five decades. When it comes to officers being assaulted in the line of duty, a familiar pattern emerges. The Law Enforcement Officers Killed and Assaulted data from the FBI (n.d. b), for example, shows that the rate of officers assaulted has fluctuated but does not appear to be sensitive to use-of-force incidents (see also Carriere & Encinosa, 2017).[9] Even citizen hostility appears to occur infrequently, as research has acknowledged that it only happens in about ten percent of all encounters with the public (Reiss, 1971). Walker and Katz, therefore, professed that, "Most police-citizen interactions are routine and uneventful, with neither side exhibiting disrespect to the other or using force" (Walker & Katz, 2017, p 358).

That is not to say that there have not been any physical or verbal attacks on police. In fact, some have been directly motivated by use-of-force events, like on October 23, 2014 when a man wielding a hatchet attacked four officers on a New York City (NYC) sidewalk and injured two of them. The perpetrator, who was shot and killed by two other officers during the incident,[10] wrote in a manifesto that he wanted to attack government officials and was an advocate for Black power. Nearly two months later (December 20, 2014), contempt for law enforcement boiled over when a gunman approached an occupied New York Police Department (NYPD) patrol car and fired upon its occupants.[11] The two officers inside succumbed to their wounds and the gunman later took his life as he fled the scene. In an Instagram post prior to the shooting, the gunman wrote that he intended to kill police as revenge for the deaths of Michael Brown and Eric Garner. Similarly, two days after the death of Alton Sterling and a day after the death of Philando Castile, protesters of police use of force gathered across the country on July 7, 2016. In Dallas, Texas, the Next Generation Action Network organized a peaceful demonstration at El Centro College. This event turned deadly when a gunman fired upon law enforcement. The perpetrator was allegedly upset at the shootings of young Black men and wanted to kill White people. The gunman in this incident killed five and injured another nine officers[12] before a remote-control bomb killed the suspect.

Verbal and physical assaults on police have co-occurred with inter-professional challenges from their criminal justice peers. Police, in particular, feel that defense attorneys often question their integrity, prosecutors frequently plea-bargain serious offenses and career criminals, and judges dismiss months of casework for minor technicalities in the law (Westley, 1970; Gottfredson & Gottfredson, 1988). This was a common sentiment expressed in our own field notes and among the interviewed officers. Jennifer, an officer with the Needle City Police Department, illustrated this point when she concluded that "the whole system is flawed" because criminals "are not being punished or made to pay for their crimes and they're being released to just do it again." Lenient sentences were also discussed frequently by the participating officers. John, a detective with 25 years of experience with the Queen County Sheriff's Office, alleged that most criminals only receive, "a slap on the wrist." A consequence of these interactions is that many officers think they have to compartmentalize their role in the criminal justice system. Joshua (from the Coconut County Sheriff's Office) and Calvin (from the Needle City Police Department), with a combined 22 years of law enforcement experience, held that cases are often "out of our [their] hands" (see also Deuchar et al, 2019).

Officers have been further frustrated by a belief that effective crime-fighting tools are being taken away from them. Several officers in our sample, for example, decried that the evidentiary standards for SQF have evolved, making it unconstitutional. Jennifer, an officer with four years of law enforcement experience, felt that changes in SQF would result in a spike in crime. During an interview, she argued,

"They [gun carriers] used to know that officers were going to stop them and jump out and check they weren't carrying them. I mean they would always have them somewhere, they have them hidden, they had them but they weren't just blatantly standing on corners with them. Where now, they know that officers are a little more unsure of the laws and a little bit more timid and know that we don't necessarily have the political support that we need and so officers have pulled back a lot in that aspect. And that's dangerous for officers and the community ... I know it's against people's human rights in some ways but that's not always a reason to stop doing it and just let crime happen." (Jennifer, officer, Needle City Police Department)

While the police regard SQF as a legitimate and effective crime-fighting tactic, it has the unfortunate history of marginalizing segments of the public (Ridgway, 2007). To that end, some police assume they are justified in targeting minorities and claim that they are overrepresented in criminal activity. As Walker and Katz explain, however, there is circular reasoning in this justification. They note that "racial and ethnic minorities are stopped and arrested more often than Whites, producing higher arrest rates that, in turn, justify higher rates of stops and arrests" (Walker & Katz, 2017, p 404). Moreover, traffic enforcement and self-report surveys find a somewhat negligible difference in law violations across racial and ethnic groups, certainly not enough to explain the targeting of racial minorities (Lamberth, 1994 and Department of Health and Human Services, 2007, respectively).

Law enforcement accountability

Law enforcement accountability, especially in the post-Ferguson era, has been a heavily debated issue, in part because officers sense they are being targeted in somewhat questionable use-of-force events by overzealous and politically motivated prosecutors and activist lawyers (Hylton, 2016). Logan, a detective in our sample with six years of law enforcement experience, stated that, "If we do something that they don't agree with, they're already convicting us before we even go to trial," and that, "officers are getting sued for doing their job and doing it right" (see also Deuchar et al, 2019). The news media has certainly latched onto this phenomenon, as well, for example in the highly publicized trials and guilty adjudications of officers in Chicago, IL, for the death of Laquan McDonald, and in North Charleston, SC, of officer

Michael Slager for the death of Walter Scott. In fact, the year following the death of Michael Brown in Ferguson, prosecutions of officers had surged. While the annual average number of officers charged with murder or manslaughter between 2005 and 2014 was approximately five, in 2015 a dozen officers had been charged prior to the year's end (Simpson, 2015). These rates unfortunately underrepresent actual perpetration of police misconduct. Specifically, 40 percent of officers in Barker (1986) self-reported that they had used excessive force at times. Similarly, Weisburd et al (2000) found that 24.5 percent of officers reported that "it is sometimes acceptable to use more force than is legally allowable to control someone who physically assaults an officer" (Weisburd et al, 2000, p 2: see also Westley, 1970; Carter, 1985).

Empirically, however, officers are only rarely held accountable by their agencies for brutality, excessive use of force, or extralegal police aggression. Contrary to citizen demands, police have traditionally been somewhat hostile to receiving complaints. Novak et al (2017) deduced that,

> citizens do not complain about the police because they do not think it will do any good or because they are afraid the police will retaliate. Some departments make it difficult for citizens to complain by creating a cumbersome complaint process and by the negative (e.g., unfriendly, rude, curt, discouraging) behavior of officers when citizens attempt to complain. (Novak et al, 2017, pp 347–8)

African Americans also tend to be overrepresented in complaints about law enforcement but underrepresented in the rate they are sustained (Pate & Fridell, 1993). Complaints that are sustained often do not result in any formal officer discipline, according to the Philadelphia Integrity and Accountability Office (2003). When they are disciplined for on-duty abuses, it infrequently results in termination. In a study of the NYPD by Kane and White (2009), only two percent of officers were terminated during a 21-year period. Of those, only 4.8 percent were terminated for on-duty abuses, which translates to less than a tenth of a percent of officers employed during the period of observation (less than 0.01 percent). Even when disciplined, half of officers declined to partake in some or all of their remediation plans according to a 2003 analysis by the Office of Independent Review (2003).

Though large agency settlements and officer convictions are shocking and often capture media attention, criminal and civil prosecutions of officers are rare because court proceedings tend to be expensive, time consuming, and difficult to win. Hughes (2001), for example, discovered that 18.5 percent of officers had been sued for an on-the-job related incident, while 74.8 percent had personally known an officer who had been sued. Officers felt, in 86.4 percent of the surveys, that lawsuits occurred even when the named officer was acting properly and had become a cost of doing business. Though officers perceive the public to use lawsuits as "get rich" schemes, research finds that plaintiffs are only awarded a tenth of their initial claims, with a median amount of $8,000 (Newell et al, 1992). Even when reform, and not financial gain or restitution, is the object of litigation, studies find they have little effect (Littlejohn, 1981). Substantively, the working relationship between police and prosecutors, the somewhat difficult standard of proof, and the sympathetic nature of juries toward police are barriers to prosecutions of officers, according to Goldstein (1967). Furthermore, the financial costs of litigation do not often affect officers or departments because unions and insurance (that is, taxpayers and members) often bear the financial burden of lawsuits. Regarding the former, police unions have felt a growing need to come to the defense of officers (regardless of guilt), while the public perceives unions as a serious barrier to positive change in police organizations (Kadleck, 2003).

Where the public has been unable to find justice with internal police, civil, and criminal processes, they have historically turned to external forms of accountability, such as news and social media outlets. Regarding the former, police have come to see news media stories as sensationalized, distorted, and in pursuit of ratings over the truth. Officers have communicated to researchers that the 24-hour news cycle has encouraged networks to be first to report events as opposed to gathering all the facts. To this point, during an interview with Jack, a detective with 15 years of law enforcement experience, he stated:

> "Unfortunately, the media and the public don't give law enforcement the same, I wouldn't necessarily say rights, like a Joe Shmoe citizen ... they're always undermining our split-second decisions. They're already saying we're guilty, 'Why are you violating people's rights?' We all have families that we want to go home to every day and we do have a split second to make life altering decisions." (Jack, detective, Queen County Sheriff's Office)

Substantively, officers were mindful of the impact of media. Luke, the outgoing chief of police in the Needle City Police Department, parenthetically expressed that "you don't want to be on the six o'clock news" (see also Fallik et al, 2019).

Furthermore, police believe that members of the public have been empowered and become activists with social media, which has been accelerated by the conveniences of video-enabled smartphones. With more and more people getting information online, police see social media as amplifying divisions and further isolating them from the communities they serve (Matt, 2014). Police, therefore, are overwhelmingly distrusting of all forms of media because they believe they are unfairly scrutinized and do not want to become the star of a career-ending viral video (Davis, 2015). In summation, officers are more aware of the negative publicity that surrounds their career choice and mindful of the public's ability to video record their interactions (Deuchar et al, 2019).[13]

Harm to officers

Though actual threats to officers' health and well-being may be infrequent, the omnipresence of danger and frequency of hostility from the public has taken a toll on police.[14] Officers tend to recall unpleasant or traumatic experiences (Groger, 1997; Ridgeway et al, 2006) and as a consequence, these events have been accompanied by a growth in fear, cynicism, and apprehension, and a decline in morale and motivation among law enforcement (Wolfe & Nix, 2016; Torres et al, 2018). This is not simply conjecture. Torres et al, in an online survey of law enforcement, found that the events in Ferguson have had a psychological impact on those performing the job, like when an officer (Robert) in Adams (2019) admitted that today, "it's harder emotionally to do the job" (p 1754). Additionally, research finds that the negative publicity surrounding policing in the aftermath of Ferguson was associated with lower levels of officer self-legitimacy and that the majority of officers feel like there is a war on cops in America (Nix & Wolfe, 2016; Nix et al, 2018, respectively).

The state of contemporary policing may also be exacerbating existing on-the-job stressors, which are uniquely acute for law enforcement. The top two stressors, according to Violanti and Aron (1995), for example, are "killing someone in the line of duty" and a "fellow officer [being] killed." In one study, 26 percent of officers suffered from posttraumatic stress, which was especially intense in the wake of a critical incident (Martin et al, 1986). In dealing with anxiety and depression brought on by job-related stress, many officers cope with alcohol (Swatt et al, 2007). Binge drinking, in particular, occurs more frequently among law enforcement, which has contributed to higher rates of alcohol-related liver disease deaths when compared to the general public (Davey et al, 2000 and Richmond et al, 1998, respectfully). Likewise, research shows that rates of suicidal ideation among law enforcement are greater than in the general public, and that this appears to be on the rise in some agencies (Violanti, 1995; Loo, 2003).[15]

Officers who seek social support, according to Patterson (2003), have lower levels of work stress and/or emotional distress. In that context, law enforcement belong to a unique albeit informal occupational culture that at times embraces values and norms in conflict with mainstream society that inform their attitudes and behaviors (Doyle, 1980; Goolkasian et al, 1985). According to Westley (1970), policing values secrecy, solidarity, and violence.[16] The development of these values begins with the recruitment of likeminded cadets, is instilled during academy training,[17] and reinforced in daily interactions with the public. The latter is perhaps the most meaningful element, as police often have selective contact with the population they serve. More specifically, they perform society's dirty work and do the tasks that no other profession will take on. In doing so, they often encounter the public on the worst day of their lives and deal with extreme human suffering. Police–public encounters are often negative because police rarely meet people without problems or individuals who do not begrudge their presence. Even more fleeting traffic encounters often leave the public hating the police. These experiences accumulate over time, and officers bond over shared, often negative, understandings of humanity. In many ways, this causes police to see the public as the "enemy" and to view police–public encounters with an "us vs. them" outlook (Adams, 2019). Substantively, their daily activities and the way in which they carry themselves in public engagements may be perceived as abrasive. Hostility toward the public can also reinforce group solidarity or a "same team" mentality among officers.[18]

One way officers have expressed a unified front in the post-Ferguson era is through the development of their own countermovement. Blue Lives Matter, as it's known to its advocates, promotes the prosecution and conviction of cop killers with hate crime statutes. Louisiana, in 2016, became the first and only state to pass this type of legislation. Public empathy and support for law enforcement, nevertheless, has adopted the Blue Lives Matter mantra. Moreover, augmented American flags with thin blue lines set on a black and gray background have come to represent this cause.

In any case, officer loyalty to one another is nearly absolute, as is made evident by the "code of silence" when it comes to discussing officer misconduct.[19] Nearly half of the officers surveyed in Barker (1986), for example, reported that they would not tell on a peer who used excessive force (see also Westley, 1970). A more recent national survey found that 52.4 percent of officers agreed with the sentiment that "it is not unusual for a police officer to turn a blind eye to improper police conduct by other officers," while another 17.5 percent considered the "code of silence an essential part of good policing" (Weisburd et al, 2000, pp 3, 5). Westley, along these lines, surmises that "illegal action is preferable to breaking the secrecy of the group" (Westley, 1970, p 113). To that end, officers believe they are justified in their protection of fellow officers because they feel as though the hostility they receive from the public is undeserved. Secrecy, according to Westley (1970), can further devolve into outright lies. This has the unintended consequence of insulating poor and/or criminal officers from scrutiny, and further detaches police from the public. The code of silence, therefore, is perhaps the biggest obstacle to police accountability in contemporary times, but remains a prominent feature of police culture.

A galvanized police response

Though it is unlikely that the police culture will discourage officers from engaging with the public altogether, several scholars have contended that they are understandably more cautious with activities they have no mandate to undertake and, substantively, have withdrawn from proactive policing duties (MacDonald, 2016a, 2016b; Wolfe & Nix, 2016; Nix et al, 2018; Nix & Wolfe, 2018; Adams, 2019; Deuchar et al, 2019). De-policing, as it is more commonly known, suggests that in the post-Ferguson era, police are less willing to put in the "extra effort," follow more discretionary pursuits, or be hands-on in their day-to-day activities. Policing's consciousness around such endeavors, according to Novak et al (2017), has been rationalized by officers as reducing their chance of being named as a defendant in a lawsuit and/or being suspected of racial bigotry (see also Wolfe & Nix, 2016). Ryan, a county sergeant with nearly 20 years of law enforcement experience, to this point, stated the following (see also Deuchar et al, 2019):[20]

> "There are cops out there that, they're afraid ... somebody's going to throw in the towel, what we call the 'race card' – 'Oh, you're stopping me because I'm Black,' 'You're stopping me because I'm Hispanic.' Whereas reality is, 'No,

I stopped you because you're committing a crime.'...I think it causes hesitation, hesitation not only to make the stop but hesitation to act, you know, with any kind of force. You know, I think instead of being primarily concerned with their own safety, that hesitation comes into play as to 'How am I going to be viewed?'" (Ryan, sergeant, Coconut County Sheriff's Office)

Evidence of de-policing, however, is less clear than expected. Wolfe & Nix (2016) reported that negative police publicity has decreased officers' willingness to engage community partners (see also Mourtgos & Adams, 2019).[21] Likewise, Andrew, a county detective with 26 years of law enforcement experience, concluded that police are fearful of street-level encounters with the public (see also Deuchar et al, 2019):

"Bottom line, you now have officers being less proactive. You know, a drug dealer standing on the street, these guys – I'm not saying all – but you got officers who are not gonna go out of their way to push them off the corners because it's going to end up in a fight, and with the things that have happened, the people on the street feel more and more inclined to not follow your instructions." (Andrew, detective, Queen County Sheriff's Office)

A similar trend has been observed in traffic enforcement. Shjarback et al (2017) found that law enforcement made fewer traffic stops in their pre- and post-Ferguson analyses of 118 Missouri police departments.

Engagement with community partners, street-level encounters with the public, and traffic enforcement are, however, low-visibility aspects of policing. Alternatively, arrests and the use of force are more highly scrutinized and, therefore, lack similar levels of officer discretion. In a seven-year study by Slocum et al (2019), low-level arrests declined following the events in Ferguson but have returned to expected levels for only Black members of the public. This indicates that de-policing may have a half-life for only certain portions of the population (see Novak et al, 2003 for an alternative finding).[22]

When it comes to the use of force, research is even less consistent with de-policing, and suggests it occurs far less frequently than media reports may conclude. The Bureau of Justice Statistics (BJS: n.d. b) estimates that police use or threat of force occurs in less than two percent of all encounters with the public. Among these instances, Adams (1995) estimated that two-thirds are justified. Moreover, the number of fatal police shootings pre- and post-Ferguson has remained remarkably unchanged, which indicates police have not been outwardly impacted by the events in Ferguson (Buehler, 2017; Campbell et al, 2018). This finding is complimented by Bollinger (2018) and Fields (2019), who found that the Ferguson Effect did not prevent officers from performing their sworn duties.

The reality of police use of force, however, is much more nuanced. Though the number of people killed by officers may not have changed, Black males tend to be overrepresented among these figures. In 2016, for example, they comprised 6.1 percent of the US population but accounted for a quarter of the people killed by police, according to the American Community Survey (2016) and a *Washington Post* (2015, 2016) database, respectively. Additionally, approximately 14 percent of the Black males killed by police in 2016 were unarmed (*Washington Post*, 2015, 2016). These disparities, Skolnick (1968) hypothesized, are due to increased officer suspicion and/or fear of racial and ethnic minority male members of the public (see also Payne, 2001; Correll et al, 2002; Holmes & Smith, 2008). Nevertheless, when the rate of police–public contacts, arrests, and resistance to or attacks on the police are controlled in research, use-of-force racial disparities tend to dissipate (Fyfe, 1988; Geller & Scott, 1992), and an overwhelming amount of evidence implies that officer decision-making is informed by lawful – as opposed to extralegal – factors (for example, Engel, 2008).[23]

Perhaps the greatest post-Ferguson concern among officers is that these events would create doubt in their training, causing potentially deadly hesitation. Our ethnographic field notes captured this phenomenon when Officer Brad was asked (informally and outside the context of an interview) about the events in Ferguson.[24] He said, "I think there are quite a lot of guys out there who are getting trigger-shy because of the media attention, and that can actually cause more of a risk in some situations, if they hesitate" (see also Deuchar et al, 2019). Hesitation concerns have also been amplified by a perceived lack of support from police administrators.[25] Emily, a police chief with more than two decades of law enforcement experience, stated that "some of our guys might be hesitant to do it [perform stops with the public] because they're concerned with 'Am I going to be supported if something goes bad?'" (see also Deuchar et al, 2019). Similarly, an officer (Samantha) in Adams said, "I think that they would rather throw the officer under the bus on that one than they would to take the public scrutiny [sic]" (Adams, 2019, p 1757). Novak et al (2017) hypothesized that command-level officers sought "to insulate themselves from litigation," but noted that they should be willing to deal strongly with de-policing (p 86).

Agencies have also responded in the post-Ferguson era by fortifying their departments with military-style tactics, operations, and weaponry (Kraska & Paulse, 1997). Though traditionally separate from the military in the US, policing's cultural shift has some believing there to be mission creep, whereby officers are tasked with activities traditionally performed by the military and vice versa. This erosion has been shown to inflame police–community tensions, as the public often perceives a militarized police force as an occupying army. Showing force has been particularly problematic in the wake of high-profile use-of-force incidents, because the public does not understand the need for armored vehicles and riot gear during peaceful demonstrations. Moreover, public and militarized-police confrontations have become a visual reminder, through news and social media, of the confidence crisis in law enforcement.

These results suggest that the Ferguson Effect is much more nuanced than simply de-policing. While officers believe they are more heavily scrutinized by the public and media, research reports that officer safety has improved in the post-Ferguson era. Officer beliefs, however, have prompted them to disengage in lower-visibility aspects of policing (for example, engaging with community partners, street-level encounters with the public, and traffic enforcement). Less discretionary police activities, such as the use of force, remain largely unchanged in the post-Ferguson era, according to research. Nevertheless, law enforcement fear, cynicism, and apprehension continue to grow among the ranks, leading officers to hesitate in their sworn duties and agencies to fortify themselves against perceived public and social media scrutiny.

Impact of the Ferguson Effect

Some researchers contend that the Ferguson Effect has had an impact on crime. The unintended consequence of de-policing, they argue, has caused a widespread reduction in formal social control and guardianship, which emboldens criminals (Levitt 2002; Braga et al, 2014). The public, for example, believes that crime rates are high and rising according to Pew Research Center polling (Gramlich, 2019). This belief is reinforced by increases in news and social media stories on lawbreaking (Ditton & Farrall, 2017). Crime, in the last 25 years, has been at somewhat historical lows (FBI, n.d. a; BJS, n.d. a) but recent, albeit slight, upticks have prompted researchers to look more closely at the potential connection between de-policing and crime.

Anecdotes from officers seem to agree that de-policing has increased crime. Logan, a detective with six years of experience, illustrated this point during an interview (see also Deuchar et al, 2019):

> "A lot of officers, I think, have taken a step back and aren't being so proactive, and I think the criminals and gang members see that ... Before, where you could sit out, you know, and do whatever you want to on the street corner and you'd get stopped by a police officer or at least questioned or, you know, a police officer would intervene ... now, they're just driving by and the criminals know that." (Logan, detective, Queen County Sheriff's Office)

Officers in our study were thus particularly concerned that de-policing would empower gang members. When explored empirically, however, research has not made this connection. Rosenfeld, for example, evaluated monthly property and violent crime rates before and after the events in Ferguson. He found that "only the timing of the change in property crimes is fully consistent with the Ferguson Effect ... [but] temporal consistency is not a sufficient condition to establish substantive proof" of a Ferguson Effect on crime (Rosenfeld, 2015, p 3). Likewise, Pyrooz et al (2016b) explored the Ferguson Effect on crime in their evaluation of index crimes in 81 cities pre- and post-Ferguson. They reported no change in property, violent, or overall crime rates.[26] More specifically, in NYC public scrutiny from the events in Ferguson was found to predict de-policing, according to Capellan et al, but de-policing did not predict increases in crime in their multilevel mediated analysis of monthly crime rates. Rather, they ceded that rises in NYC crime were due to "alternative causal mechanisms" (Capellan et al, 2019, p 14).

Though there is some agreement in this research that the events in Ferguson did not cause more crime, the methodological rigor of this research has been frequently called into question. MacDonald (2016a), for example, sharply criticized Pyrooz et al (2016b), and by default Rosenfeld and Wallman (2019). She contended that analyses using aggregations of cities mask crime fluctuations of cities with larger minority populations. These cities, she argues, would be the first to experience a Ferguson Effect on crime. Moreover, she noted that "cities with large Black populations, smaller white populations, and already high rates of violent crime" had "the highest homicide surges ... exactly what the Ferguson Effect would predict." Even if crime is not currently on the rise, some have argued that the real impact of the

Ferguson Effect on crime would be lagged and not happen overnight (for example, Deuchar et al, 2019).

While there may be disagreement on the Ferguson Effect's impact on crime, research appears to agree that de-policing has actually increased law enforcement efficacy. Shjarback et al (2017), for example, noted that the "hit rate" on contraband during traffic enforcement tended to be higher in the post-Ferguson era despite a decline in the number of traffic stops. This suggests that the ability of law enforcement to intervene in criminal activities was unlikely to have been impacted by the post-Ferguson era's de-policing in traffic enforcement. Similarly, Rosenfeld and Wallman (2019) found that the post-Ferguson era's decline in arrests in 53 of America's largest cities had no impact on these cities' homicide rates. In addition to increasing officer efficacy, de-policing may also alleviate some police–public discord by reducing the prevalence of more aggressive policing tactics. However, Novak et al (2017) argued that over time the effects of de-policing would fade and enforcement would likely return to normal/expected levels.

Chapter summary

In this chapter, we have combined a review of the extant literature on the Ferguson Effect and de-policing with insights from our own empirical data arising from interviews with law enforcement officers in Palm State. We have established that the lasting impact of the Ferguson Effect is difficult to predict. It is clear that in the post-Ferguson era, tragic use-of-force events have come to be viewed through a different lens as the nation becomes entrenched and mobilized in social activism. By occupying the no-man's-land of social conflict, police have become casualties of public discord. The constant bombardment of news and social media coverage of use-of-force incidents has, according to law enforcement, prompted de-policing and militarization. Moreover, their inability to carry out their impossible mandate has undermined law enforcement legitimacy in the post-Ferguson era, and left few contemporary opportunities for law enforcement to police by consent. Though the Ferguson Effect on crime continues to be debated by researchers, de-policing may have unintendedly eased police–community relations, which is explored further in subsequent chapters.

In the next two chapters, we turn more specifically to the issue of police–community relations. We chronicle the law enforcement approaches we uncovered during our fieldwork, and relate these to the guardian-versus-warrior debate.

4

Proactive Policing
of Gangs: Cops as "Guardians"

Across the next two chapters, we turn specifically to the issue of police–community relations as they pertain to predominantly Black and Hispanic neighborhoods. We chronicle the law enforcement approaches we uncovered during our fieldwork, and relate these to the guardian-versus-warrior debate. In this chapter, we draw on the context of gang culture as an illustrative context for our analysis, and begin by discussing the reactive and proactive approaches that have been used to police gang violence and criminality in minority US neighborhoods over the years. In the main body of the chapter, insights from participant observation of police deployments and interventions at our fieldwork sites are shared, complemented by the voices of law enforcement officers captured via semi-structured interviews and informal conversations. We illustrate how an increased conceptual awareness of procedural justice had emerged among these officers. Case studies of proactive, community-centered policing approaches are shared that illustrate the active attempts that officers were making to enhance positive relationships, particularly with young Black men, and prevent violence in gang-affected neighborhoods. These insights are used to illustrate the ways in which officers were increasingly viewing themselves primarily as "guardians" in their approaches to the policing of gangs and the remaining challenges.

Reactive and proactive approaches to the policing of gang violence

As we outlined in Chapter 2, racial animus between police and residents has long been a problem in the US, largely due to a "normative police practice that targets Black individuals" (Cobbina, 2019, p 5). Aggressive policing strategies are disproportionately concentrated in disadvantaged communities populated by Black and Hispanic populations, and young men often describe their repeated exposure to unwelcome police contact and report less favorable evaluations of the police in comparison to their White counterparts (Brunson & Weitzer, 2009; Solis et al, 2009).

As we noted in Chapter 1, young Black and Hispanic men are also twice as likely as Whites to self-report gang membership in adolescence, and two to four times more likely to do so in adulthood (Pyrooz & Densley, 2018a, and see Chapter 6 for further discussion on gang culture and racial discrimination). Negative perceptions of and reactions toward the police by young men who reside in low-income communities have thus traditionally arisen from reactive policing approaches that have often been used to deal with issues of gang violence within their local neighborhoods. For instance, zero-tolerance policing was introduced in 1993 at the hands of Bill Bratton, the then chief of the NYPD (Deuchar, 2013). The strategy was informed by the "broken windows" thesis, which asserts that an unrepaired broken window sends a message that nobody cares and, therefore, leads to more damage (Wilson & Kelling, 1982). The strategies put in place in New York City and the variations of them that were implemented in other locations were, therefore, based on the assumption that a police presence that targets petty offenders on the streets can help to reduce violent crime (Deuchar, 2013). Applying this to the policing of gangs, aggressive person-based approaches such as SQF were often put in place to blanket city areas with pedestrian stops as a way of deterring potentially violent individuals. However, these reactive, targeted enforcement approaches were especially felt by juvenile minority males, who were disproportionately subjected to police surveillance and SQF strategies. In turn, the strategies often had a harmful impact on community relations in disadvantaged neighborhoods (Mastrofski et al, 1995; Skogan, 2006; Brunson, 2007). As Gau and Brunson (2010) reported, police–community relations are already strained in many cities and neighborhoods (particularly in minority communities), and aggressive order maintenance focused on attempting to curb gang-related criminality "could hit these shaky alliances particularly hard" (p 273).

As the 1990s progressed, an increased focus on problem-oriented approaches to the policing of gang violence began to gain traction. Originally coined by Herman Goldstein, problem-oriented policing places an emphasis on grouping incidents as problems and the need for systematic inquiry, analysis of multiple interests in problems, and focusing on an uninhibited search for tailor-made responses (for a review, see Deuchar, 2013). This approach began to replace the primarily reactive, incident-driven "standard model of policing" with a model that required the police to be proactive in identifying underlying problems in hot-spot areas that could be targeted to alleviate issues such as gang-related crime (Weisburd et al, 2010, p 140). Related to this, focused-deterrence strategies began to emerge that sought to change offender behavior by "understanding underlying violence-producing dynamics and conditions" that sustained recurring gang violence, and through the strategic application of "enforcement and social service resources to facilitate desirable behaviors" (Braga & Weisburd, 2015, p 56). Focused-deterrence operations, often framed as problem-oriented exercises, normally drew upon a process of selecting a particular crime problem (such as gun violence related to street gangs), conducting research to identify key offenders, framing a special enforcement operation (such as the drawing of all legal tools or levers to sanction specifically active groups), matching these enforcement efforts with simultaneous efforts to direct services and the moral voices of affected neighborhoods that emerged via police–community partnerships to the same group of offenders, and communicating directly and repeatedly with targeted groups of offenders to let them know they were under scrutiny, what they can do to avoid enforcement action, and what the positive, community-centered alternatives might be (Kennedy, 2012; Braga & Weisburd, 2015). First used in the Boston Ceasefire project during the mid-1990s and later expanded to several other US locations (Braga et al, 2001; Deuchar, 2013), the operations traditionally narrowed the focus of law enforcement to those at the highest risk of becoming a perpetrator or victim of violence and to police–community partnerships, thereby adding legitimacy to the approaches (Deuchar, 2013).

Over the last two decades, there has been an increasing recognition that, while minority targeting and profiling by the police through aggressive, reactive strategies can break down trust and cooperation – and in turn increase crime rates – strategies that enhance police–resident collaboration and problem-solving can develop the type of positive relationships needed for the prevention of neighborhood problems such as gang violence (Mazerolle & Wickes, 2015). Accordingly, there has been a growing awareness that reducing gang-related crime can perhaps most effectively be achieved through approaches that focus not only on problem-solving but also on viewing community members as partners, with the added advantage of increasing positive community-police relations in the process (Connell et al, 2008).

In response to the high-profile incidents of officer-involved shootings and the increased tension between American law enforcement and ethnic minority citizens that we outlined in Chapter 2, the President's Task Force on 21st Century Policing (2015) emphasized the need to improve police–neighborhood relations in disadvantaged communities (Wolfe & Nix, 2016). The task force noted that community-oriented policing (COP) had consistently shown promise in "improving the public's support for and relationship with the police" (McLean et al, 2019, p 1). In the COP model, officers are seen as "clinicians" who engage in problem-solving with the clientele they serve. They take a proactive, long-term, preventive approach to solving problems such as gang violence as opposed to a reactive, short-term approach (Dejong et al, 2001, p 32), and this approach requires not only problem-solving and community partnership but also "organizational transformation." In short, the traditional hierarchy of the police department needs to be "flattened" in order to delegate decision-making to frontline officers who directly engage the community, view them as "co-producers" of public safety, and involve them actively in identifying and understanding the social issues that create crime, disorder, and fear (Gill et al, 2014, p 400). In spite of limited evidence from systematic reviews, an overall decline in the percentage of police departments using full-time community-oriented police officers began to emerge at the turn of the 21st century (Weisburd & Eck, 2004; Gill et al, 2014; Graziano et al, 2014).

Procedurally just policing is a related approach that is often used in tandem with community-oriented interventions. As we outlined in Chapter 2, procedural justice is based on the understanding that the criminal justice process is as important as criminal justice outcomes. Citizens will also be more likely to defer to police authority in instances of police–citizen interaction and to cooperate with the police (Tyler, 2004), including in relation to gang violence, if they view the police positively and as legitimate (Cobbina, 2019). While there is limited evidence for the crime-reduction benefits of community-based interventions, it is generally accepted that demonstrating concern for community welfare and ensuring that procedurally just processes are in place can provide some immunity to violence and crime in disadvantaged neighborhoods and encourage the co-production of crime solutions (Gill et al, 2014; Cobbina, 2019).

In addition to placing a strong emphasis on the need for increased community engagement, the President's Task Force (2015) also expressed a need for a renewed emphasis on procedural justice in policing. In particular, the task force called for a shift in officer mentality away from that of a "warrior" – an officer who sees himself as a "crime fighter battling evil" – to that of a "guardian," who "protects citizens through partnerships with the community" (McLean et al, 2019, p 2; and see the following chapter for further discussion). In particular, the guardian mindset prioritizes "service over crimefighting," and these officers are seen to emphasize building relationships with the community through non-enforcement contacts, thus increasing the public's trust in law enforcement as a critical element of democratic policing. McLean et al drew attention to the fact that the shift from "warrior cop" to "guardian officer" implies the need for cultural changes within police agencies (McLean et al, 2019, p 5). In the context of policing gangs in America, this may mean an increased need for officers to engage in building positive relationships and establishing trust with male residents. As a by-product of this approach, young men may begin to view law enforcement as more legitimate (Maguire & Katz, 2002).

Insights into proactive approaches in Palm State

During our fieldwork, we placed an emphasis on exploring how procedural-justice principles and the embracing of the guardian mentality within the context of COP approaches were prevalent in our officer narratives and in observed operational activity. Given the recognized and increasingly prevalent gang-related issues present at our fieldwork sites (which became apparent during our fieldwork), we explored these issues within the particular context of law enforcement approaches relating to gang culture. The remainder of this chapter, therefore, focuses on presenting insights from participant observation of police deployments in Palm State, complemented by the voices of law enforcement officers captured via semi-structured interviews and informal conversations that assisted us in exploring these issues (see list of participating officers, Table 3.1). In the following sections, sub-themes are explored and case studies are presented of specific police interventions that were observed in some of the neighborhoods visited.

People-changing, environment-changing "guardians" and "peace dealers"

The intertwined issues of joblessness, poverty, lack of parental guidance, and gang culture became apparent during participant observation of police ride-alongs in local neighborhoods in different parts of Palm State. Illustrations of this can be seen in the following field notes (see further insight into this from the perspective of wider practitioners in Chapter 6):

> As I ride along with Jack, a detective from Queen County Sheriff's Office, we enter one of the most socially deprived areas of Canary City. We pass by a large launderette, with multiple washing machines and people busily doing their laundry. "There are a few of these places here," Jack explains, "people just don't have room for washing machines in their houses and they can't afford them." As we move along the next street I can see large groups of young African American men hanging around on street corners on both sides of the road. It is dark and difficult to make out what they are doing, but I suspect that they may be in the middle of some drug deals. "The six shootings that have taken place in the last few days here are all related to gang feuds," Jack explains, "animosity between rival gangs ... There are no jobs out here – no tax base, no income sources. There are a lot of decent families but they are surrounded by these other guys who have no self-respect and no respect for each other – they are raised by moms on their own, with no father figures and no discipline; they are basically growing up on the streets, and learning behavior from TV." (Field notes, deployment with Queen County Sheriff's Office)

> While riding with officers in Coconut County, the police car weaves into Orange Avenue and the guys explain that this is where the 'hood really begins. "So, this is where the 'hood really starts. You'll notice a change in the buildings, and a real increase in the number of people outside, walking and sitting in the yards," Joshua explains. As I look around I can see what he means – many people of color are walking around or sitting in their front yards. Joshua points to an empty table in one of the front yards and explains that people will often sit there playing dominoes at all times of the day and night. The guys explain to me that there are lots of Haitian gangs around here. (Field notes, deployment with Coconut County Sheriff's Office)

In the presence of multiple forms of marginality (Vigil, 1988; and see further discussion in Chapter 6) and during informal conversations while on police deployments and rest breaks, officers alluded to the influence of negative role models such as rappers in encouraging gang violence and how social media was often used as a platform to glorify weapons:

> During an informal conversation with Lieutenant Samuel from Queen County Sheriff's Office, he explains that the county's gangs are neighborhood cliques that adopt some of their values and attitude from rappers who have staked a claim on Bloods membership. "They are influenced by Chris Brown and Soulja Boy, who both claim to be Bloods but neither of them actually grew up in Los Angeles ... so the guys who follow that are looking to be cool, claiming Blood. It can get them lots of money, but they mostly die young. They don't think about making it to 40 or 50, they are in it for now. Some of them are walking around with four bodies on them – they've killed four people ... it's literally self-hate, the shootings are promoted in the music and the videos. I mean, what is going on? They're slaughtering each other for nothing!" (Field notes, informal conversation, Queen County Sheriff's Office)

> Officer Daniel from Needle City Police Department explains that many young men are guided by a strong street code, where disrespect cannot be tolerated. Social media, according to Daniel, has amplified this focus where rival members continually "diss" each other on Facebook and Snapchat. As I watch the screen he scrolls through several Facebook pages of known local gang members, including a young man known to him, who is only 18 but is posing in photographs with AK-47 assault rifles along with his friends. (Field notes, informal conversation, Needle City Police Department)

In response to the prominent and evidently growing issue of gang culture and the tendency for much younger men to become involved in it, some officers were very clear on the need for proactive violence-prevention approaches. As a senior officer with over 40-years' experience, Jacob (deputy chief in the Queen County Sherriff's Office within Palm State) bemoaned the way in which the focus on COP, which had been prominent in the 1990s, had apparently dissipated during the last two decades in favor of a return to reactive "task forces fighting crime." This, he believed, had been counterproductive.

In a wider sense, he felt that the psychology tests used to judge the suitability of candidates entering American law enforcement had become overly focused on the need for rule-oriented approaches, the following of orders, and responding to targets, and were underplaying the importance of discretion and "self-thinking."

However, younger (but still senior) officers expressed their commitment to proactive, community-oriented approaches, and described why they encouraged officers to be autonomous, flexible, and to treat local citizens with dignity and respect. For instance, Samuel (a lieutenant in the same county as Jacob, and who had 20 years of police experience) claimed that he always told his officers to "treat [every local citizen] like it was your own family member." Emily (newly appointed chief of the Needle City Police Department within the same county) specifically drew attention to the need to be a "guardian," to help prevent crime in communities by supporting the youth "outreach." Many other participants also noted the importance of engaging with and responding to the community, showing concerns about social issues affecting families of gang-related offenders, and the need to connect them with relevant resources:

> "We engage the kids, the offenders, but our main component is engaging the families, engaging, like, you know, brothers, sisters, aunts, uncles, mom, dad, whoever is at the house and trying to work with them on what we can do to make the situation better, whether it is helping the offender maybe get a GED, which is high school diploma, getting him college assistance and getting some type of subsidized employment. If the offender doesn't want the help ... our secondary way of doing it is maybe the house needs some help with child care ... maybe the house needs some help with some other aspects, whether it is getting brother and sister in the school or something, whatever they need ... not just the offender but the offender's whole family." (Daniel, sergeant, Needle City Police Department)

Forman argues that community policing aims to mobilize the resources within a community, and that it rejects the discredited "warrior" approach (Forman, 2004, p 2). The above sentiments from officers like Samuel, Emily, and Daniel reflected a community-oriented focus on the need for "people-changing and environment-changing" (Mastrofski & Ritti, 2000, p 184). They appeared committed to collaborating with disadvantaged families and helping to address and reduce the impact of the complicated blend of social strains that could inflict them (Agnew, 2006) in order to mobilize and extend their assets and prevent re-offending (Deuchar et al, 2018b). During informal conversations with Daniel, he estimated that there had been a drop in violent crime in recent months due to the community-oriented and multi-agency work his department had been involved in, placing an emphasis on intervention and engagement. Senior officers in Queen County Sheriff's Office also discussed why they often engaged in wider forms of "community assistance," including sending colleagues to help paint people's houses or clean out their yards, and also playing recreational sport with youngsters and drawing on this as an opportunity to steer them in positive directions: "The community policing has to get out there and pick up a basketball and shoot with the kids and then turn around and tell the kid, 'If you do something wrong, this is the consequence of your action'" (Noah, sergeant, Queen County Sheriff's Office).

Jonathan, an officer with specific responsibility for coordinating youth justice strategy in Needle City, drew attention to how he and his colleagues increasingly collaborated with mental health counselors. They referred highly traumatized young people on for support, especially when they had challenging home lives and community contexts characterized by gang violence:

> "Literally you are living in an area where there is gunfire nightly ... a lot of our kids in this community have witnessed, you know, violence daily, you know what I mean, so a lot of times if you don't have the avenue to get it out, to talk to somebody, it gets worse ... a lot of times we've noticed that a lot of the young people that we deal with, they just need an avenue to get stuff out, and we realize without mental health professionals ... the mental health aspect, I think, that is partly our best tool that we've started using within the last year and a half." (Jonathan, officer, Needle City Police Department)

During wider discussion with Jonathan, he reflected upon his position as a Black officer taking responsibility for policing predominantly Black neighborhoods. He discussed why he felt that he was "hated and then loved." While some local residents saw his presence as a good thing and felt that there were not enough Black officers, others felt that he should not even be in law enforcement. This complements Cobinna's (2019) insights into the ambivalent views of residents in Ferguson regarding Black officers; while some Black residents in her study felt these officers were better able to understand minority communities, others reported experiences of being treated more harshly by them and resented them more than White officers. The opposition Jonathan experienced from minority residents presented him with additional opportunities for discussion, reflection, and engagement:

> "There are times I go out there on calls and people are like, 'Man, you are not even Black, you are not even Black anymore, you don't understand what we go through.' ... So I tell them, 'Listen, I was born Black, I was Black before I became an officer, I am an officer, [but] while I am an officer I am still Black, when I am retired I am gonna be Black, so it doesn't change anything.'" (Jonathan, officer, Needle City Police Department)

As Cobbina (2019, p 64) argues, the diversification of police departments in and of itself is "insufficient to improve police–minority relationships." The focus among officers, both Black and White, was thus on adopting a social-work-oriented, discursive, people-changing, and environment-changing approach to policing that involved collaborating with other agencies and discussing and attempting to build trustful relationships with minority young men and families, even in the face of hostility. Daniel also described the way members of his department actively participated in peace walks where they displayed community solidarity and actively re-engaged disadvantaged, marginalized young people, parents, and families (see further discussion in Chapter 6):

> "Once a month right now, we are still doing our peace walks, which is basically the law enforcement gets with different people from the community ... we walk along the streets and we hand out documentation that's geared towards assisting with subsidized employment, education, different types of after school programs ... they try to bring in parents and community members to speak at different things like that." (Daniel, sergeant, Needle City Police Department)

Although a reduced focus on COP had emerged within some areas of Palm State, and some evidence suggested that the cultural aspects of policing still reinforced the need for officers to view themselves as "warriors" (see further discussion in Chapter 5), many officers demonstrated a commitment to longer-term proactive approaches to prevent, for example, gang-related crime through community engagement and partnership working. Officer narratives reflected a need to demonstrate concern for the most disadvantaged, to help to reverse the negative forces that led to social exclusion, and to actively show local residents solidarity and support. These officers evidently viewed themselves as guardians and protectors of the neighborhoods they policed, "peace dealers" who placed emphasis on building relationships through "positive, non-enforcement contacts" (McLean et al, 2019, p 4). In spite of the national repercussions from Ferguson, there appeared to be an abundance of motivation among officers, at least in some areas of Palm State, to partner and engage with low-income communities that were often characterized by gang-related activity (Wolfe & Nix, 2016).

Street dialogue, "surrogate parenting," and democratic policing

As we have alluded to, the approaches previously described by officers were set within the context of local neighborhoods that had experienced high levels of gang-related feuds and shootings. These neighborhoods were also ones where Black and Hispanic young men had traditionally had negative perceptions of unfair treatment from the police (Cobbina, 2019). In contrast with Coconut County, the majority of Needle City police officers, as well as those in wider Queen County, had routinely become equipped with body-worn cameras (BWCs). Some of these officers talked about the ability of BWCs to foster a culture of accountability for both officers and citizens, and that this helped to de-escalate potentially contentious encounters with racial minority men (for further discussion, see Fallik et al, 2019; White & Malm, 2020). However, beyond the issuing of BWCs as a means of building trust and reducing confrontation, the President's Task Force (2015) had also recommended the need for building relationships with the community through non-enforcement contacts. As such, Sergeant Daniel (from the Needle City Police Department) suggested that officers in his department were actively involved in building social bridges between law enforcement and families in the neighborhood (Deuchar et al, 2018b).

Box 4.1 illustrates our observations recorded in field notes that focus on how Daniel (as a White officer) was actively involved in stepping out of his car, building rapport, and making attempts to divert young Black men away from street violence by steering them toward work schemes. At the same time, the field notes also illustrate how Calvin (an African American officer from the same department) was adopting an active role in supporting whole families with "surrogate parenting" and pastoral requirements.

Box 4.1: Police use of street engagements and "surrogate parenting" with young racial minority men

On Wednesday afternoon, as we drive into Third Street, the car slows down as I notice a group of young African American men standing on the street corner. Daniel, the White sergeant I am shadowing from the Needle City Police Department, rolls down his window and shouts, "What's up?" The guys respond by acknowledging him as he slows up. As we pull into the side of the road I notice that there are two young men on my side of the car in their 20s, and three younger men who are in their late teens on Daniel's side. All are dressed in T-shirts and jeans. "Hey, what's this vehicle you're in?" the boys on my side ask him. "Hey, man, it's fuckin' terrible. I told them I need a truck – it feels like two pounds of sausages in a ten-pound wrapper!" Daniel jokes loudly with them as they laugh, and I am immediately struck by the relaxed approach that this officer has with the young men and the rapport he has obviously built. "Hey, man, if you're interested in getting into a work scheme for 18–24-year-olds, I can get you into a program for construction, hair cutting, and all sorts of things – I got 35 spots and can get you in." The boys seem interested in the potential scheme, and Daniel tells them he will come back with more details the next day.

The next afternoon, during my second ride-along with Daniel he weaves into the parking lot for a gas station with a store attached to it. We both get out of the car and go in and get some cold drinks. As we are leaving we meet a young Black guy with dreadlocks and a smiley face who Daniel seems to know well. "Hey, you want a job?" Daniel asks the young man, and again explains to him about the job-readiness program. The guy is animatedly talking back to Daniel and laughing and joking, and they clearly have a good relationship. "Hey, I know you do a lot of rapping – what's your name again online brother?" Daniel asks, and the young man laughs and tells him his name. "Ok, I'm gonna look your shit up," he says. Again, I am struck with the strong rapport that Daniel is building with this young man.

A week later, I am in the car with an African American officer, Calvin, who tells me he needs to go and visit one of the children in the local neighborhood we are in, in Needle City. The boy's mother had called him earlier and asked him to talk to him because he has been in some trouble at home and at school. We turn into Sabal Street and park outside a local house where I can see a woman in her 50s who looks like she could be the boy's grandmother sitting on the front porch. We get out of the car and she shouts out the boy's name, Zak. The front door opens, and an African American boy of around ten years of age appears and walks up the front path toward us looking very sheepish. "Good afternoon, young man," Calvin opens, and the boy shakes his hand respectfully and says, "Good afternoon, sir." Calvin asks Zak to stand in front of him at the back of the police car, and I watch and listen to the dialogue unfold.

Calvin:	I want to ask you, young man, is there a problem with anything?
Zak:	No, sir.
Calvin:	No? There isn't a problem with anything? So what happened at school then?
Zak:	I don't like people talking about my family. I only have one friend.
Calvin:	So what do you do when things like that happen?
Zak:	I go into the bathroom and hit the wall.
Calvin:	Are you suspended from school right now?
Zak:	Yes, sir. (At this point the boy looks ashamed and I can see he is holding on to some emotion, trying hard not to cry as the officer continues to ask him questions and speaks to him very firmly.)
Calvin:	What about your grades at school?
Zak:	I took a test in reading, I got a C. I got an F in reading and an F in writing.
Calvin:	Ok, so what are you gonna do to make this problem better? I mean, I'm looking to see what the problem actually is here – you got a grandmom and a mom who really care about you, but your behavior has not been good has it? And now it's got to a point where I need to get involved – so it's clearly gone too far, am I right?
	(The boy nods and again looks upset.)
Calvin:	I'll tell you, you just can't get mad anytime you like – people call me names all the time and I can't do anything about it. So, when it happens to you, you tell someone about it or figure out how to deal with your anger. You write about it or you go and listen to music. Look at me, look into my eyes and pay attention to me – you got issues at home, haven't you?
	(The boy shakes his head.)
Calvin:	Grandma, does he listen to you at home? (The officer turns toward the grandma, who is still sitting on the porch.)
Grandma:	No, he don't listen to no one – Zak does what Zak wants to do.
Calvin:	What about your mom – if your mom asks you to do something, do you do it?
Zak:	Yes, I do it.
Calvin:	Well, obviously not, because I'm here! Okay, you're going back to school tomorrow?
Zak:	Yes.

Calvin: Okay, I'm going to come into your school tomorrow. (At this point the officer leans forward and, still speaking calmly and in a measured way, he looks right into the boy's eyes and talks in an extremely firm tone.) I *dare* you to mess up again, to disrespect your mom or your grandma – if you do I will find out, so I *dare* you to do it. Now, you go and you kiss and you hug your grandma.

At this point, Zak runs over to the porch and to his grandma. He reaches out and cuddles her, and immediately bursts into floods of tears. We walk over to the porch, and Calvin begins to have a conversation with the grandma about Zak's previous involvement with wrestling classes and the possibility of him getting involved in this again. "I'll look into that and see if we can get you involved," he says to Zak in a much more friendly tone this time. "Now, you help your mom and your grandma," Calvin says to Zak before we get ready to leave.

Evidence suggests that, post-Ferguson, some police departments have placed an emphasis on accelerating positive community engagement and efforts to be seen as humanitarian guardians within communities, in order to address their often-challenging relationships with ethnic minority youths (Solis et al, 2009; Deuchar et al, 2018a). Wider evidence has illustrated the way in which officers who adopt a community-oriented perspective in their work can sometimes take on the role of "surrogate parent" through acts of emotional support and nurturing behaviors toward children and young people in family contexts (see, for instance, McKenna et al, 2016). Box 4.1 provides illustrations of all of this. Daniel attempted to build rapport and redirect ethnic minority young men away from gangs and delinquency by actively leaving his car and engaging in humorous but supportive dialogue that also provided street-oriented young men with opportunities to find a route back into employment. Calvin went a step further, and actively played the role of surrogate parent. He disciplined a child from an African American home – on the request of his mother and perhaps in the absence of biological father – while also finding ways to nurture him through initiating the opening up of avenues for active participation in community sport (Richardson, 2009; McKenna et al, 2016).

In their own ways, the officers in the Needle City Police Department were actively building partnerships with their communities, serving as clinicians, and engaging in problem-solving in relation to neighborhood problems (Dejong et al, 2001). They were highly visible and accessible, and committed themselves to open discussion and friendly engagement, nurturing assets and capacities through early intervention and signposting to diversionary activities and positive destinations (Deuchar, 2013). They viewed themselves as protectors of society (McLean et al, 2019). In addition to their aim of keeping boys and young men away from anti-social behavior, delinquency, and crime, implicitly their approaches reflected recognition that, as agents of the State, their behavior needed to be approved by the people they served. Forming relationships and increasing the local community's trust in police were therefore seen as critical in their focus on democratic policing (McLean et al, 2019). In some cases, interviewed officers in this department articulated an opinion that suggested that working intensely to break down community barriers might help to prevent the type of public reaction that emerged in Ferguson, even when officer-involved shootings did take place in Needle City in the future.

Outreach, education, and dialogical workshops

In addition to street engagements and surrogate parenting, officers referred to more structured, partnership-oriented, community-based approaches to fostering open dialogue between police and minority ethnic juveniles. For instance, officers across both counties talked about working in schools and local youth centers. They referred to their active involvement in Gang Resistance, Education, and Training (GREAT) and Drug Abuse Resistance Education (DARE) programs. Within these interventions, some talked about drawing young people's attention to issues of peer pressure and the need to resist negative influences within their neighborhoods. However, some officers in the Coconut County Sheriff's Office felt that gang-resistance education needed to begin earlier (for further discussion, see Chapter 6), and welcomed the idea of having inputs in elementary schools:

> "Me personally, [we have] GREAT programs, which is gang resistance, education, and training ... in our middle schools ... it should actually be flip-flopped in my experience because kids in middle school, those kids are already full, you know, or knee or waist deep, in the gangs. A cop is not going to turn their head you know, make them see the light. So, it's to the point now where people don't realize that you have to catch them at a younger age to help prevention." (Joshua, officer, Coconut County Sheriff's Office)

As we illustrate in Chapter 5, our data generally indicated that there was more of a traditional focus on enforcement in Coconut County, where officers like Joshua and his partners principally viewed themselves as "soldiers on the front lines" (McLean et al, 2019, p 4), focused on the "real" police work of search, chase, and capture (Van Maanen, 1978; see also Chapter 6). However, some officers, like Joshua, clearly welcomed the idea of longer-term, proactive early intervention strategies to prevent the issues associated with gang culture (Dejong et al, 2001). Officers in Coconut County also spoke about organizing special events like "fun fests" where they brought children and young people from different communities together to try and integrate them and break down barriers. Some alluded to the need for forming partnerships with local outreach services in hot-spot crime areas. While they saw this as building community partners and agencies as "co-producers" of public safety (Gill et al, 2014, p 400), they also viewed it as a means of enhancing enforcement strategies by cultivating informants. In short, Ryan described how some of his department's community partners would simultaneously try to redirect young gang members down more positive paths by signposting them to relevant agencies while also keeping officers informed of potential escalation in 'at-risk' behavior:

> "We support and work with a group that's been put together called "Regenerating the City." And basically they try to find, identify these guys that are out there committing violent crimes, gang crimes, or at least are gang members – and they're trying to draw them away … They take them to the housing authority, they'll then take them to school, they use outreach workers that are guys from the community that they live in who made the right choices … we work with them … we meet about probably once a month with them … they're able to see and hear things that we're not able to see and hear because they're really part of the community, and they'll turn around and tell us, 'Hey, you know, this guy, he's dangerous, he's armed, he's talking about doing this or doing that,' and they'll drop us a heads-up or a warning."
> (Ryan, sergeant, Coconut County Sheriff's Office)

In Queen County, community partnership was viewed more squarely through the lens of social support and prevention, rather than placing a collateral focus on finding informants. A dedicated civilian gang prevention coordinator (who had a social work background) was posted there; she worked closely with the Needle City Police Department to identify families whose children were involved in (or on the periphery of) gangs, and worked with parents to help signpost these young men into after-school, diversionary, recreational, and educational programs with the help of wider agencies and institutions.

As the chief of the Needle City Police Department, Emily was particularly focused on partnership work, on early intervention, and on helping young people to progress in positive directions. She recognized that community engagement and partnership should be seen as an end in itself, a means of nurturing legitimacy in the eyes of the public, rather than (as perhaps was the case in Coconut County) something that was covertly still tied to enforcement agendas and underpinning "warrior" mindsets (McLean et al, 2019):

> "We're in the schools, we're in the parks, we're in programs all over the place. Our city is very progressive when it comes to trying to create opportunities for people to better themselves. Whether it's work, trying to get jobs for people, or work training, trying to help them get GED's, trying to do all these different things. So, if the police department works in conjunction with our civilian city leaders, that just shows that we're all tied together and working for the same thing ... I think people are starting to understand it's not us versus them. You know, we only have the power that the community gives us ... transparency is huge, so that there's no secret spy mission behind the scenes to be tough guys all the time." (Emily, police chief, Needle City Police Department)

Box 4.2 illustrates our observations of one of the Kids and Cops dialogical workshops initiated by the Needle City Police Department. Within these settings, young people who were often on the edges of gang-related crime and actively involved in juvenile justice community service programs met and engaged in open discussion with officers, public defense lawyers, attorneys, and representatives from juvenile justice, community outreach, and the clergy. This was projected by law enforcement officers and their relevant partners as a means of building bridges and trust while also educating young people about alternatives to crime.

As we have previously presented (see Chapter 2), procedural justice involves treating people with dignity and respect, being neutral and transparent in decision-making, and conveying trustworthy motives (Mazerolle et al, 2013). Some research (Carr et al, 2007) suggests that young people care about procedural justice even more than adults, and simply want officers to be professional, responsive, honest, and fair.

Box 4.2: Kids and Cops workshop in Needle City

As I gaze around the large meeting room in the local town hall, I notice that there are seven law enforcement officers around the table. There is also a female staff member from the attorney's office, seven young people (all young males, who are around 14–17-years-old, and all but one of whom are Black or Hispanic), two public defenders, two members of the juvenile justice department, a local outreach worker (Dwayne), and Paul, a religious pastor, with both of the latter facilitating the session. The purpose of the workshop is to bring juvenile first-time offenders to participate in discussion with members of law enforcement and the criminal justice system as part of the conditions of their community service programs. If the young men participate actively and well in all sessions, they can have their attendance recognized as being part of their community sentencing conditions.

Sergeant Daniel talks about how he works on the basis of forming positive relationships in the communities: "Things like this meeting for me are the norm, they should be integrated into policing. But I think officers need to be more diversified, and move more toward community outreach. That is definitely the direction we are going in with our new chief." Daniel then turns toward one of the young men sitting at the table, "I mean, I talked to you today on the streets – did you enjoy it when we just talked – rather than having someone just harassing you on corners?" The boy looks up and begins to nod. One of the other cops asks him if he trusts the police and the young man replies, "Yes, I do." Dwayne then turns and looks around the table "What about the rest of you?" Mick, a young African American boy, looks up. "No, I don't – there's too many stories, when the police come I just get paranoid and I don't know why." One of the White police officers asks him why he feels that way and if he has had any experiences that have influenced this reaction. The young man goes on to describe an incident when the cops were chasing him and his friends with dogs. "They caught us, and one of my friends got bit. I got on the floor and I wasn't resisting, but the cop punched me on the floor – so now I am wary." One of the other Hispanic young men who is at the opposite side of the table then speaks up, "I don't trust them, the police lie in their reports." Several of the other young men then talk about how they feel paranoid when they see the police: "In here they are okay ... but on the streets, when you see them the first thing you think is ... they're coming for me," they add.

Paul sets up the flip chart and asks people to consider what makes a good police officer. He asks Robert, one of the young Hispanic men, to contribute first. "Sharing respect for the community," he comments. Jermaine, a young

African American man with dreadlocks, then comments, "They need to lead by example." Jennifer, a White female officer comes in: "I think caring about the community is important – if they don't care, they shouldn't be there." Donny, one of the other young Black men talks about the need to "read people their rights." And one of the public defense lawyers, Lisa, adds, "Giving equal treatment – it doesn't matter what color you are." Ricardo, a young Hispanic man, then comments, "They need to follow proper procedure – you know, citizens have rights; most police don't go by that – they still search you even if they have no warrant." Christine, one of the public defense lawyers, talks about the fact that good officers are those who do not just do the job for the money. Keith, from the juvenile justice department, then adds, "He needs to know his community, the families and people who live there. If someone comes in and doesn't see activity for what it is, he will arrest you." Finally, Lyndsay, who works for the attorney's office, adds that there needs to be "integrity – they need to have a moral compass and be honest."

Paul then asks the group what they see as a police officer's job. "We haven't heard from Mr Gray tonight," he says in a rather authoritarian tone as he turns toward one of the young White men, Brandon. The young man smiles and says, "They need to get to know people." "Okay, and Mick – it looks like there is something on your mind …" he says as he turns toward Mick. "Well, instead of being angry at people if they catch someone, they should want to help – instead of going against us, they shouldn't be mad and do extra stuff to help us." It occurs to me just how insightful this young man is. However, Candice, from the juvenile justice department, clearly did not hear the boy well from the other side of the room. "Are you talking to yourself or to the officers? Speak up – let's all get it – the whole reason we are here is to hear one another." I feel she is a little unfair on the young man since speaking in front of these professionals would be daunting for adults let alone for juveniles like him.

Paul then asks the young men if they feel they can approach cops when incidents happen. One young man responds, "I can't do that." Lyndsay asks if it might be different if the beat cops were out on foot rather in their cars. Mick responds, "No, I don't think people would feel comfortable with the police walking around." At this point, Calvin, a Black officer, begins to laugh somewhat cynically. "I'm sorry, but people say they feel uncomfortable with us walking down the street?" he says incredulously, and I can feel the tension emanating from him. "We're human beings! I wave at people and see people spit on the ground sometimes – I don't care who you are or what color you are … I wave at people, I engage with them, but I know my approaches are not of the norm … I'm not out there harassing people. But the times I've got out of the car to talk to people and they've walked away ..." I sense that this officer has had a nerve touched, and he is beginning to sound defensive. There is silence in the room.

Jennifer, the White female officer, then breaks the silence: "If I see an officer mistreating someone, I feel I need to point that out – I will say, 'Hey guys, knock it off,' but equally if I see a citizen being disrespectful I'll jump in – we all need to respect each other. In these sessions, we put names to faces and then it's harder to be disrespectful. Like with Larry," she says turning toward one of the young Black men in the room, "I'm not going to disrespect him because I know him."

Sergeant Daniel then asks the young men to ensure that they begin to speak up more next week. "I know a lot of you on the streets, and you're loud – so do speak up," he says. Paul summarizes that he feels we are all part of the community and we have all got to be "committed to the work." As I look around the room, I note that even after a two-hour session the young men are still engaged – still listening and attentive, even although it is now 8 pm and they have been participating in this workshop for almost two hours.

However, although experiences of procedural justice can evidently improve young people's perceptions of police legitimacy and their willingness to engage with officers in a wider sense, as we alluded to at the beginning of this chapter, a wide range of evidence in the US has illustrated the way racial minority males often feel that they are treated with suspicion in the eyes of officers and are subjected to heightened, disproportionate, and unwarranted police scrutiny (see, for instance, Mastrofski et al, 2002; Alpert et al, 2005; Skogan, 2006; Gau & Brunson, 2010).

As Box 4.2 illustrates, the predominantly ethnic minority young men who participated in the Kids and Cops workshops expressed a considerable degree of mistrust in officers due to previous experiences of perceived injustice in the way police reports on their behavior had been handled, instances of police brutality, or apparently unwarranted and/or unexplained experiences of SQF (Mastrofski et al, 1995; Skogan, 2006; Brunson, 2007; Deuchar, 2013). This had evidently led to the described feelings of tension and paranoia among the young men when the police entered their neighborhoods as a result of anticipatory anxiety that officers may use aggressive confrontation strategies or treat them disrespectfully (Deuchar et al, 2018b). The young men had evidently become involved in minor offending behavior, and had been referred to participate in the workshops as a condition of their assigned community service. Within this context, officers in Needle

City evidently viewed the workshops as a means of mobilizing the youth resources within the community, building cooperative ties and networks with the young men, and enhancing perceptions of police legitimacy (Forman, 2004; McLean et al, 2019). The officers were at pains to draw attention to themselves as human beings, not just officers. They were keen to highlight their ongoing work in the community and their commitment to being approachable, treating people with respect, and helping to care for local citizens. These goals were often also conveyed to us as researchers during wider interviews and informal conversations with officers who participated in the workshop sessions, although practitioners beyond law enforcement sometimes had different views on this (see discussion, Chapter 6).

Through partnerships formed with outreach workers, criminal justice representatives, and the clergy, the Kids and Cops workshops presented police with an opportunity to give disadvantaged young men a voice, to ascertain their views on the police, and to bring an array of perspectives to the table. On the surface, the workshops presented opportunities for practitioners and youth to be brought together in unconventional ways to foster deliberative dialogue that lent itself to active listening, critical thinking, reasoned argument, potential reciprocity, and trust (Deuchar et al, 2015). However, it was also evident that the institutional power dynamics remained fundamentally unchallenged. Some officers, like Calvin (who we noted earlier was also actively involved in elements of surrogate parenting in minority family contexts), displayed a sense of defensiveness against any perceived negative reactions toward police presence in local neighborhoods. Practitioners in the room, some of whom were partners of law enforcement (perhaps with the exception of public defense lawyers), seemed unaware of the intimidating ethos that the young men were being exposed to, insisting that they "speak up" or pointedly addressing them in authoritarian tones and forcing them to contribute to the discussion.

Although officers with the Needle City Police Department and their community and judicial partners were attempting to signal their commitment to proactive, emancipatory practices that empower, a web of social control (Friere, 1972; Giroux, 2005), stigmatism and oppression still permeated the underpinning rationale for and dialogue within the workshop sessions (Deuchar & Bhopal, 2017; see further illustrations in Chapter 6). Young men were brought to the sessions as a condition of their community sentences and therefore were expected to contribute and perform as part of a judicial system that tends to oppress them rather than empower them. Furthermore, the young men highlighted largely negative and challenging experiences with officers beyond the workshop, and such sentiments were often left hanging and not adequately addressed – or in some cases, rebuked by individual officers.

As we discussed in Chapter 2, procedural justice is promoted when the "agent of authority listens or otherwise receives input, maintains a neutral stance, and treats parties with respect" (Taylor & Lawton, 2012, p 417). Although the workshops were premised on police demonstrating an active ability to listen, neutrality was still lacking. It could be argued that the young men – in spite of willing attempts on their behalf to participate actively in a somewhat intimidating environment where they were surrounded by agents of social control – were in some cases still treated with a degree of coercion as opposed to compassion, persuasion, and responsiveness (Atkinson, 2003; Woof, 2016). In a wider sense, although many of the officers in our sample articulated a strong commitment to listening to, and communicating and building relationships with, members of disadvantaged communities, several also acknowledged ongoing challenges in terms of police investigations that relied on citizen cooperation and engagement. As we alluded to in Chapter 3, referencing the perspective of Sergeant Ryan, members of local communities were evidently still reluctant to engage with officers during their investigations relating to gang-related shootings. This was due to the stubborn persistence of the "no snitching" rule (see also Chapter 6) and the perception of police as authoritarian figures in society:

> "You take places like [Canary City], you can go in there and have a [gang-related] shooting, over a hundred rounds fired, six houses shot, five cars hit, a hundred misses – and nobody saw anything." (Andrew, detective, Queen County Sheriff's Office)

> "Still a lot of issues, always gonna be issues. We're not liked. I hate to say it, that's just my personal opinion, we're not liked. We're not liked. In low-income areas, we're not liked." (Calvin, officer, Needle City Police Department)

Herbert stated that "the dilemma of legitimacy plagues no other state institution more doggedly than the police" (Herbert, 2006, p 481). In the post-Ferguson period, it was evident that law enforcement officers – at least in some of our fieldwork sites – displayed a commitment to procedural justice and were very keen to ensure that communities of color regarded their agencies as legitimate. In their attempts to police gang culture, they were evidently making active attempts to adopt a guardian mentality, engaging in pastoral and trust-building interventions to foster reconciliation. This was particularly evident in the Needle City Police Department in the form of dialogical workshops, street dialogues, and surrogate parenting approaches. However, the historical legacy of racial animus between police and residents within our fieldwork sites (as discussed in Chapter 2), combined with the tendency of some law enforcement officers to display authoritarianism and defensiveness against perceived criticism, may help to explain why evident distrust emerged that still hampered police investigations related to gang-related crime. As Calvin himself admitted, and repeated four times during the above extract, there was a lingering feeling among officers that they simply were "not liked."

Chapter summary

In this chapter, we have briefly reviewed the reactive and proactive approaches that have been used to police gang violence and criminality in the US over the years. We have discussed how the President's Task Force on 21st Century Policing recommended the re-emergence of COP strategies to help improve relations between officers and communities while also emphasizing the importance of procedural justice and the privileging of the "guardian" officer mindset. The latter prioritizes community partnership and service, whereas the "warrior" cop mentality focuses exclusively on crime fighting (McLean et al, 2019). The main body of the chapter has presented insights from participant observation of police deployments and interventions in Palm State, complemented by the voices of law enforcement officers captured via semi-structured interviews and informal conversations.

Procedural justice principles and the embracing of the guardian mentality within the context of COP approaches were particularly evident in one of our county divisions, Queen County, and were most acutely prioritized in one of its police departments – Needle City. As we will explore further in the next chapter, officers in Coconut County principally viewed themselves as warriors focused on enforcement, although some still clearly welcomed the notion of longer-term, proactive early intervention strategies to prevent the issues associated with gang culture and to build community reciprocity and trust. However, some of these same officers also viewed the latter as a means of enhancing enforcement strategies through creating informants.

Conversely, Queen County appeared to place more of a genuine emphasis on community partnership as a means of violence prevention and of building trustful and reciprocal relationships that would enhance police legitimacy (Tyler, 2004; Cobbina, 2019). In the Needle City Police Department, this was expressed in eclectic ways, including through the use of street dialogues with young Black males, surrogate parenting, partnerships with local agencies and practitioners, and providing community assistance for families and recreational activities for juveniles. Officers actively served as clinicians, engaged in problem-solving, and prioritized the building of community trust and re-engagement of young men to get them away from the grip of gang activity by nurturing their assets and signposting them toward positive destinations (Deuchar, 2013; Deuchar et al, 2018b). In addition to their aim of keeping boys and young men away from gangs and delinquency, the officers' approaches implicitly reflected a recognition that, as agents of the State, they needed to enhance their sense of legitimacy in these communities by demonstrating procedural justice values, perhaps in order to avoid a Ferguson-type incident emerging in the future (Tyler, 2006).

Although our data suggested that an increased conceptual awareness of procedural justice had emerged among the sampled officers, even in Needle City, where the guardian officer mentality appeared most prioritized among the officers we worked with, there were continuing challenges. During organized, structural dialogical workshops with young men that appeared to be guided by democratic policing (McLean et al, 2019), institutional power dynamics remained fundamentally unchallenged. Social control, stigmatism, and oppression still permeated the underpinning rationale for the dialogue within the workshop sessions. The overarching concerns of the participating young men regarding differential, aggressive treatment at the hands of law enforcement were never fully addressed during the dialogues (Deuchar & Bhopal, 2017).

Although the dialogues elucidated that more could be done, solution-based responses were lacking. Furthermore, the young men were expected to contribute as part of a judicial system that still oppressed rather than empowered them, and were treated with some degree of coercion (Atkinson, 2003; Giwa et al, 2014; Woof, 2016; Deuchar & Bhopal, 2017). Wider officer narratives suggested that the historical legacy of racial animus between police and residents in local racial and ethnic minority neighborhoods still led to levels of distrust that hampered police investigations related to gang-related crime. This was perhaps due to enduring issues relating to police culture that supported the "warrior" tendencies among police officers (McLean et al, 2019). It is to this issue that we turn our attention in the next chapter.

5

Reactive Policing
of Gangs: Cops as "Warriors"

In this chapter, we build on the previous discussion by exploring the "warrior" mindset in policing. This mindset is reflected in the highly controversial militaristic strategies that have characterized contemporary policing in many of America's disadvantaged crime-prone communities. Residents in these locations are often the recipients of disorder-enforcement, SQF, and zero-tolerance crackdowns. The conceptualization of warrior policing underlines the concern that officers who see themselves principally as warriors ignore the inherent consequences of forcible approaches in these communities. Here we define the contrasting roles of police as guardians and as warriors, followed by a critique of warrior policing and the impact of aggressive, and often reactive, enforcement strategies. We also explore the history of militarism and aggressive enforcement in the US, along with further insights from interviews with our sample of police officers and from our participant observation during deployments.

The warrior/guardian framework

In the 1960s, psychologist Abraham Maslow stated that "it is tempting, if the only tool you have is a hammer, to treat everything as if it were a nail." (Maslow, 1966, p15). Maslow's hammer refers to a form of confirmation bias involving an overreliance on a familiar tool. When someone acquires a tool or a skill, there is a tendency to be influenced by its function and utility, which leads one to see opportunities to use that tool or skill everywhere. There is also a tendency to see the world through the narrow lens of one's profession. Policing is not the only occupation that is susceptible to this bias, but due to the high stakes associated with police work, the overreliance on the use of force is an ongoing concern. This heavy reliance on force also recognizes the role of organizational culture in shaping norms and sustaining the practices that influence the behavior of personnel (Paoline, 2003). Within this framework, police leadership may tacitly encourage officers to adopt behaviors that are consistent with the guardian or warrior policing orientations (Stoughton, 2016).

The overreliance on force can be understood within this context. Research suggests that the warrior mindset is a main catalyst for the problematic police–citizen encounters that have elicited increasing public outrage (Pyrooz et al, 2016b; Wolfe & Nix, 2016; Nix & Wolfe, 2016, 2017; Shjarback et al, 2017; Nix et al, 2018; McLean et al, 2019). There is also empirical support for the inference that strategies reflecting the police's role as guardians will help to ameliorate tensions between police and residents and ultimately improve legitimacy perceptions (Tyler & Wakslak, 2004; Stoughton, 2015). As suggested in the previous chapter, this is a view held by an increasing number of police officers, as many support the use of community-oriented strategies for effectively engaging with residents. This is noteworthy given that the police-as-guardian philosophy is driven by the principles of community policing.

There is a great deal of support for the notion that police will not be able to do their jobs effectively without the support of the community, and that they must therefore take intentional steps to use "softer" and more humane methods when interacting with residents (Deuchar et al, 2019; McLean et al, 2019). Consistent with this notion is the police's role as guardians. As referenced in the previous chapter, these officers defend the community by operating as part of the community, and they demonstrate empathy while utilizing procedural justice principles during encounters with residents (Rahr & Rice, 2015). While the guardian mindset might not be an explicit part of agency policy, it can be evident on an individualized basis through the conduct of officers who embrace this mindset. This is reflected in the following excerpt from an interview with Jonathan, an officer who functioned in the role of juvenile coordinator within a special community-response division in the Needle City Police Department:

> "This is a different way of giving back to the community. This is different because this is more of a community-based program, so you ... interact with the community ... interact with families at different levels. [Unlike regular police patrol] this is more the long-term program where I get to really know the families, I get to know the inner

workings of the families, the makeup of the family, I get to know the kids' birthdays, family events, you know, I get to go to the schools and interact with the youth there, I also interact with the siblings as well … I can leave a lasting impression on them that can help to breach that gap between law enforcement and the community." (Jonathan, officer, Needle City Police Department)

This perspective highlights the importance of building trust in the community through community outreach programs. Jonathan embraced the guardian mindset and saw great value in developing relationships within the community, despite the absence of an agency-wide policy on community policing. This is also consistent with research regarding officers who embrace the guardian mindset and are inclined to make warm connections with residents. Such activities can elicit public trust, and as a result, people might be more inclined to be forthcoming with information to assist police with their investigations (Manning, 1984; Tyler & Fagan, 2008; Tyler et al, 2014).

Conversely, the cops-as-warriors orientation prioritizes officer safety and crime fighting as the main mission of police, which is gradually ingrained in many officers during academy training (Van Maanen, 1974; Skolnick, 2011). Stoughton stated that the warrior mindset refers to a "deep-bone commitment to survive a bad situation no matter the odds or difficulty, to not give up even when it is mentally and physically easier to do so" (Stoughton, 2015, p 226). This reflects the valorization of self-sacrifice and grit which is often coupled with a militaristic brand of heroism. The warrior mindset also relies heavily on the use of force. It elevates legally sanctioned force as the guiding principle of policing (Stoughton, 2016), given that police officers are constantly engaged in a battle between good and evil, with the survival of law enforcement officers as a primary objective (Stoughton, 2016; McLean et al, 2019). The following quote from Officer Calvin depicts the importance of the use of force as a key tool for law enforcement:

"You have to have it though. It's like a child. You tell a child something and they don't listen, and then you discipline them. They remember: If I do this again, here's my consequence, here's what's going to happen. You need community-based policing … to try and help the community, but on the other hand you don't want it to be a crutch or something for them to say, 'Okay, well they're all about the community, if I do this I'll be able to get away with it.' So, I think that's where the enforcement side comes in." (Calvin, officer, Needle City Police Department)

A deterrence analogy about parenting was used here to draw attention to the principal role of police as law enforcers. It is a belief among some officers that too much community policing could embolden criminals. They believe that what is needed is a strong focus on the war against criminal forces, which is one of the hallmarks of warrior policing. This rationale undermines effective community relations, and depending on the types of enforcement strategies used, it could also undermine trust by promoting a battle between *us* and *them*. In some communities, this warrior mindset seems to uphold a complex of superiority in which police sustain a condescending distinction between themselves and civilians (Rahr & Rice, 2015).

This framing of the warrior cop is consistent with the traditional policing mindset discussed by John Van Maanen and others in the 1970s. Traditional policing was characterized by forceful and uncompromising conduct, which is an essential part of "real police work" (Van Maanen, 1978, p 227). Police attain an exclusive status that only law enforcement personnel can understand, which creates a divide between police and residents. Van Maanen (1978) also typifies police interactions with the public as encounters with "suspicious persons," "assholes," and "know-nothings." The following quote from a veteran patrol officer summarizes the "asshole" sentiment:

> "I guess what our job really boils down to is not letting the assholes take over the city. Now, I'm not talking about your regular crooks. They're bound to end up in the joint anyway ... What I'm talking about are those shitheads out to prove they can push everybody around ... They're the ones that make it tough on the decent people out there. You take the majority of what we do and it's nothing more than asshole control." (Van Maanen, 1978, p 222)

The conduct of officers who embraced this perspective was often characterized by activities of coercion and control. This also impacted how citizens' complaints were viewed by police, as many officers saw themselves as above reproach based on the notion that police are different from regular people and uniquely trained to risk their lives and battle crime.

There is also a racial component to this framework. While warrior policing is typically presented in race-neutral terms, its focus on responding to the threat of violence may reinforce a social context that conflates Black communities with violence (Collins, 2004; Welch, 2007; Russell-Brown, 2009; Muhammad, 2011; Anderson, 2012; Epp et al, 2014; Owusu-Bempah, 2017). The socio-political context of race in America has been shaped by the policing of drugs and violence, and the need for warrior policing was cemented in the American consciousness (Forman, 2017). The crack epidemic of the 1980s helped to perpetuate this need, as images of Black men being arrested became a part of the nightly news. The war against drugs, particularly as it relates to the crack epidemic, enshrined the notion that "police must be warriors, aggressive and armored, working ghetto corners as an army might patrol enemy territory" (Forman, 2017, p 156).

In addition to concerns about the social construction of race, aggressive masculinity symbolized by warrior garb and weaponry is often enacted and justified through warrior policing. Kraska (2007, p 506) used the term "hypermasculinity" as a way of referring to the masculine skills and personality traits associated with crime fighting. This presents a picture of the street cop as a courageous and heroic "hard charger" who has mastered the art of violence (Hunt, 1984; Herbert, 2001). The following field notes, based on the researcher's observations of a gang unit in Palm State, show the frustration that some officers feel due to public constraints that prevent them from engaging in the tough, "masculine" police work that they believe is required in certain situations:

> I ask the guys if they can still do car chases, since the messages from [Coconut County] seemed to suggest otherwise. "We still do chases," Joshua replies, "if you run from us we would chase you, and we would crash you out if you are a known felon, but with the new policy being brought in the chase has to meet certain criteria. You know, our job is to catch the bad guys, and we end up having to let some of them go – they have to be a known felon involved in violence – but once we get on you, you won't get away, and we'll bring in helicopters and dogs." It occurs to me that these guys are somewhat frustrated at the lack of opportunity for robust physical action in policing nowadays and feel they have been disempowered. (Field notes, informal conversation, Coconut County Sheriff's Office)

Here, the notion that "bad guys" were being let go due to new rules and guidelines was a growing source of frustration. In this vein, the officers being interviewed here conform to the image of the warrior cop who embraces a masculine persona, and would therefore not respond enthusiastically to the current environment that scrutinizes the conduct of police officers. Among those who adhere to this ethos, policing is mythologized as a test of agility and strength, as interactions with citizens are viewed as a contest of masculinity, with clerical tasks involving paperwork being devalued as "feminine" (Hunt, 1984; Herbert, 2001; Cooper, 2008; Carlson, 2019). The valorization of this notion of warrior masculinity further entrenches and legitimizes the aggressive policing of people of color and raises concerns about the consequences of police militarization in America.

Police militarization

Police militarization provides a context for understanding the role of police as warriors and the overreliance on the use of force. Police militarization refers to the tendency of law enforcement agencies to take on the characteristics of the military. Researchers have stated that modern policing began to look more and more like the armed forces as they incorporated military characteristics, weapons, uniforms, technology, equipment, organizational hierarchy, language, values, and behavior (Kraska & Cubellis, 1997; Kraska & Kappeler, 1997; Kraska, 2007; Balko, 2014; Lieblich & Shinar, 2018). Militarism, the conceptual foundation for militarization, refers to the beliefs, values, and assumptions that emphasize violence and the threat of violence as the most appropriate and effective means for problem-solving and reducing crime (Eide & Thee, 1980; Bergbahn, 1982; Kraska, 2007). The following excerpts from an account about drug raids in Coconut County highlight officer reliance on militaristic approaches and the use of force:

> As the police truck pulls out onto the main road, I can feel a rush of anticipation and slight anxiety as I don't know what lies ahead. I begin to strike up a conversation with the officer who sits beside me in the back of the crowded vehicle. His name is Steve and he is around 35, with a lean appearance and a black beard. He tells me he spends time regularly going out with the SWAT [Special Weapons and Tactics] team, and I ask him whether he has ever shot someone. He says he has and I ask him how it felt. "It doesn't feel good at the time, but I knew there was no alternative and I took comfort in that. There are

honestly no issues lingering in me from it because I know that we did everything we could and we protected the lives of other innocent people by using deadly force ..."

I ask the officers in the truck why the unit would take firearms with them on a house operation of this kind. Dave, another young officer sitting next to Steve, responds: "If there are drugs involved and there is a known dealer, when they know we are arriving and they are being taken into custody they will either try to destroy the evidence or will fight back. So, we have our Glock 21 pistols with us, but we also have longer-range submachine guns and spray – the situation can escalate or de-escalate depending on the reaction of the people involved." The guys explain to me that the people who are selling the drugs could be gang members, but as far as they know they are only selling marijuana ...

The truck stops alongside the front yard of the house, and as one of the cops opens the side door I can feel the anticipation of what is about to happen building up inside of me – adrenaline begins to kick in as we all pile out of the vehicle. There are around seven guys in front of me – one at the front with a large black shield with "Sheriff" emblazoned on it, who is holding a semiautomatic machine gun, and another six behind him. As we move towards the house I notice that Steve, Dave, and several of the other guys deliberately point their Glock 21s towards the windows of the house as we pass, just in case anyone begins to shoot from there. We reach the front door of the house and the officer at the front taps the door. I realize it is open and the battering ram is not required. The guys move swiftly in through the door, shouting "Sheriff's Office, we have a search warrant. Sherriff's Office, no one move!" (Field notes, deployment with Coconut County Sheriff's Office)

These observations depict the use of a militarized approach involving tactical units and strategies that are like a military operation. Police were deployed in a disadvantaged area to raid a house where marijuana was reportedly being sold. This deployment was deemed to be a success given that the officers made arrests without having to use deadly force; however, the need to use this militarized approach reflects a theme in American policing.

In the deployment of militarized policing there is a presumption of threat that is reflected in the anticipation of violence and the forceful response that follows. Police militarization is often not directed at individuals as it relies on collective assumptions about the potential for violence in the community. One of the most obvious signs of police militarization is the acquisition of military equipment, vehicles, and weapons (Kraska, 2007; Campbell & Campbell, 2010; Balko, 2014), as evidenced in the gradual development of military-styled policing throughout the US (Maguire & King, 2004).

The growth of paramilitary policing units in the post-civil-rights era was documented by Kraska and colleagues as they addressed the development of Special Weapons and Tactics (SWAT) teams, which typically use surplus military weapons and equipment. SWAT teams were created to respond to dangerous criminal events, terrorist attacks, and hostage situations (Beck, 1972; Kraska & Cubellis, 1997; Kraska & Kappeler, 1997), and as these units became more common in the 1980s, they were increasingly used for law enforcement activities such as proactive patrols and the serving of warrants (Kraska & Cubellis, 1997; Dobrin et al, 2018). This trend is now well integrated into contemporary policing in terms of practice and in popular depictions of policing in art and entertainment.

As stated previously, some have argued that militarization was empowered through the war on drugs and later through the war on terror, which led to a process of police militarization (Lieblich & Shinar, 2018). It was suggested that American policing sustains this war mentality, with SWAT teams conducting frequent raids on private homes (Balko, 2014). It was also concluded that the vast majority of these raids are for public order offenses, which are consensual crimes involving willing participants, and where the victim is the State, the judicial system, or society at large (Balko, 2014). Furthermore, such forcible responses were once reserved as the last option to defuse a dangerous situation, but they are increasingly being used as a primary problem-solving tool and the first option to apprehend criminals (Balko, 2014; Lieblich & Shinar, 2018).

Recent criticisms of the militaristic tendencies of police cite the increasing public outrage regarding the police response to the civil unrest following the deaths of Michael Brown in Ferguson, Missouri, in 2014, and Freddie Gray in Baltimore, Maryland, in 2015. In the aftermath of these tragic events, the militaristic deployment of police sparked a national debate about aggressive police strategies and the unintended consequences of militarization (Moule et al, 2019). As these events unfolded, news broadcasts depicted footage of heavily armored police wearing camouflage and combat gear pointing military-style weapons at civilians (Dolan et al, 2014; Cobbina, 2019).

While some argue that a militaristic response is necessary in order to effectively deal with potentially violent demonstrations and maintain public safety (Madhani, 2014; Turner & Fox, 2017), others have expressed concern about civil rights violations, the impact of military force on civil liberties in local communities, and the potential damage to public trust in the police (American Civil Liberties Union, 2014; Lynch, 2014; Madhani, 2014; Paul, 2014; President's Task Force on 21st Century Policing, 2015; Cobbina, 2019). Public trust is linked to the effectiveness of police, and if people are concerned that law enforcement is encroaching upon their civil liberties, they will be less inclined to be supportive of police actions in the community (Davis & Silver, 2004; Moule et al, 2019).

The reasons for the increasing reliance on militaristic strategies are unclear. Studies show that crime rates do not predict the increased use of paramilitary units (Kraska & Cubellis, 1997; Kraska & Kappeler, 1997). Alternatively, some suggest that federal funding initiatives might explain this trend given that they provided local police with increased access to surplus military equipment (Pennella & Nacci, 1997; Balko, 2014). One such initiative is the 1033 Program, enacted as part of the National Defense Authorization Act of 1997, to facilitate federal equipment exchanges and enable police departments to gain more access to military equipment (US House Committee on Armed Services, 2014). Moreover, after the terrorist attacks involving the loss of thousands of lives on September 11, 2001, additional federal funding streams were created to develop and implement new technologies and acquire more military equipment for local law enforcement (Balko, 2014; Chaffetz & Cummins, 2016). According to recent studies, 80 percent of US counties received equipment through the 1033 Program between 2006 and 2013 (Delehanty et al, 2017; Radil et al, 2017), and as of 2018, almost 50 percent of police agencies in the country had participated in the program (Defense Logistics Agency, 2018).

It is noteworthy that President Barack Obama issued an executive order in 2015 curtailing access to some surplus military equipment and weapons that were made available through the 1033 Program, due to concerns about the impact of aggressive militaristic policing (Korte, 2015). Two years later, President Donald Trump rescinded Obama's executive order due to concerns about public safety and the safety and effectiveness of police officers (Goldman, 2017). Attorney General Jeff Sessions also criticized the Obama-era executive order, claiming that the restrictions on the police went too far, and that concerns about the police use of military-style weapons in local communities were superficial and should not be prioritized above public safety needs (Ebert, 2017).

Warrior policing in the "hood"

While aggressive policing strategies have received support from politicians and a segment of the public (Balko, 2013), increasing scrutiny and negative publicity in the post-Ferguson era has led to more public outrage toward this style of policing than ever before (Deuchar et al, 2019). The degree to which law enforcement has been criticized by the public through emerging forms of media is unprecedented, as controversial encounters between police and citizens, often involving the deaths of young Black men, have sparked an ongoing national debate and shaped the politics of the past decade (Cobbina, 2019). These controversial and often tragic encounters reflect the aggressive forms of policing that are now almost ubiquitous across the landscape of law enforcement, and which have also become deeply rooted in police culture (Carlson, 2019).

The *hood*, a colloquial term used to describe urban ghettos, essentially comprises a suspect class of recipients of this forceful style of policing. Such vulnerable neighborhoods are often viewed by police, and the wider society, as hotbeds of criminality, and the people who live there are deemed a class of "usual suspects" in criminal investigations (Lucas, 2015). Residents are affected by a range of structural forces that perpetuate disadvantage, including pervasive unemployment and joblessness, ineffectual social support systems, and crippling physical disorder (Wilson, 1996). Ironically, these neighborhoods are located in many of America's sprawling urban centers, such as New York City, Los Angeles, Chicago, and Baltimore. The perspectives of African American residents in many of these areas are shaped by a history of negative experiences with police and governmental authority in general, that fuels attitudes of distrust toward law enforcement. They also tend to view police as an occupying force rather than as public servants (Brunson, 2007; Balko, 2013).

These concerns are reflected in a DOJ report following its investigation of the Baltimore Police Department stemming from the death of Freddie Gray at the hands of the police. The report found there to be several challenges, including the finding that Baltimore police frequently confront complex social problems that are rooted in poverty, racial segregation, and deficient educational, employment, and housing opportunities (US Department of Justice, 2016). The report also found there to be contrasting community perspectives on policing. The DOJ's Civil Rights Division conducted numerous interviews with city leaders, practitioners, and community members and found that residents in the city's wealthier and predominantly White neighborhoods perceived officers to be respectful and responsive to their needs, while many individuals living in largely African American communities found that officers were often disrespectful and did not respond promptly to their calls for service.

It is noteworthy that the Baltimore Police Department's response to the increasing crime problem in the 1990s was to encourage zero-tolerance enforcement on the streets, which led to large numbers of stops, searches, and arrests. According to the report, there was insufficient oversight regarding these activities, and this led to repeated violations of constitutional and statutory rights which eroded the community's trust in the police. Members of the city's largely African American communities felt they were subjected to unjustified stops, searches, arrests, and excessive force. These issues were compounded by a lack of accountability in cases of police misconduct and the lack of data collection and analysis of officers' activities, along with findings that police were not provided with sufficient guidance, training, equipment, and resources to do their jobs effectively (US Department of Justice, 2016).

The aggressive overpolicing of low-income neighborhoods is not a new feature in American policing. Some may hold the view that warrior policing is warranted due to high levels of criminality in inner-city communities, and due to the problems posed by youth involvement in gangs. From a conservative policy perspective, the use of blanket enforcement strategies in crime-prone areas may seem like an appropriate and reasonable approach for addressing public safety concerns (Tonry, 1995). Still, it is an important concern that highly publicized incidents involving the use of excessive force, which often stem from such approaches, can undermine police effectiveness in the long term (Sunshine & Tyler, 2003; Ekins, 2016; Mock, 2017b).

Warrior policing is also reflected in the tough-on-crime approaches promoted by some politicians. As the national discourse on strategies for reducing gang-related crime grew in intensity, President Trump, an ardent supporter of tough-on-crime approaches, often shared his opinions on crime fighting at his political rallies. The two excerpts below depict Mr Trump's remarks to an audience of law enforcement officials in 2017 and at the International Association of Police Chiefs in 2019, respectively:

> It's essential that congress fund another 10,000 ICE officers — and we're asking for that — so that we can eliminate MS-13 and root out the criminal cartels from our country. Now, we're getting them out anyway, but we'd like to get them out a lot faster. And when you see these towns and when you see these thugs being thrown into the back of a paddy wagon — you just see them thrown in, rough — I said, please don't be too nice. Like when you guys put somebody in the car and you're protecting their head, you know, the way you put their hand over? Like, don't hit their head and they've just killed somebody — don't hit their head. I said, you can take the hand away, okay? (White House, 2017)

> I've told them to work with local authorities to try to change the terrible deal the city of Chicago entered into with ACLU [American Civil Liberties Union], which ties law enforcement's hands, and to strongly consider stop-and-frisk. It works, and it was meant for problems like Chicago. It was meant for it. Stop-and-frisk. (White House, 2019)

In the first quote, Mr Trump referred to Mara Salvatrucha, widely known as MS-13. This largely Salvadoran street gang originating from poor neighborhoods in Los Angeles in the 1980s has influence that spans from Central America to Europe. MS-13 has been in the news frequently in recent years due to a spate of violence in both Los Angeles and New York City (Queally & Ormseth, 2019), along with the heated political discussions based on growing concern about an immigration crisis on the Mexican border (Dreier, 2018). In this context, Mr Trump encouraged the police to use force to break up criminal cartels such as MS-13, and recommended aggressive, strong-arm tactics when arresting suspects in general. Many commentators were not only concerned about the President's tone and the nature of his opinions, they were also concerned about his description of making arrests and throwing suspects into paddy wagons (police vans), and his eliciting laughter from the audience (Swanson, 2017). Mr Trump also expressed concern about civil rights organizations such as the American Civil Liberties Union (ACLU) and their role in preventing law enforcement from doing their jobs effectively. He suggested that the way to deal with the crime problem in cities like Chicago is to rely on "stop-and-frisk."

SQF is relevant to the notion of warrior policing in minority neighborhoods. Stops, frisks, and arrests are tools police use reactively to address crimes reported to them and to investigate suspicious behavior. They can also be used proactively for anticipating and preventing crime (Weisburd et al, 2014). SQF, based on the legal authority stemming from the Terry v Ohio 1968 case,[1] also refers to police powers to perform a frisk (or pat-down) on an individual if during a lawful stop they have reasonable suspicion that the person is about to commit, is in the process of committing, or has committed a crime (Sherman & Rogan, 1995; Weisburd et al, 2014). The practice of SQF has become one of the most controversial policing strategies because police directly interact with citizens and use intrusive policing powers.

In 2013, federal judge Shira Scheindlin ruled that the way police officers were stopping and frisking individuals amounted to racial discrimination. As a result of this decision, along with legal challenges by the ACLU and various forms of public advocacy, an investigation was launched into the enforcement tactics employed by the New York City Police Department (NYPD) (Mock, 2017a). Despite the controversy and growing criticism from civil rights groups, the proponents of law-and-order policy have continued to support the use of SQF within the context of strong-arm policing approaches that reflect the warrior policing mindset (Mock, 2017a). The following quote from an interview with Jennifer, a police officer from Needle City, reflects the frustration that some officers feel regarding the public condemnation of SQF:

> "Yes, it's scary when stop-and-frisk is phased out – between you and I, I know it's against people's human rights in some ways, but that's not always a reason to stop doing it and just let crime happen ... we can't even chase cars now unless it is a known violent felony – and people know you can't do these things, they tell you on the streets. It's a mess."
> (Jennifer, officer, Needle City Police Department)

This perspective also reflects concerns about the ability of police to do their jobs effectively in a social climate that vilifies police for conducting lawful stops and searches. Furthermore, it should be noted that SQF is one of a range of policing tools often incorporated into a larger zero-tolerance program. Crime-reduction strategies that target gang violence often utilize SQF along with other approaches, and many of the tactics used on the streets are forceful or aggressive in nature and clearly invested with the values of militarism. Supporters of gang-suppression policies also frequently promote militaristic deterrence and incapacitation measures as the main tools for reducing youth violence (Fritsch et al, 1999; Klein, 1993; Trujillo & Vitale, 2019).

This is evident in cities such as Oakland, Los Angeles, and Chicago where police have used intensive surveillance techniques along with militaristic deployments to suppress gangs, despite the increasing concern that such approaches have done little to curb the rise of gang-related violence in some problematic areas (Brotherton, 2015; Trujillo & Vitale, 2019). Critics suggest that these approaches have spawned the unintended consequence of enhancing youth identification with gang life, and may also lead to greater numbers of youth being recruited into gangs (Klein, 2004; Green & Pranis, 2007; Brotherton, 2015; see further discussion in Chapter 6). There is also a need for more civilian oversight and accountability regarding the conduct of specialized gang units (Trujillo & Vitale, 2019). Moreover, the absence or avoidance of oversight can be a prescription for corruption and abuse.

Warrior policing and gang suppression

Regarding anti-gang initiatives and the need for oversight, there are several high-profile examples. The Los Angeles Police Department (LAPD) implemented an anti-gang unit in the 1990s called Community Resources Against Street Hoodlums, which was responsible for widespread human and civil rights abuses. More than 70 officers who were associated with the unit were implicated in misconduct ranging from falsifying arrests to dealing drugs and using excessive force (Domanick, 2015; Felker-Kantor, 2019). More recently, it was reported in January of 2020 that at least a dozen LAPD officers who were assigned to the Metro Division crime-suppression unit were being investigated for falsifying information gathered during stops that wrongly portrayed people as gang members in order to boost stop statistics (Winton & Puente, 2020).

In addition, in two separate examples from the city of Chicago, there were troubling details of a "midnight crew" of rogue detectives accused of torturing more than 100 Black men, from 1972 to 1991, in order to secure confessions. The alleged victims, many of whom were purportedly engaged in gang activity, were shocked with cattle prods, smothered with typewriter covers, and had guns shoved into their mouths (Ackerman & Stafford, 2015). In another case from Chicago, there was a federal probe in 2018 into allegations that police officers attached to a gang unit known as Area Central robbed drug dealers and allegedly sold the drugs in the Chicago area (Meisner et al, 2018). These are glaring examples of malfeasance and abuse which draw attention to agency and civilian needs for oversight and accountability within law enforcement.

Warrior policing and the use of blanket enforcement techniques are an ongoing concern, and Portland, Oregon, provides an example of the questionable use of aggressive gang-suppression strategies. In response to an official review, the Portland Police Department disbanded their Gang Enforcement Team when it was found that the approaches used created a racial disparity in the targeting of neighborhoods and the overpolicing of Black men. These methods were also criticized for utilizing high numbers of improper pretextual traffic stops that ultimately did not reduce crime (Portland City Auditor, 2017). Similarly, the NYPD, in the aftermath of its "We Own the Night" campaign, which targeted predominantly Black and Brown inner-city neighborhoods, had to shut down its Street Crime Unit due to the high-profile killing of Amadou Diallo, an unarmed Black immigrant.

The Diallo killing, which predates the events in Ferguson by more than a decade, was a catalyst for negative public sentiment toward aggressive violence-reduction approaches, and drew attention to a need for more scrutiny of police encounters with residents. Diallo was a 23-year-old immigrant from West Africa, and according to a timeline presented in the case against the officers, worked as a peddler in lower Manhattan selling videotapes, socks, gloves, and other items from a spot on the sidewalk. He had returned home to his Bronx neighborhood around midnight on February 4, 1999, and discussed a utility bill with one of his roommates. The roommate went to bed and Diallo, for reasons that are not known, went downstairs to the lobby of the building. Four White officers from the Street Crimes Unit were dressed in street clothes and patrolling in an unmarked car. The unit had been established to patrol high-crime areas in an effort to prevent property crimes and curb violent gang activity (Fritsch, 2000).

One of the officers testified at trial that Diallo was acting suspiciously and that he fitted the general description of a serial rapist, but he also acknowledged on cross-examination that he could not see Diallo well enough to determine his race. The officers also suspected that Diallo might have been a lookout for a push-in robber.[2] The officers approached Diallo to question him and reported that he did not respond to their commands to stop, did not keep his hands in sight, and that they believed he was reaching for a gun. They then fired 41 shots, striking Diallo 19 times as he retreated inside. When he finally slumped to the floor a wallet fell out of his hand. There was no gun. The officers acknowledged that they had made a mistake, but also said that Diallo was largely to blame for his death (Fritsch, 2000; Meminger, 2019).

The district attorney in the Diallo case suggested that Diallo may simply have been reaching for his wallet to hand it over to what he thought was a gang of robbers, or he may have been trying to show the officers his identification. Many Bronx residents believed that the officers made a snap judgment about Diallo when they first saw him, and that they showed a recklessness and a lack of concern for his life. After the four officers were acquitted there were intense demonstrations and incidents of civil disobedience throughout the city (Fritsch, 2000; Trujillo & Vitale, 2019). This case is yet another example of the excessive use of force and its potential impact on legitimacy perceptions in communities of color. It also highlights the warrior mindset in terms of how police are often inclined to view their roles in the community principally as enforcers of the law engaged in a good-versus-evil battle that often leads to a narrow and often flawed moral judgment of the people who live in their jurisdictions.

Two decades later, these concerns are still relevant. The NYPD conducted highly reactive and expansive gang raids in West Harlem in 2014 and in the Bronx in 2016 that were widely condemned by residents and progressive commentators. After the NYPD raid in Harlem in collaboration with the Manhattan District Attorney's Office, it was reported that five hundred police officers in military gear, under the watchful view of police helicopters, raided the Manhattanville and Grant high-rise developments and surrounding buildings in a coordinated pre-dawn operation. This sweep was meant to address the ongoing problem of rival gangs terrorizing neighborhoods in Harlem (Hattem, 2016). These warring gangs were allegedly responsible for ten murders, 46 non-fatal shootings, and 27 incidents of shots being fired, and the raids were deployed to get at the root of the problem. A large gang takedown was implemented and this led to the arrest of 103 mostly young Black and Hispanic individuals (Goodman, 2014; Hattem, 2016).

It was assumed that those arrested were gang members, and this was reported widely in many of the major news outlets. After the raid, parents of the young men arrested held a protest outside the Harlem State Office Building complaining that the police pointed guns at them, their children, and senior citizens living in their homes. A similar raid occurred in the Bronx in 2016, when the NYPD collaborated with several federal law enforcement agencies to execute another large gang takedown operation. The raid led to the detention of 120 individuals, and it surpassed the West Harlem raid to become the biggest gang raid in New York City history (Alcorn et al, 2016; Immigration and Customs Enforcement, 2016).

A 2019 report from the CUNY School of Law showed that two thirds of those indicted were not convicted of violence, a third were convicted of marijuana-related crimes, and about half of those indicted were not even alleged to be gang members by prosecutors themselves (Howell & Bustamante, 2019; Trujillo & Vitale, 2019). While there were some positive crime-reduction effects, meaning that the sweep did reduce violence in these neighborhoods, critics have argued that the opposite effect has occurred as the raids succeeded in skimming a layer off the top of the gangs and opening a vacuum for the next generation to fill (Hattem, 2016).

In addition to these concerns about the impact of aggressive gang raids, there was widespread criticism over the NYPD's use of a gang database as part of its Precision Policing initiative that labeled over 18,000 individuals as active gang members (Trujillo & Vitale, 2019). It was reported that some individuals included in this database were as young as 13-years-old and approximately 99 percent of the people in the database were members of racial and ethnic minority groups (Bratton & Murad, 2018). People were also not notified that their names were in the database and there was no mechanism for challenging the "gang member" label (Boyer, 2019; Trujillo & Vitale, 2019; see further reference to gang databases in Chapter 6).

These examples of aggressive, militaristic gang suppression show the pervasive reliance on force as a mechanism for crime reduction. The precepts of warrior policing are also favored by law enforcement agencies when it comes to dealing with increasing violent crime among young people in inner-city neighborhoods. An important critique of such militaristic strategies is that the police will not be able to solve the problem of youth violence in the absence of a coalition of law enforcement and community agencies to help in the development of programs that support community-oriented approaches along with carefully prescribed, evidence-based enforcement solutions.

The assumption that police must either see themselves as warriors or guardians and choose between distinct orientations might not have practical veracity. It is likely that most officers do not think about policing in terms of discrete categorical roles. Most will agree that the ability to use force is an important tool for effective police work, despite the harsh and excessive manifestations of force that were employed in the examples provided here. However, it is also clear that the role of police as guardians is crucial for achieving sustainable improvements in problematic communities, as stated by Emily, a police chief in one of the jurisdictions studied (namely Needle City): "You've got to find the balance between that guardian and warrior. People call us to be the guardian, they call us to be the warrior. I think you could be a little bit of both."

According to perspectives that support a blended approach to policing that includes an amalgamation of warrior and guardian orientations, good officers must be crime fighters who value forming partnerships with the community. It is also suggested that police officers who seek to do their jobs effectively must define themselves as both warriors and guardians (Blake, 2016; Cullum, 2016). This sentiment was echoed in the words of police sergeant Daniel from the Needle City Police Department:

> "I believe that every officer has to have a warrior mentality 'cause how many professions wear a bulletproof vest? When you leave your family in the morning and give your baby a kiss goodbye and your wife a kiss goodbye … you have to have this warrior mentality 'cause at any time things can go bad. But I am definitely a firm believer in the guardian, you know, mentality … not only are we here as a warrior to protect you but we are here to be a guardian and to help nurture you, to do what we can to bring the community back towards what it needs to be. I am a firm believer in that but I do believe that it's a two-sided coin, you need to have both aspects. It can't be one or the other and I think that is the direction community policing needs to go with both aspects … it has to be both, it has to be a happy meeting, it can't be one or the other, it has to be both. But I am a firm believer in a middle ground between the two, because I think the warrior is too robotic and hard core and I think the guardian can be [like taking] my kindness for weakness … So, I think the two need to be nurtured as one." (Daniel, sergeant, Needle City Police Department)

Some have argued that the distinction between warriors and guardians is purely semantic and does not represent real differences in officer attitudes or behaviors (Schwartz, 2015; Cullum, 2016). Stoughton (2016), for example, indicated that guardian-oriented officers are also responsible for fighting crime. However, such officers do not view criminal activity as inherently evil or requiring law enforcement to constantly adopt a warrior posture against all social problems. As outlined in Chapter 4, during participant observation and interviews, we noted that officers on the whole were becoming increasingly conscious of the need to become guardians as opposed to warriors and to rebuild and repair historically troublesome relationships with community members. Yet, it was clear during conversations with participants that warrior policing approaches were needed and, in some cases, there was a preference for the "old style" of policing that allowed officers to be aggressive crime fighters.

Chapter summary

This chapter has explored the overreliance on aggressive police strategies in disadvantaged communities and described the characteristics of warrior policing and its implications for police legitimacy. We discussed the trend of gang-suppression strategies and the need to curb youth violence within the broader context of police militarization. This phenomenon is linked to political movements that created the war on drugs, as residents in impoverished locations became the focus of frequent enforcement activities. It is also a concern that effective community relations were often not seen as a priority due to the constant emphasis on militarism and violence reduction. Somewhat paradoxically, such efforts may reduce violent crime in the short term but they may also inflict further damage on minority families, particularly when social support programs and community institutions are weak or dysfunctional. Moreover, the primacy of warrior masculinity in policing further legitimizes the targeting of racial minority men and increases the luster of street gangs in the eyes of disenchanted youth.

Despite the impact of enforcement strategies on community relations, some police officers interviewed in our study continued to rely on aggressive strategies, whether they be proactive or reactive. Still, a growing number of officers did not see the warrior/guardian roles as an either/or proposition. Rather, they saw the two philosophies as two sides of the same coin that are integral to effective policing. Findings from research in other places show that many officers also see the warrior/guardian roles as part of a largely intuitive and discretionary process that occurs while conducting their duties in public. There were also illustrations from a drug raid in a poor neighborhood in Coconut County, along with findings from around the country of continuing frontline enforcement strategies in the form of gang-related drug raids and the targeting of young Black men to challenge gang-related associations. Although community engagement had grown in favor as a means of reducing crime and enhancing police legitimacy in areas of Palm State, the continuing emphasis on enforcement activity and the aggressive perspectives of male officers reflected an interesting juxtaposition between contrasting roles of police.

In the next part of the book, we turn our attention to exploring the perspectives of non-police practitioners and young minority men in our fieldwork sites. We examine and unpack their views and experiences of policing and police–community relations in the post-Ferguson period.

PART III

Practitioner and Youth Insights on Police–Community Relations

6

Police as "Guardians" and "Warriors": Non–Law Enforcement Insights

In this part of the book we turn our attention to practitioner and youth perspectives on policing and police–community relations in the post-Ferguson era. In this chapter we begin by placing the spotlight on the voices of non-police practitioners who worked closely with racial minority youths in one of the counties studied. Drawing on data from semi-structured interviews, we outline the insights we gained into the current challenges faced by young racial minority males in local communities and the relationship between some of these issues and gang-related violence and crime in their neighborhoods. Insights are presented into the type of community-centered interventions in place within the county to prevent violence and to re-engage disadvantaged young men (including those involving law enforcement), as well as practitioners' reflections on their nature and impact.

The prominent role or apparent absence of police in these interventions is considered, drawing on the perspectives of practitioners, and supplementary insights from youth focus groups shed light on justice-involved young men's continued distrust of law enforcement. We draw implications from practitioners on the challenges stemming from the policing of young men located in gang-affected neighborhoods, and how this may have evolved in the post-Ferguson era. Given the prominence of street gangs in the locations where fieldwork was conducted, we begin the chapter with a brief overview of some of the existing literary insights on gangs in the literature. Specifically, we focus on the literature on gang involvement among racial minority males and their relationships with the police.

Racial minority men, gangs, violence, and the police

Since the time of the early work conducted by Frederic Thrasher (1927) and the Chicago School of Sociology, many academics have analyzed and described how poverty, unemployment, social disorganization, and oppression can help to stimulate gang culture among groups of young men (Shaw & MacKay, 1942; Whyte, 1943; Cohen, 1955; Cloward & Ohlin, 1960; Anderson, 1999; Decker et al, 2013). Some contemporary scholars (Anderson, 1999; Alonso, 2004; Hagedorn, 2008) believe that young Black men are the most prominent casualties of advanced marginality in American towns and cities, and that this may stimulate their violent offending (see Wacquant, 2008; Deuchar, 2013, 2018). For instance, Anderson (1999) has argued that the profound social exclusion of African Americans has arisen from historical prejudice, discrimination, and the lingering psychological scars emerging from the legacy of slavery (Du Bois, 1953; see also our discussion in Chapter 2).

Others have also recognized the differential effects of joblessness, residential segregation, and public service availability on communities of color and how gangs have increasingly been viewed as contexts where young men can achieve alternative social status (Adamson, 2000; Alonso, 2004; Wacquant, 2008). Adamson (2000) and Alonso (2004) document how significant migration of African Americans and Hispanics to cities in the Northeast and Midwest during the late 19th and early part of the 20th centuries promoted street-oriented clubs. Subsequent sustained exploitation and White violence by agents of social control led to the collapse of the Black Power movement at the end of the 1960s, and young men of color becoming instruments of their own oppression (Deuchar, 2018). The continued exclusion of Black and Hispanic young men from legal jobs led to increased violent gang feuding in many disadvantaged communities across the US throughout the last century (Adamson, 2000; see also Anderson, 1999; Alonso, 2004).

Key authors in the field have also documented how many minority young men in low-income communities often grow up in environments where there is a paucity of adult male role models (Anderson, 1999; Harper et al, 2008); this can and does lead to a felt need to emphasize outward displays of toughness, physicality, and gang-related violence (Harper et al, 2008). As discussed in Chapter 1, although the term "gang" has been debated since the early work of Thrasher (1927), no agreed-upon definition of a gang actually exists (Pyrooz & Densley, 2018b). However, many criminological analyses of American gang culture have emphasized the centrality of territorial conflict, the upholding of a code of respect through violence, and the perpetual focus on attempting to gain economic security from the lucrative drug trade (Deuchar, 2013).

As we also alluded to in Chapter 1, research has demonstrated that gang-involved youth tend to have disproportionate rates of involvement in criminal acts, including elevated rates of gun violence (Curry et al, 2002; Melde & Esbensen, 2011; Decker & Pyrooz, 2010; Decker et al, 2013; Huebner et al, 2016; Pyrooz et al, 2016b; Densley & Pyrooz, 2020). Given that socially disadvantaged Black men and boys are disproportionately represented within American gang culture and related street violence and criminality, some have suggested a direct relationship between racial discrimination and the perpetration of neighborhood street violence within gangs as a coping strategy (Reed et al, 2010).

As we discussed in earlier chapters, it has long been recognized that a major source of racial discrimination in many disadvantaged American neighborhoods is the presence of aggressive police practices that target young Black men (Fine et al, 2003; Cobinna et al, 2008; Cobbina, 2019). In fact, Adamson notes that these practices may have contributed to inner-city gang problems through the "harshness and irrationality of certain of their responses" (Adamson, 2000, p 288). He argues that by disproportionately arresting Black men for drug-related offences and ensuring that they account for much of the fourfold increase in the proportion of drug offenders in US prisons, Black teenagers have in turn been deprived of parental guidance (see also Anderson, 1999). Simultaneously, the huge incarceration rate of Black teenagers has led directly to their future joblessness and exposed them to gang influences behind bars. As we described in Chapters 2–3, evidence suggests that reactive enforcement approaches have often been particularly targeted at juvenile minority males, and excessive force used disproportionately against them. Young Black men have also been found to be overrepresented in the compilation of police gang databases, thus reflecting an entrenched policing philosophy that still criminalizes the most marginalized (Densley & Pyrooz, 2020; and see previous discussion in Chapter 5).

In addition to their direct experiences of racial discrimination at the hands of law enforcement, Brunson also draws attention to "vicarious" experiences that can influence their evaluation of the police (Brunson, 2007, p 73). Victims may often share accounts of racial bias with family and friends, which creates a domino effect of anger and resentment within communities of color. Accordingly, Brunson (2007) argues that perceptions of the police among Black youths are often negatively shaped not only by their own experiences of injustice but by others' experiences as well, in turn negatively impacting their views of police legitimacy (see also Fine et al, 2003; Cobbina et al, 2008; and see Chapter 2 for a detailed discussion on the rubric of procedural justice and police legitimacy perceptions).

When law enforcement officers continue to be viewed largely as warriors within minority communities (as in our analysis in Chapter 5), this may perpetuate not only continued gang violence but also wider collateral consequences such as the entrenchment of the "no snitching" rule. Clampet-Lundquist et al (2015) argue that the "no snitching" rule is an "exhortation for the whole community to keep quiet, to not trust in, talk to, or cooperate with law enforcement," and most commonly becomes prominent in African American and Hispanic neighborhoods (p 266). Anderson (1999), for example, stated that "stop snitching" is an "outgrowth" of the street code that often emerges in poor urban communities, that emphasizes the need to have matters settled without recourse to formal structures while encouraging the use of violence to maintain reputation and exert informal control (Clampet-Lundquist et al, 2015, p 268; see also Parker & Reckdenwald, 2008). In Chapter 4, we drew attention to the President's Task Force on 21st Century Policing's (2015) recommendations regarding COP strategies as a means of improving relationships in communities of color, with a focus on procedural justice and the privileging of the "guardian" officer mindset (McLean et al, 2019). As we indicated in that chapter, including a commitment on the part of officers to view racial minority males as assets to be developed rather than problems to be managed may help to reduce gang violence while also enhancing young men's views on police legitimacy (Taylor et al, 2004; Gau & Brunson, 2010).

Insights from practitioners and from participant observation in Queen County

In Chapter 4, we illustrated how the guardian mentality was being embraced by officers in our fieldwork sites, especially in Queen County. It was evidently prioritized in terms of law enforcement strategy in the Needle City Police Department. In Chapter 5, however, we also documented some of the enduring issues relating to police culture that still produced warrior mentalities among officers and the observations of this we made in Coconut County (McLean et al, 2019). As such, it was important for us to explore wider evidence beyond police narratives and observations of police deployments and interventions.

We wanted to consider community perspectives on the continuing issues facing young men of color in Palm State, including their views on law enforcement, policing styles, approaches and interventions involved in youth engagement and violence reduction.

In the next chapter, we consider the views and perspectives of young men who belong to racial minority groups and who have had contact with law enforcement and the criminal justice system themselves, drawing on semi-structured interviews conducted in a county jail and local neighborhoods. The remainder of this chapter presents insights from semi-structured interviews conducted with practitioners outside of law enforcement in Palm State and participant observation of community-centered interventions. As outlined in Chapter 1, interviews were conducted with a total of 16 practitioners for this part of the research, all of whom were based within Queen County: five public defense lawyers, two social workers, two outreach workers, one juvenile justice worker, one youth prevention manager, one religious pastor, and four youth coaches (see Table 6.1 for a listing of practitioners). Two focus groups were additionally conducted with a total of ten adolescent men between the ages of 12 and 16 years of age, who were actively and regularly participating in the activities offered within an after-school youth-engagement program at one of our fieldwork sites within the same county. We include some reference to the insights gained from these focus groups as part of a case study in subsequent sections.

As we referred to in Chapter 1, the purpose of the practitioner interviews was to explore and examine their perspectives on the current challenges faced by young racial minority men and the relationship between some of these issues and gang-related violence and crime. We also explored practitioner perspectives on law enforcement in the post-Ferguson era and the degree to which they believed that policing styles had changed and evolved in relation to young Black men in particular during recent turbulent times. Participant observation enabled us to gain a deeper insight into the nature of proactive, community-centered engagement exercises and programs within the county. Practitioners' reflections on the presence, extent, and relative effectiveness of police interventions were gleaned from interviews, while youth focus groups enabled further supplementary insights to be gained into the impact of after-school intervention strategies on young Black men (see further details on other young men's perceptions in Chapter 7).

In the following sections, sub-themes are explored with the presentation of extracts from interview transcriptions and field

Table 6.1: Interview participant description – practitioners

Name	Professional role	Years of service	Location
Anne	Youth coach	4.5	Needle City, Queen County
Candice	Juvenile justice worker	4	Needle City, Queen County
Charles	Youth coach	7	Needle City, Queen County
Dakari	Youth prevention manager	10	Needle City, Queen County
Jack	Youth coach	20	Needle City, Queen County
Jamir	Outreach worker	10	Needle City, Queen County
Mark	Youth coach	5	Needle City, Queen County
Paul	Religious pastor	11	Needle City, Queen County
Betsy	Assistant public defense lawyer	20	Queen County
Camilla	Assistant public defense lawyer	1.5	Queen County
Cheryl	Public defense lawyer	14	Queen County
Danny	Public defense lawyer	18	Queen County
Dwayne	Outreach worker	11	Queen County
Elijah	Social worker	42	Queen County
Ken	Social worker	27	Queen County
Lucas	Assistant public defense lawyer	2.5	Queen County

notes, and a small case study focused on insights from one specific after-school program.

Young racial minority men, multiple disadvantage, and gangs

As with officers (see Chapter 4), all of the practitioners acknowledged that the young racial minority men who they worked with often grew up in contexts defined by disadvantage (Vigil, 1988). They referred to how many were raised in single-parent homes, where the absence of fathers was prevalent and mothers were stressed, and where they subsequently found themselves neglected (Anderson, 1999). They also alluded to young men's exposure to worklessness and abject poverty (Decker et al, 2009). These factors, combined with a perceived need to uphold levels of hegemonic masculinity within their neighborhood contexts (Connell, 2005; Deuchar, 2018), led them to seek out gang membership and engage in violence:

> "It obviously starts with home, single-parent homes, usually single mother ... I think originally gangs at a younger age, it

was reaching out for that family atmosphere and I know that's kind of a cliché. So they group together and look for these groups." (Danny, public defense lawyer, Queen County)

"It's a lot of single-parent households, that took a lot of fathers out; because of the drugs, whether they died, or whether they went to jail, or they just left … [So] now, I have to posture, protect myself, protect my family and protect my property 'cause I don't want people to run in and out of my house stealing stuff because they feel I'm soft." (Dwayne, outreach worker, Queen County)

Decker et al (2013) drew attention to the relevance of macro-level factors in producing street-gang activity. This was reinforced to us when Ken, a Queen County social worker we interviewed, summed up the views of many by describing how young racial minority men were often so lacking in employment opportunities that they increasingly recognized that if they were unable to "make a dollar the legal way" they simply became compelled to "make the dollar in an illegal way." Several interviewees also described the extensive and increasing instances of mental ill-health that they came across in communities of color. Jamir, an outreach worker in Needle City, acknowledged the way this was often fueled by poverty and subsequently became intertwined with drug addiction and gang violence:

"Mental health is probably the beginning because I believe they're all suffering from some type of depression … it comes before the violence. Violence is a way of dealing with it, the drugs is a way of dealing with it. Some of the kids, you may have a 16-, 15-year-old on heroin. So, we're dealing with the poverty, the depression." (Jamir, outreach worker, Needle City)

Similar to officers' views (see discussion in Chapter 4), the practitioners we interviewed in this part of the research acknowledged the influence of negative role models such as rappers and the images that young men regularly become exposed to on social media. They believed this exposure influenced weapon-carrying and lethal violence through a focus on "broadcasting badness" (Lauger & Densley, 2017, p. 816):

"Rappers … they're good storytellers, maybe they weren't necessarily involved, some of them, some maybe might

have been, but it's them telling a story. It may be a made-up
story, or sensationalized, but they're talking about something
that is actually happening. We may try to discredit them
as much as ... 'oh it's just entertainment,' but it happened.
I was listening to a rap song and he was talking about the
trust and how you always have to walk around with a gun."
(Dwayne, outreach worker, Queen County)

"Social media plays a big part in a lot of crime. It broadcasts
it. If I didn't know how to rob somebody, I could go to social
media and see what's going on. I can also communicate
to streets and other neighborhoods through social media."
(Jamir, outreach worker, Needle City)

Several interviewees also drew attention to their belief that guns had
become much more accessible to young men (Huebner et al, 2016;
see also Chapter 4) and that this had been combined with a general
decline in moral values and "respect":

"There's more guns now ... it's easier to get a gun out on
the street than to get a gun at a store. So, it's more accessible
to the kids now ... when I was growing up, we had little
handguns. Now, we got 10-, 11-, 12-, 13-year olds with
assault rifles ... and no guidance." (Jamir, outreach worker,
Needle City)

"There is no respect for older people now. It was a time
when you saw someone's grandma walking down the
streets, people wouldn't act like they're doing something.
They would help carry her bags to the house even though
everyone was selling drugs, doing whatever they were
doing. It was still that ounce of respect. That is totally gone.
Some of these kids would slap their own grandmother that
raised them." (Dwayne, outreach worker, Queen County)

According to many practitioners, underpinning much of the
disadvantage were issues relating to race and class (Wacquant, 2008).
Like many other parts of the US, they observed that communities of
color in Queen County tended to be populated by the lowest-income
families and were also subjected to the greatest volume of police
surveillance (Fine et al, 2003; Cobbina et al, 2008; Cobbina, 2019).
Lucas, an assistant public defense lawyer in Queen County, summarized

the perspectives of many by stating the fact that "active patrol" among law enforcement officers in Queen County was often viewed as being synonymous with "looking for people that look suspicious – kids of color, who are hanging out together." Others agreed, and evidently believed that continuing antagonistic relationships with the police often exacerbated these young men's involvement in gangs and violence.

Young men and the police in racial minority communities

Practitioners believed that relationships between racial minority young men and law enforcement were still very problematic. As an outreach worker, Jamir had some mixed feelings about the style of policing he witnessed within local neighborhoods. Reminiscent of the illustration we outlined in Chapter 4 of Officer Calvin, who adopted a disciplining approach to "surrogate parenting" in an African American home, Jamir had observed some officers in Needle City adopting a "guardian" approach in their dealings with young men and their families. However, although he had not become aware of the levels of antagonism and confrontation in Needle City that had been reported in other counties or states within the US, he acknowledged that many young men he worked with were still hostile toward law enforcement:

> "I've seen a lot of [officers] who have good relationships [with young men] ... we have a lot of officers that come in here [the outreach center] ... who work with our kids. They have good relationships with our kids, but then it goes back to knowing their families – their daddies, their granddaddies, where they come from ... I've seen a rise in people shooting back at the police, so a lot of departments kind of lose that respect from the community ... but ... in the city of Needle City I haven't seen that, not yet. [But] I think they all hate the police the same." (Jamir, outreach worker, Needle City)

Other practitioners were less ambivalent in their views, and believed that officers in the county still tended mainly to be adversarial "warriors." They felt that minority young men could sometimes be seen as committing "police-created crimes" by disrespecting officers. This reflects wider insights by Deuchar (2013, p 103) who found that young Black men are often seen to be held in "contempt of cop" by officers who feel disrespected by them during street encounters. Although a minority of officers in areas like Needle City might have been trying to build trustful, reciprocal relationships that enhance police legitimacy perceptions (Tyler, 2004; Cobbina, 2019), some practitioners in our sample believed that the public awareness of publicized officer-involved shootings, combined with vicarious experiences of procedural injustice, perpetuated resentment and distrust (Brunson, 2007):

> "In my opinion, it will take many, many years, I think because the progress that has been made ... I guess you could say that it has been deteriorated by recent shootings ... any strides that have been made, I think with what is happening [nationally] to African Americans, it has just been eroded – the trust." (Elijah, social worker, Queen County)

> "I don't see any improvement ... it's certainly still a relationship where the people who are policing these communities are not part of the communities. They're antagonizers in many ways, and they're seen as opposition ... and so you get, especially in [young men], a lot of what people refer to as 'police-created crimes,' which will even be a 'resisting without violence' charge that comes from a police officer's initial interaction with someone being aggressive; and kids are afraid of the police, especially in these neighborhoods, informed by the experiences they've had growing up and the experiences of those around them ... [even where someone has had] interactions ... with a police officer who's been friendly to them, there's five to ten other experiences that have been relayed to them by others where they've been treated unfairly." (Lucas, assistant public defense lawyer, Queen County)

As discussed previously, Clampet-Lundquist et al draw attention to how low-income urban communities of color have been targeted for mass incarceration over the last 40 years as a result of the so-called "war on drugs" and the drive to reduce gang violence (see also Deuchar, 2013). They argue that it is unsurprising that there has been a backlash including witness-intimidation incidents. They highlight the presence of the push to "stop snitching," which is more than just witness intimidation but an "exhortation for the whole community to keep quiet" (Lundquist et al, 2015, p 266). In spite of police efforts to reignite the trust and cooperation of young men and to place an emphasis on community partnership as a means of violence prevention (particularly in areas such as Needle City), our interviewed practitioners acknowledged the continuing high levels of distrust in law enforcement that existed. In some ways this had increased as a result of the publicizing of high-profile incidents such as Ferguson, and the prominence of the "no snitching" rule within the communities they served (Anderson, 1999; Clampet-Lundquist et al, 2015; see also Chapter 4):

"These last two years, when the kids can go on Facebook live and watch somebody get shot by a police officer live, it kinda hardens [them] towards police officers." (Charles, youth coach, Needle City)

"I just know that a lot of clients are still distrustful. You know, they don't want to call, they don't want to help. You know, if they see something happen they're not going to put their name forward ... it's been going on for years, where it's directed at minorities ... you know, they definitely target minorities ... they've been living with it forever but now it's become more publicized." (Cheryl, public defense lawyer, Queen County)

There were certainly nuanced perceptions about the proactive, community-centered policing approaches that were being implemented in some parts of the county, and about their potential impact on gang-related crime reduction and the building of police legitimacy in communities of color (Tyler, 2004; Cobbina, 2019).

Reflections on proactive, community-centered policing approaches

Critical perspectives on community engagement and officer-youth dialogues

Some of our research participants drew attention to the limited backlash within neighborhoods with local use-of-force incidents. Some associated this with the relatively transparent way some officers were engaging with communities. Paul, who was a religious pastor and who now worked on behalf of the mayor in Needle City to help improve experiences and outcomes for young Black men in the most disadvantaged neighborhoods, drew attention to initiatives such as Coffee with Cops and Shop with the Cop that had emerged in recent years. He believed that such community engagement exercises had created opportunities for law enforcement to make deposits that enhanced their resiliency when negative eventualities occur in the future:

> "It's like making deposits … so when you make these deposits in the community, you kind of build that account so if something negative does happen that's a withdrawal … I think they are making an intentional effort to make positive deposits, particularly in this area of the city." (Paul, religious pastor, Needle City)

Paul also talked about the way he and other members of the clergy regularly engaged in peace walks alongside officers and local citizens in Black neighborhoods (see earlier discussion on this in Chapter 4). He believed that this provided a signal to local citizens that the police were on the side of the disadvantaged and wanted to support community safety. However, Danny (a public defense lawyer in Queen County) was more skeptical of this and believed that "you can't just tell people to love and be at peace," and that officers had to have frank conversations with local citizens (including young men) about how they could work together to prevent violence. In relation to such frank conversations, in Chapter 4 we presented insights into the Kids and Cops dialogical workshops initiated by the Needle City Police Department. Young men who were often on the edges of gang-related crime and actively involved in juvenile justice community service programs regularly met and engaged in discussions with officers, public defense lawyers, attorneys, and representatives from juvenile justice, community outreach, and the clergy. Although these sessions appeared to be guided by democratic policing (McLean et al, 2019), our observations led us to believe that institutional power dynamics remained fundamentally unchallenged and social control still permeated the underpinning rationale for and dialogue within the workshop sessions.

Some of the practitioners we interviewed were involved in these dialogue-based workshops, and articulated various opinions about their value. For instance, Dakari was the manager of the Youth Prevention Project in Needle City, which was partially funded by the city council but also relied on grant funding. His project partially funded the Kids and Cops dialogue workshops along with funding from the city. As such, he clearly believed that the sessions helped to build bridges between officers and youth and to sow the seeds of trust (Giwa et al, 2014). In addition, Candice (a reform specialist worker in the juvenile justice department in Needle City) felt that the sessions helped to reduce triggers among officers and young men:

> "I think it's a tremendous help ... [pointing toward photographs] it's tremendous what the Kids and Cops program is doing, just to get them together like that. Up here on the board behind you, those are all Kids and Cops activities. There's police having a conversation with a couple of youths. You can see the one with a hoodie over his face – he's got a look on his face like he's angry, but he's still listening. That's the first bridge right there ... they leave there with an understanding that not all cops are bad, and they never get into the system – that's the prevention side of it." (Dakari, youth prevention manager, Needle City)

> "There are triggers, and so we all have to know that kids and officers have triggers. We have officers that have been in situations, and been just like our kids and came from some of the same neighborhoods and now they're officers – and they have their own triggers. [So] you need Kids and Cops dialogues on both ends." (Candice, juvenile justice worker, Needle City)

Certainly, some of the workshop observations illustrated how discussion sometimes allowed bridges to be formed by drawing attention to commonalities, as opposed to differences, between officers, other adults, and young men – albeit with the support of attorneys who actively appeared to reinforce the messages the police wanted to put across (Deuchar et al, 2018b, and see also Box 4.2, Chapter 4):

> "OK we are going to do an exercise to start us listening to each other," Paul, the religious pastor, announces to the group during the second Kids and Cops workshop. He asks for two adult and two youth volunteers. One man, Anthony from the juvenile justice department, and one Hispanic officer, Manny, volunteer. Paul then asks Brandon and Dylan, two of the young men, to also participate. He then invites the four volunteers to describe themselves:

Anthony: I like the beach, riding motorcycles, shooting. I like to start projects, get my hands dirty, and play football.

Dylan:	I like to play football and basketball.
Brandon:	I like playing basketball.
Manny:	Like Dylan and Brandon, playing ball – when I was their age I was into the same things. But now I prefer to have a quiet lifestyle and not such an active lifestyle.

> Paul then encourages the group to reflect on how they found the exercise. He asks Brandon first. "Good, it's good to hear what others said." Manny makes the observation that perhaps some would think he should develop more hobbies rather than working all the time, and then adds, "When I am in the patrol car, in uniform, people … only see the cop." Dylan observes that it felt good to hear about other people playing basketball. Finally, Anthony comments that he felt good about expressing how he tends to use his "downtime" to others. Paul then asks if the other members of the group who were observing have any further comments. Lyndsay from the attorney's office answers first: "I thought it was interesting to see more similarities than differences between the kids and the adults." Paul then sums up: "This is a safe space, where people can be open – there's a lot in common." (Field notes, observation of Kids and Cops workshop)

Dwayne and Paul, as racial minority males who both regularly helped to facilitate the dialogues on behalf of the city council and in partnership with the Needle City Police Department, firmly believed that the sessions held strong potential to build more trust between youth and officers. However, while Dwayne believed strongly that the sessions could enable young men in communities of color to begin to regard officers as being approachable and legitimate, Paul offered a cautionary note. He drew attention to the defensiveness he had witnessed in officers in response to negative feedback and comments regarding racial discrimination, and the way in which Officer Daniel from the Needle City Police Department had been keen to exclude public defense lawyers from participating because they openly challenged police perspectives:

> "Me and Sergeant Daniel have this debate all the time, they have a real problem with the public defenders … two

weeks ago, [Daniel said] 'we should really look at kicking out the public defenders, it's always negative, I just don't think it's good for the groups.' I'm like, "Well, Daniel, I hear what you're saying, but on the flipside you all love the state attorney, they're very pro–police ... you know, that's why they're called dialogues, it's not really 'you all do great stuff" ... it's not about just hearing that, you got to be willing to hear tough experiences, or tough comments ... everybody's experience hasn't been positive ... it can get hard. The last group we had, I mean it was a sergeant, one of the young men was just talking about how mass incarceration now, it's a lot like slavery and there's been a lot of oppression. And this [sergeant], he just pounds the table, 'Slavery is over and you all need to get over it, your neighborhood is a mess!' It was like, 'Wow!' So, I'm sitting there holding my tongue." (Paul, religious pastor, Needle City)

As an assistant public defense lawyer in Queen County, Camilla had engaged in the workshops on several occasions (including several of those observed in Box 4.2, Chapter 4). She believed that the dialogues were simply a mask for officers to encourage young men to "snitch," and that officers were unwilling to reflect upon their own entrenched practices (see also Giwa et al, 2014):

"I think it is important for the public defender's office to be represented there because otherwise you have a prosecutor and a bunch of cops telling kids to snitch ... I think they should just be advertised for what they are ... this is not a community-building exercise, this is very clearly for the benefit of the mayor's office and the Needle City Police Department ... I don't think it was for the benefit of those kids at all ... what they're saying is that in order for the community to be better, these kids have to come forward and do all this stuff. Then when I said something about officers, they were like, 'Thank you for your input, that's not gonna happen.' So, it's like, okay, these cops don't have to change anything that they're doing. The kids have to rat people they know, that might be dangerous, and that's gonna fix our community, okay!" (Camilla, assistant public defense lawyer, Queen County)

During participant observation, some evidence of what Camilla was describing emerged. While Camilla herself tried to draw attention to the risks associated with "snitching," officers appeared to be subtly encouraging the young men to cooperate with them, to not be afraid of becoming informants, and to view this as a means of protecting their community (Dodge, 2006):

> During the third Kids and Cops workshop, Paul asks if the "no snitching" rule is real, and all of the young men nod. Sergeant Daniel then comes in: "I want to break this to you – people *do* snitch; the police don't do everything themselves." One of the public defense lawyers, Camilla, then adds: "If you snitch against a gang member, even if the gang member is in jail, they will still come after you." Manny, a Latino officer, then speaks up: "These people thrive off fear. The thing about 'snitches get stitches' – I have never actually seen this happen. As Sergeant Daniel says, a lot of people talk to us. Once a community decides they want the community back, it's not seen as snitching – it's seen as working together to get the community back." (Field notes, observation of Kids and Cops workshop)

Lucas, an Assistant public defense lawyer in Queen County, agreed with Camilla's views and believed that there needed to be more of a focus on raising young men's awareness of their rights and encouraging officers to listen more:

> "I would think on the kids side it [should] be [about] informing them what their rights are and how to stay safe in an encounter ... I would like to talk more with the officers to kind of try and bridge that relationship, [rather] than trying to address scared kids whose only experience has been fear from these sentinels of their neighborhood. So, I would maybe try and open up that line of dialogue with the officers listening, more than thinking that they're teachers." (Lucas, assistant public defense lawyer, Queen County)

Beyond their critical reflections on the dialogue-based workshops, during interviews practitioners also shared their opinions about law enforcement gang interventions and violence-prevention strategies.

Police involvement and absence in outreach, early intervention, and prevention

As an outreach worker in Needle City, Jamir drew attention to the good *attempts* officers like Sergeant Daniel were making to get out of their cars and actively build positive relationships with racial minority men (examples of which are captured in our field notes in Chapter 4). He had also observed the recreational activities that other officers had become involved in that helped to build trust within communities. However, he stated the fact that his own presence was often still needed as a mediator between officers and young Black residents (Deuchar, 2013), and that those officers who were hitherto stationed in less disadvantaged areas, but who were occasionally sent into communities of color, often struggled to display a suitable level of empathy and understanding:

> "I go out on Saturdays for the programs that we offer here … just give a hand that helps the police department because a lot of times they don't speak to the police department unless I'm there … [but] I would want to see … the police more involved in the community, which they're going at right now, but maybe a little more … and maybe some training because lots of times you get a police officer from the west come over here … not used to what goes on here or the level of someone's voice when they're talking. They think they're yelling or screaming … it's a lot different here than what goes on over there." (Jamir, outreach worker, Needle City)

Previous research has suggested that police partnerships with Black clergy can help to improve police legitimacy in minority communities and enhance youth-violence prevention strategies (see Deuchar, 2013; Brunson et al, 2015). As a Black religious pastor in Needle City, Paul described how members of the clergy regularly collaborated with officers. For instance, they had collaborated on developing Workforce Development programs with a range of other partners, and actively referred disadvantaged youths who may have gang-related offending histories into education and employability initiatives (for illustrations of police engagement in this, see Chapter 4). However, some participants believed that many minority young men had become so deeply entrenched in gang-related offending because they had a lack of moral guidance in communities from "old heads" (reflecting earlier insights from Anderson, 1999, p 145) due to mass incarceration and the emergence of minimum mandatory sentencing in Palm State. In spite of officer narratives presented in Chapter 4 that suggested heavy police involvement in youth education, practitioners believed that officers needed to be more involved in early intervention initiatives in schools than was currently the case:

> "When the judges had more discretion, they could review and look at [cases] ... now they're faced with minimum mandatories. 'If you do A, you get B, no question.' ... That's what caused the initial downfall of the youth, because initially you and I are old criminals, old con-artists. We go in and out of prison, but we're there kind of talking to the kids. It's kind of a weird Mafia-style guidance, 'Hey, you don't wanna do that, that's just freakin' stupid.' Not morally, but it's just stupid ... once those seniors were sentenced to those long sentences, once they started getting 15–20 years, you eliminated a whole generation of guidance ... how do you tell a 12-year-old that can make $200 a day to not do it? They're gonna be like, 'Pfft' ... we need to reach in at a younger age. I can't even imagine trying to take today's teenagers and try to convince them to have a relationship with police officers. That's so rotten right now ... 'If I'm losing the battle so bad, I need to go back over there and prevent them from getting to here.' Whatever it takes. Whatever happened to having police officers going into schools and talking to kids?" (Danny, public defense lawyer, Queen County)

However, given that school may not always be the source of the most positive experiences among disadvantaged youth, after-school clubs may also play an alternative role in early intervention and prevention. The Boys and Girls Clubs of America is one of the oldest and leading community-based youth-development organizations in the US, and currently serves over 4.5 million youths nationwide (Fredricks et al, 2010). Drawing on observations, interviews, and focus groups, Box 6.1 illustrates our insights into the work and apparent impact of the Boys and Girls Club based in Needle City, the views of some of the enrolled young men on issues relating to law enforcement, and the staff members' observations about the declining police presence within the club in recent years.

Box 6.1: Case study – Boys and Girls Club of Needle City

Reflecting the overarching national mission of the Boys and Girls Clubs of America, the club based in Needle City aims to provide a positive and safe place for children and young people where they can reach their full potential as responsible citizens (Aberton et al, 2005). The club is one of 13 within the wider Queen County; around 80 percent of the enrolled young people in the club are from disadvantaged areas and single-parent households, and a sizeable majority are ethnic minorities (Black, Hispanic, Asian, or mixed race). The majority of employed coaches also come from communities of color in order to represent the cultures of the enrolled student population. Although the club does not adopt a formal syllabus, all young people participate in a wide range of activities that promote personal confidence, self-esteem, and active, responsible citizenship with an underlying focus on crime prevention in local surrounding neighborhoods.

During an interview, the club's head youth coach, Jack, described viewing the club as a place where children and young people can have a voice and experience a sense of inclusion. For teenage boys, he saw it as particularly important to be on the lookout for negative, gang-related influences and to provide them with opportunities to avoid offending lifestyles and prison:

> "If their dress code is one where they have their pants down here and they're showing their underwear, we know that [influence] is not coming from here ... they may come in with certain headbands. I saw one the other day and I said, 'Why are you wearing that?' The guy had a ... red handkerchief around his foot, with one pant leg rolled up ... he said his foot was hurting ... a few moments later, I saw another one and asked him, 'Your foot is hurting too?' ... Later I found out that it's something from the outside about belonging to a gang. I said, 'You know, it's not okay in here!' ... Our role is not necessarily to change them but to give them options, and to make them know that they can come to a place where they're heard ... I believe that we are the front end of the prison system. I really do believe so." (Jack, head youth coach, Needle City)

Youth coaches viewed themselves not only as coaches but also as counselors who could and should listen to young people's problems and build positive relationships. They recognized the importance of providing positive male role modeling to those who may be lacking father figures:

> "Instead of them going home to play in the streets and finding their gang friends, they have a secure place to come to that keeps them out of the

streets ... a lot of our boys don't have the father [figure]. They have the man in their household who either dates their mother or is in and out of their lives ... they [run] to Eddie [a male coach] as soon as they get here because they want that father, and he's caring and he's there, he listens ... they know they can come talk to him." (Anne, youth coach, Needle City)

During focus groups with justice-involved young men, many drew attention to their positive, trusting relationships with coaches and how they enabled them to share their personal concerns they had, to deal with anger issues, and to avoid becoming involved in delinquent activity:

Group: I have a good relationship with [the coaches] ... they have made a big impact ... I consider them like family, and anything they need from me I'll give back to them ... because they help me with stuff. If I have a situation at home, I can talk to Mr Charles about what happened ... I used to have anger issues, but I got better ... like [Mr Charles] just told me, no matter what, whatever you're going through, just don't hold it in ... if you have any problems, just talk about it, let it all out ...

Interviewer: How might life be different if you had never come to the club?

Group: I would have dreads, smoking on the side of the road ... I would have had lots of fights ... [and] be super bored.

        (Focus Group A, with six young men aged 12–15)

However, many of the young men also expressed their continuing distrust of law enforcement and how they believed that officers were racist because of the stories they had heard and what they had observed or experienced in local neighborhoods. In addition, they also drew attention to the "no snitching" rule and the fear of retaliation they might have if they did report anything to the police:

"It's not just me but the people I hang around, they think the police are racist against people ... the only time I see people, like, experience police is when they get pulled over ... somebody might come back and shoot you [if you snitch]." (Focus Group B, with four young men aged 14–16)

"I ran away once, [and] the police grabbed me, and just moved my arm and he was like, 'I'll choke you, I'll punch you in your face right now!' ... They think you did something, just because of your skin tone ... certain police officers [are killing] Black people ... for no reason ... there's no point of you trying to get involved in something that you don't have nothin' to do with, then you have drama at your house, people coming to your house … because you snitched … it's an unwritten rule … people nowadays are relentless, they're rebellious, they don't care, they'll kill you for the smallest thing … basically, snitching is too much work." (Focus Group A, with six young men aged 12–15)

Although at one time officers might have had a physical presence within the Needle City club in the role of guardians, this was no longer the case:

"We had funding for five years where a police officer would come every day, but funding ran out. It was good … [it] helped to change the perception about what the police officer is all about because he didn't walk around with a gun at his side. It was one of relationship-building, it was like community policing." (Jack, head youth coach, Needle City)

"We used to have a gang violence program … we used to have an officer here three nights a week when I first started, and he would do anything that we asked in terms of crime prevention, gang violence. He would talk to all the groups. I don't know where that fell through the cracks, but we did have it." (Charles, youth coach, Needle City)

"The police haven't come over here in a while. Only if something, you know, really bad is going down or whatever." (Mark, youth coach, Needle City)

Relationship-building, partnership work, and the recognized need to focus on crime prevention among disadvantaged youth was very much to the fore within the club, and the staff also talked of actively expanding a focus on providing educational support activities for parents and families. However, it seemed that the involvement of law enforcement in the routine club activities was now very much missing.

Previous research (St Pierre et al, 1992) has drawn attention to the potential for after-school organizations such as the Boys and Girls Clubs of America to provide prevention programs that are tailored toward youths' individual needs, ethnic/cultural backgrounds, and life circumstances. This can be particularly important in cases where school is not a positive experience for young people and/or for those who live in communities with a heightened presence of neighborhood risks (Fredricks et al, 2010). The case study outlined in Box 6.1 shows how the Boys and Girls Club of Needle City placed an emphasis on prevention of criminal engagement among young men. For adolescent members of the club in particular, there was an emphasis on coaches being responsive and supportive, building positive, trusting relationships, and enabling youth autonomy. The young men in the club were clearly benefitting from being exposed to positive male role models who empowered them in the face of obstacles (Harper et al, 2008).

However, the perceptions of the young men in relation to law enforcement remained negative, and their lack of trust in the legal system evidently increased their identification with the "no snitching" rule. In this book, we have drawn attention to the scholarship suggesting that officers who demonstrate concern for community welfare and actively strengthen community relationships can encourage the co-production of crime solutions and provide some immunity to neighborhood offending, including gang violence (Gill et al, 2014; Cobbina, 2019; and see review, Chapter 4). Although there had evidently been a fairly strong police presence in the Needle City club in the past, with a focus on building relationships with young people and on delivering violence-prevention workshops, this had disappeared due to apparent funding cuts (either on the part of the police or the club itself – this remained unclear). Given the club's close proximity to justice-involved Black youth and their parents, a renewed emphasis on police involvement in "guardian" roles within the club, where officers place an emphasis on positive, non-enforcement contact with young men of color and their families, could enhance the existing focus on preventing gang culture and violence in Needle City that is an inherent part of the club's ongoing work.

Police focus on "guardians" and a remaining, entrenched "warrior" culture

Beyond the use of after-school programs, several of our sampled practitioners still believed that officers across the county were poor at communicating effectively with young racial minority men and understanding the extreme issues of trauma and other disadvantage they often experienced. There were some noted exceptions to this, where some police departments within our areas of geographical focus were enhancing their awareness of mental ill-health and trauma and how to respond to it, sometimes acting as "guardians" in partnership with others (also see officer perspectives in Chapter 4):

"The majority of our kids, 70 percent, have mental health diagnoses. Probably 80 percent have some sort of trauma in their lives ... we [juvenile justice department and police officers] were talking the other day about 'Stick them outside where they can see the stars' ... they're in an environment that's not conducive for seeing stars, whether they're human stars or not. So, we give them the opportunity to take ... them out of this environment." (Candice, juvenile justice worker, Needle City)

Even alongside encouraging practices, many suggested that remaining challenges associated with warrior approaches to law enforcement were always present:

"As a Black male, it doesn't sit well with me because you do feel like, you know, [officers] are more apt to shoot first and ask questions later ... with communities of color, it's obvious ... I know that the officers I've been able to interact with and have become fairly close with, I know there's hope but ... how does that spread out throughout the culture? So, I mean they do training around implicit bias and procedural justice, you know, they do a lot of good stuff ... this is the kind of face of the department that we see, but there's a whole other group out there, kind of the grizzled veterans, guys that's kind of been around for a while, you know I'm sure it's a little different." (Paul, religious pastor, Needle City)

"The culture is the culture ... you give somebody a gun and say, 'Hey, we're all behind you,' and you kind of get these ego trips. It's always been that way ... [officers] have a way of thinking, 'It's just the way it needs to be done.' There's no thinking outside the box." (Dwayne, outreach worker, Queen County)

Accordingly, practitioners were evidently concerned about the potential ongoing negative challenges associated with entrenched police culture beyond those who may be dedicated to community work. Their views suggested that even in the post-Ferguson era, many mainstream officers continued to favor "real" police work associated with confrontation and hypermasculine street enforcement, akin to the warrior culture discussed by Van Maanen (1978) and Kraska (2007). This seemed to dovetail with the insights we gained from some officers, outlined in Chapter 5, that brought to light the continuing emphasis on enforcement activity and aggressive law enforcement perspectives.

Chapter summary

In this chapter we have drawn attention to the previous literature suggesting the link between gang culture and violence, social disadvantage, and racial animus between young racial minority men and law enforcement. In short, we have argued that warrior approaches to law enforcement often contribute to and perpetuate inner-city US gang problems as well as continuing negative evaluations of police among minority young men. Building on the insights from police officers captured in Part II of the book, in this chapter we have documented the views and perspectives of practitioners beyond law enforcement who worked closely to support young racial minority men throughout Queen County.

The practitioners drew attention to the continuing problematic and antagonistic relationships with the police that often exacerbated young men's involvement in gangs and violence. Reflecting the dual insights we outlined in Chapters 4 and 5 regarding the contrasting roles of police as guardians and warriors, practitioners could often describe active attempts that some officers were making to connect and engage with youth, but also recognized that young men's personal experiences of confrontation and street enforcement, combined with the vicarious experiences passed on to them by others, still bred resentment and distrust. Community-engagement strategies put in place by law enforcement had evidently built some resilience against the type of community backlash that had occurred in places like Ferguson, even when discriminatory practices and officer-involved shootings emerged. However, there was a feeling that more bridges needed to be built with young men, and strong views among some that the dialogical workshops that had been put in place in Needle City were deeply flawed and used simply as a mask to encourage more oppression and entice young men to cooperate as future informants. The moral vacuum that had emerged due to racially oriented mass incarceration led practitioners to believe that police-initiated early intervention approaches were essential, but they were in reality still scarce. As Maguire and Katz (2002) have argued, some police organizations may strive to achieve the "appearance" of legitimacy by implementing only token changes to support community-oriented approaches.

In our own exploration of the Boys and Girls Club of Needle City, it seemed that youth distrust of police was high, but police presence in the club (as a means of reversing distrust and adding an extra layer of protection against young men's future involvement in gang-related culture) had rapidly declined. More engagement of officers in programs and interventions of this kind that reach the lives of young men and their families was evidently needed. This was particularly important given our wider practitioners' views about law enforcement's general paucity of understanding and empathy relating to social disadvantage and trauma, and their thoughts on the continuing emphasis on confrontational, militaristic warrior approaches that still characterized the policing culture in the post-Ferguson era.

The next chapter turns the spotlight away from practitioner perspectives and onto the views of young men in communities of color with offending histories, in relation to police intervention and police–community relations.

7

The Post-Ferguson Era: The Lived Experiences of Young Men in Racial Minority Communities

This chapter turns the spotlight away from practitioner perspectives and onto the views of those who are often most affected by law enforcement strategies – young men in communities of color, and specifically those with offending histories. The chapter draws upon insights from semi-structured interviews conducted in a county jail and in local neighborhoods, with young men with criminal histories or those who were on the periphery of criminality. We explore the collective challenges these young men had encountered, including the impact of adverse childhood experiences, social and economic disadvantage, and (where relevant) the influence of gang culture. We also chronicle the young men's lived experiences with racial discrimination from police interventions and the wider criminal justice system. Among the generally despondent narratives shared, we also draw attention to the cautious optimism expressed by some who had recently participated in police-initiated community-engagement programs. In so doing, we draw some conclusions about the young men's juxtaposed exposure to contrasting guardian and warrior police roles, and the continuing and cumulative disadvantage they experienced via law enforcement and – in some cases – the wider criminal justice system.

Moving beyond practitioner perspectives: Interviews with young men

As we described in Chapter 1, this part of the research firstly involved the implementation of semi-structured interviews with eight young racial minority men who were currently residing in the Queen

County jail, often awaiting sentencing related to suspected crimes of violence associated with gang culture. Access to the jail was established through a formal application process to the Queen County Sheriff's Office, Department of Corrections, and once this was approved by senior officers, currently incarcerated young men were interviewed. The criteria for selection of the small group of young men was as follows: they had to be residing in the jail for offenses relating to gang-related and/or violent crime; they had to be over the age of 18; they had to be from an ethnic minority group (normally African American or Hispanic), and be willing, through a process of informed consent, to participate in an interview of up to 60 minutes in duration. Senior officers within the Department of Corrections subsequently facilitated meeting times for inmates (aged 22–35) over the course of two full days of fieldwork. The purpose of the interviews was to explore the challenges these men had faced during their upbringings, their perceptions about law enforcement, and why they believed that they had experienced hostile relationships with officers.

Secondly, a small number of additional semi-structured interviews were conducted with four young men who were residing in disadvantaged local communities of color within the county. Each of these men was on the periphery of criminality and/or had already had formal contact with the juvenile or formal adult justice system for offending-related behavior, sometimes (but not exclusively) relating to gangs. One of these men (who was aged 23) was accessed via gatekeepers within the Queen County Sheriff's Office, since he had previously engaged in a rehabilitative support program coordinated by the sheriff's office's dedicated civilian gang prevention coordinator immediately following his release from prison for gang-related offending. The other three young men were juveniles (aged 15–17). Each of these young men had been on the edges of criminal behavior, having been charged for minor misdemeanors, and had actively participated in the Kids and Cops dialogical workshops in Needle City, implemented on behalf of the city council and the Needle City Police Department. Following participant observation during said workshops (see Chapters 4 and 6), access was negotiated via gatekeepers from the county's juvenile justice department to conduct interviews with a small group of the participating young men. Members of the juvenile justice department subsequently facilitated meeting times between the author and the three young men who eventually volunteered to participate.

The purpose of conducting this second set of interviews was to further explore perspectives about law enforcement among a small number of young men who had had some involvement in police-led engagement and support programs in the community, in order to complement those insights provided by the men who were incarcerated. While three of the young men interviewed belonged to racial minority groups, one of the juveniles was White. It was felt that the inclusion of this latter participant would provide a nuanced and illuminating contrast to the wider sample, but at the same time there were areas of commonality with the other juveniles interviewed. For instance, the young man in question lived in a community largely populated by minority citizens and had many young male friends who were from minority racial groups. He had also been found to be on the edges of criminal behavior, having been charged for a minor misdemeanor, and had actively participated in the Kids and Cops dialogical workshops in Needle City.

Table 7.1 provides an outline of the 12 participants from this part of the research, including details of where they were located at the time of the interview (either in jail or within the community). As alluded to, all but one of the young men were from ethnic minority groups but, since they did not always openly disclose their specific race or ethnic identity during the interviews and we did not believe it was appropriate to infer any such specificities. Accordingly, we simply refer to the participants as "young men of color."[1]

Table 7.1: Interview participant description – young men

Name	Age	Location of interview
Brandon	15	Community
Chad	23	Community
Dylan	17	Community
Michael	17	Community
Antonio	27	County jail
Bruno	28	County jail
Edward	25	County jail
Jarvis	27	County jail
Jordan	25	County jail
Juan	35	County jail
Orlando	22	County jail
Sylvester	28	County jail

As with the data gathered during other parts of the fieldwork, audio-recorded interviews were transcribed and thematically coded manually. In the subsections that follow, the emerging themes are presented with key quotations emerging from semi-structured interviews.

Adverse childhood experiences, gangs, morality, and risk management

In earlier chapters, we illustrated police officers' and wider practitioners' views on the multiple strains and issues of marginality that often led young men into gangs, violence, and offending behavior. These included issues relating to father absence, child neglect, poverty, and lack of opportunity for education or employment. In recent years, a growing body of research has demonstrated the harmful impact of adverse childhood experiences (ACEs). ACEs commonly refer to ten specific abuse, neglect, and household dysfunction exposures, including physical and emotional neglect, domestic violence, household substance abuse, parental separation, and having family members with an incarceration history (Centers for Disease Control and Prevention, 2018). Wolff et al (2020) draw attention to the fact that many of the risk factors identified in previous gang research represent ACEs, although not always described as such (see, for instance, Howell & Egley, 2005; Esbenson et al, 2009; Pyrooz et al, 2013; Howell & Griffiths, 2019). In Wolff et al's research, drawing on a sample of over 100,000 juvenile offenders (the majority of whom were from ethnic minority groups) in Florida, a "positive and significant association between ACE scores and gang involvement" was observed (Wolff et al, 2020, p 42).

During our interviews with young men of color, particularly those who were currently incarcerated, they described having been raised in families where exposure to what could be regarded as ACEs was commonplace:

> "My momma used to abuse me ... I stayed for my family members. Like, I stayed for my brother, I'm very close to him." (Jordan, age 25)

> "My mom was incarcerated for a little while, and then when she got out she had to take care of me and my brother and my sister ... I communicate with [my father] sometimes, but we ain't got no relationship like me and my mom is ... it's rough [in Canary City]. There's a lot of violent crime and that ... the people you hang around with, that type of violence comes towards you." (Orlando, age 22)

"It was tough for me because I grew up in a home with drug abusers, my family they was doin' a lot of drugs, and you know, pretty much didn't pay me no mind. I got to do what I really wanted, and you know, they didn't care ... I never met my real dad, he was in prison for as long as I know ... but as far as my stepdad and my mom, you know, they were heavy drug users and that's how I got put into foster homes." (Jarvis, age 27)

Previous research by Melde et al (2009a) has suggested that negative life events and violent victimization are key risk factors for gang involvement. Others (Howell et al, 2017; Wolff, 2020) have demonstrated how a household member's incarceration history and foster care involvement are statistically related to gang involvement among youth, and that substance and family-related abuse may also be related to later gang association. The experiences of Jordan, Orlando, and Jarvis reinforce this, given that their early exposure to abuse, family incarceration, experiencing drug abuse within the family home, and foster care experience contributed to their involvement in gangs. Orlando also alluded to neighborhood effects – growing up in a community surrounded by violence stimulated his later involvement in gang-related street violence (Farrington & Loeber, 2000). In addition, Edward described the way his own childhood was characterized by living in a socially and economically disadvantaged, high-crime neighborhood combined with drug abuse within the family home:

"Being raised in Canary City is like being raised in a bunch of violence, drugs being sold, murders happening every two or three months ... in my family, when I grew up my mom was on drugs so it was like we struggled up until the age of 18 ... it's like really every family in Canary City goes through the same situation. The majority, their parents don't have a good job, they don't really have nothin' to rely on." (Edward, age 25)

The majority of the young men described how they had drifted into gang membership, drug dealing, and violence. On some occasions, earning an initial reputation for selling drugs led to the men being approached to become members of street gangs, where bonds of solidarity were formed based on ethnicity (Sullivan, 2005). Other times, membership of local groups or gangs was self-initiated and motivated by the young men's drive to make names for themselves as tough guys in the local community (Deuchar, 2018):

> "In high school, my last year I was dealing pot in school … two people came up to me after school one day, said they heard about me, asked me questions, asked if I wanted to join their clique … you had to be part-Hispanic to be in that, and I'm half Hispanic." (Chad, age 23)

> "I was doin' drugs, sellin' drugs, fightin', you know? Tried to make a name for myself, basically. Tried to be somebody … you have to put a name for yourself." (Antonio, age 27)

Many of the men who were in jail talked about their gang involvement and how it provided them with a sense of family and the opportunity to make "fast" money through drug dealing. Matthews (2002) discusses how crime is infused with issues of morality, while Yablonsky (2000) draws attention to the moral codes associated with gang members (see also Deuchar, 2018). Maitra et al (2018) found that certain actions are deemed morally legitimate from an offender's perspective, while others are not. In our sample, we found that several of the incarcerated young men insisted that there were some crimes (like rape and robbing local people) that were morally illegitimate in their eyes, while others (such as drug dealing) were viewed as morally acceptable because they were trying to earn money to support their families (Fader, 2016):

> "I wouldn't do rape … because there is a woman involved. It's something against our gang too, we got to respect women. I never hit a woman in my life … we have rules, we gotta respect women … I stopped robbing too. I used to rob, but I stopped doing that, I started being more independent and selling drugs." (Antonio, age 27)

> "My reason for resorting to drug dealing was because, when I was 16, I had my first daughter. My first job was in Wendy's and … the drugs, the money was faster and it helped me take care of my daughter, for the bills and everything, so I stuck with drug dealing." (Edward, age 25)

> "That's the only way I could help my momma out … I was paying the bills, I was putting food on the table … I didn't give a fuck what she thought at the time." (Jordan, age 25)

In earlier chapters, we referred to officers' and wider practitioners' beliefs that rap music was increasingly having an influence in encouraging gang violence in Queen County. However, among the men we interviewed only one of the juveniles referred to the influence of rap music. Michael was aged 17, and he had been charged with minor misdemeanors but lived in a neighborhood dominated by gang-related crime. He believed that some young men he knew had a desire to emulate rappers who had a "whole lot of money [and] guns." In Chapter 4, we also documented the insights we gained from informal conversations with officers on how social media could allegedly be used as a platform to glorify weapons and to support attempts to disrespect rival gang members. Wider criminological research has also suggested that gang members increasingly use the internet and social media to promote gang culture (Pyrooz et al, 2015), to make remarks or threats to rival gangs, and to flaunt illegal substances and weapons (for a review, see Pinkney & Robinson-Edwards, 2018). However, the men in their twenties and thirties insisted that this would not be something they would engage in. Although several openly discussed how they had gained possession of, and used, assault rifles in the past as part of gang activity, they believed that posting weapons on social media was purely narcissistic and posed too much of a risk in terms of being caught more easily. Some indicated that they had actively cautioned others against this practice in the knowledge of covert police-surveillance strategies:

> "We didn't want nobody knowing what kind of arsenal we had ... people who post images like that, to me they're a fraud ... they try to portray an image ... some of them really just think they look cool holding guns like that for the feds or the police to see them, 'Oh, he's on our radar now because he's holding a fucking assault rifle with a fucking 32-round magazine.' ... That's not the people that I've [been] known to hang around, that's not what they do." (Jarvis, age 27)

> "If I catch a shooting case and they look on my social media website, they'll be able to pinpoint everything. Can't do that ... it don't make sense. If you get caught, you get caught quicker." (Bruno, age 28)

> "I socialized with people who did that. Like, I talked to them and tell them, the same thing you got on Facebook or social network, Queen County Sheriff's Office got one too ... they got you as a friend on Facebook and they can

look at everything ... people I hang around with don't do
that." (Orlando, age 22)

Although the young men had evidently avoided the tendency to
openly flaunt their involvement in gang-related activities on social
media and attract unwelcome online attention from covert policing
(see Fallik et al, 2020), they had clearly become subjected to negative
police attention in public places. As we drew attention to in Chapter 5,
warrior policing has often been reflected in the tough-on-crime
approaches promoted in American inner-city contexts, and gang-
suppression strategies can lead to the overpolicing of Black and Brown
men (Goodman, 2014; Ackerman & Stafford, 2015; Hattem, 2016;
Portland City Auditor, 2017). Living in neighborhoods where there
were recognized and increasingly prevalent gang problems meant that
law enforcement presence had been a defining feature of the young
men's lives, both prior to and during their gang-involved years. Their
described lived experiences suggested that militaristic, warrior officer
mindsets were very much to the fore, as the next section illustrates.

Police discrimination, brutality, and repercussions from
"warrior" approaches

In her research conducted in Ferguson and Baltimore, Cobbina
conducted interviews with local citizens and explored the personal
experiences they had had with the police. She found that just over
half of the personal incidents described were negative, as were the vast
majority of vicarious accounts that they also described. Importantly,
she found that incidents reported by Black participants were more
than six times as likely to be negative compared with incidents
reported by Whites. Many Black residents believed that they had
been racially profiled and resented bring stopped by officers without
any legal justification. In the words of one of Cobbina's young Black
male participants, although one is supposed to be "innocent until
proven guilty," with Black people "you're definitely guilty until proven
innocent" (Cobbina, 2019, p 44). Participants in her study especially
disliked that officers spoke to them in a disrespectful manner.

We found similar insights emerging from the young men in our
sample. Reflecting the initial insights we had gained from the ten
adolescent men who participated in focus groups within the Boys
and Girls Club of Needle City (see Chapter 6), all of the young men
of color we interviewed in jail and in the community reported on
their long-standing experiences of racial discrimination at the hands

of law enforcement officers. The men often relayed stories about being harassed by officers while hanging on street corners, and both personal and vicarious experiences of being profiled and framed for drug possession or violent crimes because they had previously been known to the police (see also Deuchar, 2013):

"If we hangin' out on the block, they gonna come, cause they got certain little posts where they be at, and if you see us out there, they gonna try come stop us to see what we're doin' ... some of the cops are racists ... we just try to bite our tongues ... try not to comment on what they say 'cause they'll take us in for any little thing." (Bruno, age 28)

"They was definitely racial profiling me ... they would pull me over ... I got a lot of friends out there that would just, you know, call me and be like, 'Bro, you'll never believe what just fuckin' happened, like, one of these motherfuckers tried to throw some dope on me, you know what I'm saying, they tried to frame me, talking about my car was involved in a shooting on this block, the same car, or I fit the description of a murderer.'" (Jarvis, age 27)

"If someone say 'Police,' we get like paranoid ... it's almost like once they know your face, they keep picking on you." (Dylan, age 17)

Chad, a 23-year-old, summed up the views of many of the young men we interviewed when he declared that "a lot of cops are twisted; they will find something to get you in trouble." Weitzer and Tuch (2002) noted how direct experience with racial profiling can have a lasting, and adverse effect on individuals' perceptions of the police. Seventeen-year-old Dylan's feeling of paranoia whenever the police were around had clearly emerged as a result of many years of experience of being picked on. Earlier insights from Cobbina suggested that ethnic minority men can come to regard officers' aggressive policing practices as an "explicit attempt to restrict their movements" (Cobbina, 2019, p 42). In relation to this, Orlando described his experiences of being targeted if he was observed being "out of place," for instance while visiting a neighboring corner store:

"If I went up to a corner store – I can't go to the corner store without them harassing me ... 'Y'all harassing me for nothin' ... just because I'm standing on this corner, you got 12 police officers on my car come stop me ... why y'all come and target me?'" (Orlando, age 22)

Some of the young men interviewed also described previous adverse experiences of law enforcement that had impacted negatively on their family lives, and the lasting influence this had had on them. For instance, 25-year-old Edward described his father being shot and killed by a police officer when he was an infant. In spite of this, Edward was somewhat ambivalent in his views on law enforcement:

"My father passed away when I was the age of two, he was killed by a police officer ... they were trying to arrest him for drug issues, and he was resisting, he fled – and they shot him ... I'd say, yeah [I was resentful] ... but at the same time, when I was growing up I met some good cops and I met some bad cops, so I really didn't take it as all cops are the same ... it's just by the heart of the officer ... some officers are cold hearted, you get some officers that are kind and nice." (Edward, age 25)

It seemed that such resentment toward law enforcement was not always confined to young men of color. As the only young White man in our sample, Brandon (a juvenile at age 15) described living in a community where most residents belonged to racial minority groups. He had seen many of his Black male friends subjected to the aggressive use of force by police, and felt that he too was unfairly targeted by officers:

"Yesterday I was walking, and they (officers) said something to me like they're about to arrest me. I don't know why ... not all officers are mean, [but] I just grew up just not talking to them ... [they] beat up kids, Black males, shot one of them ... they tased him." (Brandon, age 15)

Jackson et al drew attention to the way in which perceptions of procedural unfairness – including "disrespectful treatment and unfair decision-making" – eroded feelings of shared group membership with authority figures such as the police (Jackson et al, 2012, p 1053). Cobbina (2019) also showed that there is a lasting negative impact of discourteous treatment by officers on young Black males. Brandon's comments implicitly suggested that the lasting effects of law enforcement biases can perhaps also be felt by young White men who live in communities of color. It is difficult to ascertain how common this may have been in the communities where we conducted fieldwork, given that Brandon was the sole White respondent.

Several of the young men of color in our sample believed that they continued to be judged negatively and treated unfairly by officers because of their previous criminal records. For instance, Antonio (a 27-year-old who was in jail at the time of the fieldwork) drew attention to the fact that he had picked up a trafficking charge on top of his gang-related offences. While he had ambitions to desist from the gang-related criminal lifestyle, to get education, and get a job when he was released from jail (or prison if eventually sentenced), he felt that having his name known and recognized by officers would hold him back. He described how, prior to going to jail, he had been frequently stopped, had suspicion directed at him, and was often subjected to having his car searched:

> "My criminal record, that's what's holding me back ... when I get pulled over, even if I don't get in trouble, they'll pop up with my name, my nickname ... they know my name ... one day they pulled me up, saying, 'Oh, you better not be recruiting.' I'm not recruiting nobody ... I want to do something with myself, I want to get trades, I want to go to school ... probably have to change my name ... as long as they see my name, they pull me over, especially now I got a trafficking charge. They want to search my car all the time ... there are some crooked police officers that put drugs on you ... 'Oh, I found some weed in your car!'" (Antonio, age 27)

Similarly, 28-year-old Bruno also felt stigmatized because he had carried firearms in the past. He described how he had then become frequently subjected to SQF by officers because officers assumed he might still be armed: "It's like my name comes up as a red light because I carry guns so they gonna search me automatically to see if I got a gun on me" (Bruno, age 28).

In their exploration of the warrior officer mindset, Mclean et al reported that officers often view themselves as "soldiers on the front lines" (McLean et al, 2019, pp 3–4). They see their role as that of crime fighters, battling evil, and their use of aggression and overreliance on force, particularly in the *hood* where neighborhoods are often regarded by these officers as hotbeds of criminality, further divides the police and public (Lucas, 2015; see also Chapter 5). In her empirical research in Ferguson and Baltimore, Cobbina (2019) found a preponderance of young Black males describing their experiences of overly aggressive and/or physically violent police encounters akin to this warrior mentality. Wider research has also shown that urban Black males are often the targets of excessive use of force and have a strong sense of themselves as "symbolic assailants" in the eyes of the police (Brunson & Miller, 2006, p 613). The young men of color participating in our research described experiencing encounters where warrior-style officers had subjected them to brutality, clearly because these officers believed that the young men were threatening or dangerous to them (Bell, 2017b):

> "I've been dragged, I've been kicked, I've been hit on the head with a pistol, I've been kneed, I've been pepper sprayed … they jumped out and blocked me off because they thought I had some stolen merchandise in the car, jumped out, the co-defendant, they shot him and shot the truck nine times, the dude almost died." (Juan, age 35)

> "Violent, guns drawn, as soon as they exit the patrol car, guns drawn, pointed at you, you know, they might rough you up, they might run down on you with the gun pointed at you, tell you, 'Turn around, put your hands behind your back!' – shit like that, and slam your head into the patrol car, you know, shit like that." (Jarvis, age 27)

In some instances, experiences of these types of overly aggressive encounters had evidently begun while the young men were still at school. For instance, Jordan described an incident that took place when he was aged 15, when officers had pulled him over because he was walking through a White neighborhood to get to school. The accusations directed at him combined with the disrespect shown by officers ignited his anger, and after attempting to flee, he was immediately subjected to physical abuse at the hands of the officers (see also Cobbina, 2019):

> "I don't know if it was my clothes that I had on, but they pulled me over, asked me where I was going. I was in the other neighborhood, I was in one of those rich White folks' neighborhoods and they pulled me over to talk to me, 'Where were you going?' 'I'm going to school.' So, you know, at the time I had dreads and gold on my arm, so they're like, 'Where you going?' 'I'm going to school.' 'No,

> you're not, you're up to no good.' ... I lost my temper ...
> I said, 'Fuck you, cracker, keep your shit trucking.' ... So,
> he's like, 'Oh, we got a smart ass? Black man, yeah we got a
> smart ass.' ... Then I kinda run, but they caught the back of
> my shirt ... they punched me in my shit, they jumped me
> ... so, every time I see the police, I run." (Jordan, age 25)

This confrontational scenario – according to Jordan – emerged because officers viewed him as a dangerous Black man walking through a White, middle-class neighborhood. He was evidently targeted because his presence was noted as being out of place since he came from an area characterized by concentrated disadvantage and a large minority population. Being seen out in "dangerous places" led officers to construe Jordan as a symbolic assailant (Anderson, 1990; Brunson & Miller, 2006; Skolnick, 2011).

Like Jordan, other participants also referred to being subjected to physical abuse if they attempted to run from officers. Twenty-eight-year-old Bruno, for instance, recalled times when he and his friends had fled from the police and had been beaten by officers when they caught them. He reflected with anger on these instances declaring, "Y'all supposed to 'serve and protect us', [but] y'all beating us and y'all making us worse." The two young men, who had participated in the Kids and Cops workshops, had also witnessed the use of excessive force against ethnic minority young men or had heard stories from others to this effect. As such, 17–year-old Michael had decided not to flee from officers when he encountered them, because he believed there was a risk that he too might be shot and end up dead or paralyzed for the rest of his life. Rather than complying based on perceived law enforcement legitimacy (Sunshine & Tyler, 2003; Reisig et al, 2007; Tyler & Fagan, 2008; Reisig et al, 2011; Reisig et al, 2012), Michael tended to obey law enforcement because he was afraid of being subjected to excessive force (Brunson & Miller, 2006; Katz & Maguire, 2020). Others in the sample also referred to being strongly aware of officer-involved shootings of young Black men that had taken place locally or nationally. They believed that these events were becoming more frequent and were racially motivated. The fact that these incidents were now being publicized more widely via social media meant that they were more acutely aware of the threat posed by law enforcement:

> "Police is shooting other people and stuff ... it's been
> happening too much ... you know, like some police
> officers drop young people on the ground and stuff like
> that." (Dylan, age 17)

"It wasn't involving me and my friend, it was just involving this one particular person who was on the corner [one day] with us, chilling. And it was a routine traffic stop … [an] officer pulled this person, it was a routine traffic stop and he jumped out of the car and was running, and he shot him in the back of the head. So, I would say with certain officers, it's a racial thing." (Edward, age 25)

"It's getting worse, shit's getting worse. I've seen, like, the White folks, killing innocent Blacks, they're killing Blacks for no reason. All types of police, they think they're bad, they'll kill them." (Jordan, age 25)

"It's publicized more, you see it on TV, a killing here, you see it's a cop that did this … if you look at events, it's predominantly Black towns, Baltimore, Louisiana where they shot the dude on the curb, all these places, it's happening, in smaller Black communities … it's happening where you got ignorant motherfuckers … ignorance is what kills, it's not the gun." (Juan, age 25)

Cobbina (2019) reports that some of her respondents found that Black police were more aggressive in their policing tactics when compared to White officers. Earlier insights from in-depth interviews conducted with residents in three neighborhoods in Washington, DC, by Weitzer (2000) reinforce this phenomenon where some participants believed that Black officers treated Black residents more harshly. Some of our participants agreed:

"I'd say, the Black officers, certain ones, because I've seen even Black, African American officers treat Black, African Americans different, like as if stereotyping with force, excessive force, so sometimes it's not always by race." (Edward, age 25)

"The Black cop is worse than the White cop … they look at the Black[s] like, 'I ain't gonna feel sorry for you … I came from that struggle too and you could have did it better. I did better.'" (Sylvester, age 28)

As Juan stated, the men in our sample believed that "ignorance" killed, and in their minds, officer ignorance (regardless of their own race) arose from their lack of regard for the disadvantage that communities of color face combined with their overreliance on force and abuse of police power (Brunson & Weitzer, 2009). As we have shown, when law enforcement officers continue to be viewed largely as warriors within minority communities, this can lead to a greater reliance on the "no snitching" rule. The findings from interviews also showed that practitioners who worked with youth believed that the "no snitching" rule had grown in prominence as a result of young people's awareness of incidents like Ferguson, that officers were highly conscious of this, and that some young adolescent men in the Boys and Girls Club in Needle City feared retaliation if they did snitch. As a result of the profound personal and vicarious experiences they had to draw upon involving police harassment, aggression, and brutality, the ethnic minority young men who were currently incarcerated were generally of the mind that they would always avoid reporting any type of criminal activity to the police. "Stop snitching" was clearly seen as both an extension of the street code within their communities and also a reflection of their deep-rooted personal values (Clampet-Lundquist et al, 2015, p 268; see also Anderson, 1999):

> "If someone is killed and there is only one witness that seen this crime happen and the police find out about it through this witness, then the whole community is going to feel like, 'Oh, they're telling' ... so, they're gonna retaliate against them ... in African American communities and in some inter-racial communities too ... that's really the rule, no snitching." (Edward, age 25)

Interviewer:	Would you ever report a crime to the police?
Jordan:	Hell, no, that'd be snitching.
Interviewer:	Is that a kind of rule within your neighborhood?
Jordan:	It's just my code, period.
Interviewer:	What would happen to you if you were to be found to be a snitch?
Jordan:	I'd kill myself, I'd commit suicide ... I don't give a fuck, that's my grounds. (Jordan, age 25)

In Chapter 6, we drew attention to the perceptions of practitioners beyond law enforcement regarding community-police engagement strategies; although some had evidently built resilience against the type of community backlash that had occurred in places like Ferguson, there was a feeling that some interventions remained deeply flawed and that more bridges needed to be built with young racial minority men. Though the young men's narrative expressed distrust for law enforcement, there was some slight but nuanced optimism expressed by some members of the sample regarding emerging guardian mindsets among officers, as the next section illustrates.

Proactive intervention, "guardian" approaches, and continuing cumulative disadvantage

The young men who were currently in the community (but who had had some contact with the juvenile or formal criminal justice system) described how they had previously engaged in intervention programs that involved the support of law enforcement. Chad, a 23-year-old, disclosed that he had been part of a subset of a prominent Hispanic gang for several years. Like the other young men who were interviewed, he described having had a troubled relationship with law enforcement officers in the past. At one point, he had resisted arrest when intercepted by officers for gang-related crime and had subsequently been exposed to six officers who used excessive force to restrain him. However, upon his release from prison he had made the decision to move away from the gang lifestyle, and decided to try and get rid of his facial tattoos to enhance his employability. He subsequently was referred to a tattoo-removal program run by Queen County Sheriff's Office and coordinated by its dedicated civilian gang prevention coordinator. This was part of a wider community-rehabilitation program, where he was also offered the opportunity to do voluntary work visiting high schools and talking to young people about the risks of gang membership and criminality. Although initially reticent about engaging in a police-associated program, ultimately his experiences were positive:

> "I was nervous, because the initiation with the program is an interview with two gang detectives and [the gang prevention coordinator] as well ... I don't have a negative feeling towards all police officers ... she offered me this opportunity to change my life and I grabbed it."
> (Chad, age 23)

Chad had encouraged other young reforming gang members to get referred to the same program, but admitted that some had not persevered with it because they were not yet fully ready to move away from the gang lifestyle or to engage with a police-affiliated initiative. Although Chad's experiences in the program had been good, and he had evidently developed more positive views of the proactive work being done by the police and their civilian partners, he also believed that it was difficult to shift long-lasting perceptions of racial bias in the minds of other young men. This was particularly hard in light of the online videos of racially motivated police violence that were now readily accessible:

> "There's not really much that the police can do, they can be proactive all they want but if the citizens of the community they are trying to be a part of don't want anything to do with them then nothing is going to work ... it doesn't change the bias in the minds of the criminals in that community that have had experiences with the cops ... because so much violence is going on, cops doing shit to citizens. You have videos of that nationwide – even though cops try to be proactive, you see some cops abusing the citizens, people are not going to want to listen to the cops ... you can have a lot of good things happening, but a fuckup ruins everything." (Chad, age 23)

Previous research has illustrated how open dialogues between officers and minority juveniles can help to generate social capital and support officers in creating better community-policing strategies that enhance police legitimacy (Solis et al, 2009; Deuchar et al, 2015). Dylan, at the age of 17, had participated in the series of Kids and Cops dialogical workshops observed during our fieldwork in Needle City (see Chapters 4 and 6). He described how he had been referred to the workshops by a probation officer as part of a community sentence. Although his impressions of the police had almost always been negative prior to this, he admitted that participating in the dialogues shifted his attitude a little because he was evidently encouraged by the way the officers interacted with him during the workshops:

> "I mean ... it changed my views about these cops ... I feel like now I got to talk to them, like I got communication with them ... like, they were different from what I thought ... like, every Wednesday for, like, four weeks, I found it helpful because I can make, like, more communication with them and see, like they changed my mindset a little bit about the police and stuff. Like, to me, I don't really like the

police, like, the police is bad to me sometimes ... but now they, like, changed my mind a little bit." (Dylan, age 17)

In addition, Michael had also been an active participant in the Kids and Cops workshops in Needle City. Like Dylan, he felt that he had got to know the officers in the workshops. Having been put into a position where he was meeting with officers on a weekly basis while they were in community service (or "guardian") roles (McLean et al, 2019), he had gradually begun to change his views about them and recognized that they were human beings with emotions too:

> "I never talked to the police except if I got arrested. But it made me kinda see when cops are not on duty and they are out and they're not working, I see they're still people ... cops have emotions too, and they go through the same things that we go through every day. At first I just thought that cops had everything, they got all their money, they got guns, they could do everything they want to and nobody wanna touch them. But, at the end of the day, you just kinda talk to them and you see where they come from." (Michael, age 17)

However, although glimpses of movement in reciprocity and trust between law enforcement and young men like Dylan and Michael may have emerged within the workshops, the latter's extended narratives indicated that this was far from being pervasive (Deuchar et al, 2018b). Drawing upon Bourdieu (1990), Chan (1997) argued that the policing *field* represents the structural conditions of police work that emerged within specific social and political contexts, while *habitus* refers to the cultural knowledge and system of dispositions that characterize practical policing. Although structural conditions are important, they do not completely determine the cultural knowledge or practice of frontline officers. Even though, theoretically, the policing fraternity in some regions, such as Needle City, may have come to embrace a focus on proactive, community-oriented perspectives and procedural justice, young men like Dylan and Michael continued to find the dominant "police habitus" in their marginalized and gang-affected urban neighborhoods to be characterized by an adversarial warrior mentality. As such, they continued to resent local officers because of their awareness of officer-involved shootings and the disrespectful way the officers continued to treat them. They believed that local patrol officers needed to communicate the way that officers in the workshops did:

> "Some police just take it to the extreme, like they shoot people when they have a knife ... they shouldn't shoot them like that." (Michael, age 17)

> "These cops [in the workshops], I feel like they're alright, like they're cool and stuff ... but, like, the other ones that patrol my area, like, it didn't really change with them ... like, the police is bad to me sometimes ... but like with these kind of police [in the workshops] and the other type of police ... they are both Queen County ... it would be better if they came together, and communicated with everybody." (Dylan, age 17)

As a 15-year-old young White juvenile, Brandon had also participated in the workshops (see Chapters 4 and 6). Like Michael and Dylan, he clearly found a difference in the dominant police "habitus" demonstrated on the streets compared with what was apparent in the workshops. In the workshops, being exposed to engaging in dialogue with officers had made him realize that they were not "as bad as they seem"; however, he still did not trust law enforcement:

> "I mean, the cops in [the workshops], I like them ... I got to know them, and I've been seeing them a lot. They're just good officers ... it wasn't that they were friendly but we got to interact anyways 'cause we in there for like four weeks so there was no choice but to talk ... [and] they're not as bad as they seem, they just gotta do their job ... out of here, I don't like no police ... out on the street, kids don't like police. You know, police talk to the kids and they walk away." (Brandon, age 15)

Although young men like Michael clearly believed that extreme use-of-force measures were still being employed against racial minorities by some officers, he also had developed a wider, more balanced view of local officers. As with the other participants in the research, he had clearly been influenced by the street code where cooperating with officers was actively discouraged under the stigmatized rubric of snitching (Rosenfeld et al, 2003; Carr et al, 2007). It also appears that the impressions he had gained in the workshops were encouraging him to interact with local officers and show them some courtesy:

> "Before, when I see police if I was walking, even if I was doin' nothing I'd turn away because I'm trying to walk away from them. But now I know they just doin' their job ... if I see police in my neighborhood, I would walk past them, 'Good morning,' shake their hand. 'Cause you never know, one day you might be in danger and that cop comes." (Michael, age 17)

Michael's views resonated with insights from Carr et al (2007), who found that, even though young people may be negatively disposed to officers based on previous lived experiences of antagonistic interventions, this may in some cases be transitory. Where they encounter professionalism, responsiveness, and honesty from officers, which are key elements of procedural justice, they may be supportive of punitive solutions to crime. In spite of Michael's isolated views, the other men continued to be sensitive to the dichotomy between what they appeared to experience in intervention programs and initiatives and what they still came across on the streets – namely, the juxtaposition between contrasting guardian and warrior roles referred to in Chapter 5.

In addition, the young men who were in jail evidently had strong perceptions of a wider sense of bias and discrimination in the criminal justice system. In particular, several raised the issue of race and how it could impact jury composition by reinforcing the discriminatory law enforcement system they had experienced for many years (Somers & Ellsworth, 2003):

> "If you're letting a person go to trial upon what evidence the detectives have or the officers have accumulated against this person, even if this person is guilty or not guilty you're having a six to 12 man jury telling him whether he is guilty or not guilty, so it's to the point where you're picking people out of the community that don't even know the law ... it's a class division and it's racially chosen because if the State picks 12 jurors ... the person that's on trial might be a Black person or Hispanic, just say the State is a White ... of course they're going to go with their race because they feel that they are more racially strong. When it comes to the choice, they're going to lean on their side. (Edward, age 25)

"Crimes in [Palm State] wouldn't be considered crimes in other states. Some of the things we get locked up here for, you're not getting locked up for in Boston ... you can rarely get a fair trial ... You're putting your fate in these 12 jurors that are from Queen County who are ... older White people ... you trippin', you'll get forever and a day ... it's systematically set up." (Juan, age 35)

Chin draws attention to the existence of racial bias at incremental stages of the American criminal justice system and how they connect to create "cumulative disadvantage for defendants of color" (Chin, 2016, p 441). Edward and Juan clearly believed that prior negative experiences with law enforcement combined with the racially motivated punitive ethos that was a feature of the system in Palm State increased the likelihood of later negative events, namely unfair outcomes from racially biased juries.

Chapter summary

In this chapter, we have explored the insights emerging from semi-structured interviews conducted with 12 young men in Queen County, the majority of whom were from racial and ethnic minority groups. All of these participants had also resided in communities mostly populated by Black and Brown residents. While the majority were being detained in the county jail at the time of the interviews, a smaller subset (including three juveniles) were residing in the community. We have discussed the impact of adverse experiences on youth who reside in communities where gang culture was prevalent. Many of the racial minority men we interviewed described how they had drifted into gang membership, violence, and drug-related crime, and many of the juveniles had recently picked up charges relating to minor misdemeanors. For several of the young men, gang-related crimes were interrelated with their moral codes in the sense that drug dealing was sometimes viewed as the only means of earning money to support their socially and economically disadvantaged families. Contrary to practitioners' opinions, the men were not always influenced by rap artists and were not inclined to flaunt the trappings of their gang lifestyles online. Although the men had avoided attracting unwelcome attention from law enforcement in a virtual environment, they had clearly been subjected to negative police attention in public places.

Reflecting insights from wider research (see, for instance, Weitzer & Tuch, 2002; Brunson & Miller, 2006; Brunson & Weitzer, 2009; Bell,

2017a; Cobbina, 2019), the ethnic minority young men interviewed presented us with many examples of how they had been exposed to racial discrimination, harassment, profiling, and physical brutality by officers. Several indicated that they had come to be regarded as symbolic assailants in their neighborhoods, and were subject to police attempts to restrict their movements in the *hood* (Brunson & Miller, 2006; Cobbina, 2019). Although our sample was limited in terms of its inclusion of only one White participant, he indicated that he too had been targeted for discriminatory treatment due to his proximity to justice-involved Black counterparts.

As with insights from previous research (Weitzer & Tuch, 2002), racial profiling had a lasting impact on the young men of color in our sample. Although a minority had ambivalent views on police, many others were highly distrustful of law enforcement and continued to adhere to the "no snitching" rule as part of a street code (Anderson, 1999). Several men described experiences of openly avoiding or even fleeing from officers on sight, and in some cases subsequently becoming exposed to retaliatory use of officer brutality. Some juveniles indicated that they would comply with officers, but rather than this arising because of positive legitimacy perceptions it was based on fear of being subjected to excessive force. In spite of officer perceptions about the emergence of de-policing (see Chapter 3), in the post-Ferguson period it appeared that the young men we interviewed were still strongly aware of officer-involved shootings and excessive use of force against young Black men. They clearly perceived there to be a continuing (and even growing) threat posed by law enforcement.

During the interviews with the young men in the community, we detected a nuanced sense of optimism and hope among those who had recently participated in police-initiated community-engagement programs. However, although some had become more positive in their views of law enforcement as a result of being exposed to officers in the role of guardian, for the most part they continued to be sensitive to the dichotomy between the police habitus they came across in workshops and their continuing exposure to warrior policing in their communities (Chan, 1997; Mclean et al, 2019). In addition, the young men who were in jail had strong perceptions about a wider sense of racial bias and discrimination that was present in the criminal justice system, which reinforced the impact of discriminatory law enforcement.

Chin (2016) argues that the reality of cumulative racial disadvantage in the contemporary justice system is less obvious and more covert than overt animus, but no less real. The positionality of the eight men we interviewed in jail reflected this, given that they were experiencing pretrial detention following a long history of exposure to racial discrimination at the hands of "warrior" police officers. Although some encouraging guardian-oriented practice was beginning to emerge among the law enforcement officers we encountered in some parts of Queen County (albeit with recognized flaws), the wounds emerging from the cumulative disadvantage experienced by men like these may take another generation to heal.

Having reached the end of the empirical sections of the book, we do recognize that the research data we have presented comprise limitations. For instance, our fieldwork was confined to one southern state within the US. The vast majority of the officers, and all of the wider practitioners, were located in one county within the state, and the insights into young men's experiences of policing were largely restricted to those perceptions put forward by a small sample of ethnic minority males who were either incarcerated or on the periphery of offending lifestyles. We also were unable to explore the experiences and perceptions of young women, and we gained access to only one young White male. Given that the latter expressed that his experience with police was similar to his Black associates, it would clearly be beneficial in the future for researchers to explore more closely the neighborhood/class effect and how this intersects with race by interviewing wider groups of young American White people (male and female) who live in communities largely populated by ethnic minority groups in different parts of the US. Future research should also perhaps unpack the way in which the issue of police–community relations plays out differently for different cultures and nationalities across the country, given that our analysis in the book has perhaps implicitly conflated multiracial experiences.

In spite of these limitations, we believe that the multi-perspective, in-depth qualitative research approach we have adopted leads us to draw attention to some important emerging issues regarding the policing of racial and ethnic minorities and make some recommendations for police–community reforms. In the concluding part of the book, we draw our discussion and analysis together and make these final observations and recommendations.

PART IV

Conclusion

8

Future Perspectives on Police–Community Relations

Findings from fieldwork conducted with police, non-law enforcement practitioners, and justice-involved young men were presented throughout the previous chapters. We explored contemporary police–community relations and discussed the historical roots of racial conflict and social decay in America. Scholarly perspectives on policing and anti-gang strategies were also discussed, and challenges related to the policing of young men in disadvantaged communities were highlighted. In this concluding chapter, we summarize findings based on ethnographic research in a Southern American state and address the implications of navigating a post-Ferguson era largely characterized by divisiveness and acrimony. We note emerging issues regarding the policing of racial and ethnic minorities and suggest approaches to foster more procedurally just practices and improve police legitimacy perceptions. In addition, we reflect on lessons learned from previous police-reform efforts and provide recommendations for police–community reforms in troubled times.

Navigating the impossible mandate

Commentators have characterized the unique challenges of police work as "the impossible mandate," or *mission impossible*, due to unrealistic public expectations (Manning, 1977; Goldsmith, 2005; Roelofse, 2010). In contexts where resources are scarce and personnel are stretched, police are expected to be effective at enforcing the law, maintaining order, and keeping crime at bay, while also garnering trust and partnering with communities. During times of crisis and social change, such wishes are even more difficult to fulfill, and given the lessons of the last hundred years it is not surprising that police often fall short of lofty ideals. For example, between the 1920s and 1940s, despite concerns about police brutality and civil rights abuses, there was an emphasis on managerial efficiency and adherence to the bidding of lawmakers (Walker & Katz, 2017); however, this was soon followed by significant developments related to the civil rights movement, as social upheaval and racial conflict took center stage. This ushered in a wave of civil and human rights campaigns comprising organized groups of racial minorities, political activists, civil libertarians, LGBTQI community members, and bohemians.

Civil rights campaigns were also launched in response to police abuses and government overreach, and they forced municipalities to reconsider the relationship between oppressed minorities and the State (Agee, 2017). This gave rise to social justice advocacy as an increasing number of community groups and leaders called for the democratization of policing and for agencies to be more representative of their communities (Walker & Katz, 2017). Police were also expected to be an instrument for the improvement of society, and as such, were expected to be accountable to the people (Walker, 2001). Furthermore, increasing concern about the discretionary actions of police officers in the face of community conflict and riots led to federal commissions, efforts to alleviate a wide variety of community problems, and a growing interest in community policing (Walker, 2001; Potter, 2013).

The common concern that seems to infuse many of these campaigns and reform efforts is the ongoing crisis of legitimacy in the US (Wallace et al, 2018). It is noteworthy that police legitimacy has been at the root of almost every policing-reform initiative due to concerns regarding the treatment of marginalized and oppressed groups, and the progressive changes in American life over time (Agee, 2017; Katz & Maguire, 2020). Ironically, the American dilemma of police legitimacy is yet to be solved. Police legitimacy is still a vexing part of the policing mandate as we move into the third decade of the 21st century, and from a critical perspective this mandate seems even more impossible today. Police leaders around the world must now contend with issues related to globalization and socioeconomic changes reflected in patterns of migration, as well as the dynamic technological changes that have diversified the landscape of policing (Ortega, 2018; Caparini & Hwang, 2019; Hoggett et al, 2019).

While increased public scrutiny may help to improve police accountability through the subjective lenses of smartphones and the sharing of online content, and also through objective forms of oversight such as public boards and commissions, they may also add a great deal of strain to an already challenging occupation. The officers sampled in our study were keenly aware of this seemingly impossible mandate, and many of them resolved to do their jobs diligently and not allow public criticism to deter them. Still, it is difficult to ignore the increasing scrutiny that police departments across the country are experiencing due to high-profile officer-involved shootings, and the intense media coverage in the aftermath of incidents involving the untimely demise of young Black men such as Michael Brown, Eric Garner, and Freddie Gray (Deuchar et al, 2019). Visceral responses to decades of perceived abuse and neglect, along with waning support for a system that routinely decides not to indict police officers who allegedly engaged in corrupt or morally questionable behavior, has contributed to decades-long police–community strife (Mock, 2017b; Cobbina, 2019).

In the midst of such conflicts, police have lamented a growing trend of biased news reporting and false pronouncements that condemn police officers based on little evidence. Our sampled law enforcement participants described such pressures and frustrations that stemmed from constantly being under scrutiny, and discussed its impact on the performance and effectiveness of police. Moreover, there was concern regarding a Ferguson Effect, meaning that police were experiencing low morale, becoming despondent, and engaging in de-policing, or a "pulling back" from encounters with residents (MacDonald, 2016b). This despondency was due to public outrage fueled by social media activism and collective engagement groups such as BLM (Deuchar et al, 2019; Fallik et al, 2020).

In this increasingly tense and at times hostile environment, some police officers were less inclined to be proactive. SQF, in their view, was an important and useful proactive tool once available to law enforcement in the past; however, now SQF was widely frowned upon and deemed by some legal minds to be unconstitutional (Weisburd et al, 2014; Fradella & White, 2017). Officers feared that proactive approaches were unfairly deemed to be racial profiling. They were also concerned that routine police work was interpreted as the intentional targeting of Black and Brown residents, which contributed to the creation of a suspect class, otherwise known as the "symbolic assailants" (Skolnick, 2011; Bell, 2017a). Furthermore, as noted in Chapter 3, there was concern that officers would withdraw from encounters with citizens and even choose not to take charge of situations where the use of force might be appropriate (Braga et al, 2014; Capellan et al, 2019). The safety of officers and civilians might also be further jeopardized given the possibility that criminal behavior was going unchallenged.

Some of the officers in our study were also concerned about the increased likelihood of experiencing disrespect on the streets while conducting their duties, particularly in marginalized and disadvantaged communities. This concern was not only a response to the public outrage, it was also based on the belief that community and family values had deteriorated, and that there was an absence of positive male role models. The result of this, as expressed by some officers, was that young people lacked discipline and showed little respect for authority. This perspective on the absence of role models is reflected in our findings from fieldwork with social workers, clergy, and other practitioners who worked with justice-involved youths. Many of the racial and ethnic minority young men that they served in low-income communities were raised in disorganized homes and deprived of positive influences, particularly the presence of gainfully employed father figures.

The non-law enforcement practitioners who were interviewed, as noted in Chapter 6, also described the prevalence of joblessness and poverty among the young men that they worked with. At-risk youth in such environments were often influenced by negative role models that reinforced criminal norms such as the carrying of illegal weapons, the use of violence to solve problems, and the need to engage in outward displays of aggressive masculinity in order to negotiate the challenges of adversarial neighborhood contexts (Anderson, 1999; Connell, 2005; Harper et al, 2008). These young men invariably encountered police officers on the streets, and in a context defined by poverty, neglect, and institutional failure, there was often a spirit of antagonism between the officer who feels frustrated and disrespected and the Black man who feels desperate, deprived, and angry.

Stark images on social media and reports of police brutality have a deleterious impact on these young men's perceptions of authority. As discussed in Chapter 2, the continually negative coverage of police conduct undermines public trust and fuels the growing disfunction in the relationship between community members and the police. This dysfunction is also reflected in the growing legal cynicism that characterizes the perceptions of the urban poor, many of whom are Black or Hispanic. Legal cynicism refers to the unfavorable attitudes that stem from weak or unresponsive legal norms (Crichlow & McGarrell, 2016), and it is a growing concern that legal cynicism will have a negative impact on citizens' willingness to cooperate with the police and report crimes to police. This problem is amplified given that police will not be effective at their jobs without the support and cooperation of the community. The following quote from Desmond et al (2016), a seminal study on police violence and citizen reporting in Milwaukee, Wisconsin, highlights this point (the "Jude effect" noted here refers to the aftermath of the severe beating of Frank Jude, a Milwaukee resident, by off-duty police officers):

> In the short run, publicized episodes of excessive police violence against unarmed Black men can activate legal cynicism within the Black community to diminish residents' cooperation with law enforcement. In the long run, such episodes likely contribute to that very cynicism by being incorporated into the community's collective memory. We believe collective memory explains why we found "the Jude effect" to be particularly strong in Black neighborhoods. Such incidents belong to a centuries-old tradition of State-sanctioned assaults on the Black body – from slavery and lynching campaigns to urban riots and mass incarceration … Against this backdrop, a violent episode carried out by the police is registered as proof and product of a violent heritage, rendering victim and perpetrator actors in a larger historical drama. (Desmond et al, 2016, p 872)

This case study refers to one of Milwaukee's most publicized moments of police brutality, and presents the analysis of data on police-related 911 calls before and after the incident. The main finding was that police violence against unarmed Black men had a significant negative impact on citizens' reporting of crime. Furthermore, in predominantly Black neighborhoods, high-profile cases of police violence can transcend the nature of individual encounters with police and produce negative effects on crime reporting, perceptions toward police and crime, and disorder across communities.

One important implication here is that in the future of police–community relations within the context of these troubled communities, there should be a renewed commitment to transparency when it comes to investigations of police violence. Moreover, beyond the promise of procedural fairness, which could yield some benefits, there is a need to address the aggressive policing of ethnic minority neighborhoods and patterns of violence among police. These issues will be discussed in the following section as we review the warrior and guardian mindsets and consider the implications for police practice.

A tale of warriors and guardians

The warrior-versus-guardian framework can be considered within America's contemporary political context. There was a view among some of the law enforcement participants that Mr Obama, the former US president, had not extended enough support to law enforcement during his tenure as President. These participants were critical of the former administration and what they believed were hastily arrived at conclusions on the culpability of police officers when incidents involving the police were reported in the news. On the day before President Trump's inauguration, this issue was discussed with several officers who believed that Mr Obama should have done more to defend and praise police. The officers believed that Mr Trump would be an enthusiastic supporter of the police, that law enforcement would garner more respect, and that public perceptions would eventually turn around (Deuchar et al, 2018a). It was also stated that the pendulum had already begun to swing in a favorable direction, and that political support for law enforcement would help to restore officer confidence and morale.

At the time of writing, there was no empirical evidence to suggest that officer morale had improved during Mr Trump's term in office. Yet, there were signs of a renewed focus on the tough-on-crime approaches of the past, which many officers support (Swanson, 2017; Dreier, 2018). Based on the policies presented by the Trump administration White House, Mr Obama's previous push for more police oversight and increased funding for community-oriented programs had been either diminished in terms of priorities or completely dismantled (Deuchar et al, 2019). This preference for tough-on-crime approaches is reflected in the observations made during fieldwork with police officers who embraced a warrior style of policing. The officers who supported this approach saw themselves primarily as enforcers of the law engaged in a good-versus-evil battle against civilians.

As discussed in Chapter 5, the warrior policing mindset is informed by police militarism and a strong reliance on aggressive, zero-tolerance approaches. The warrior policing ethos was also evident in the highly favored gang-suppression strategies that were utilized to curb youth violence in the public housing projects of the inner city. These aggressive warrior-style approaches often have a debilitating effect on police legitimacy perceptions in disadvantaged communities (Brunson, 2007), as they reflect a philosophy that criminalizes the most marginalized neighborhoods in urban areas. They also legitimize the targeting of Black men who are often overrepresented in law enforcement's compilation of gang databases (Butler, 2017; Densley

& Pyrooz, 2020). On the other hand, as depicted in Chapter 4, it was clear during participant observation that some officers were conscious of the need to become guardians rather than warriors. These officers were willing to incorporate proactive strategies to build and sustain legitimacy among community members.

One of the police departments provided a reasonably strong example of the police-as-guardians approach. In this department, there was an agency-wide commitment to prioritizing community service rather than focusing exclusively on crime fighting, and the officers seemed open to discussing early intervention strategies to engage at-risk youth, prevent gang violence, and build partnerships within the community. Street dialogue with youth, the creation of mentorship opportunities through recreational activities, and the provision of community assistance for families are some of the methods used by police officers who embraced the guardian mindset.

There had been very little backlash to officer-involved shootings within some of the fieldwork neighborhoods, and this could be attributed to police outreach efforts in the community. Despite these efforts, many of the justice-involved young men that were interviewed were still suspicious of the police and believed that officers were racist due to direct and vicarious experiences with law enforcement. One of the main concerns among these young men was the fear of retaliation if they were to violate the "no snitching" rule by reporting crimes to the police. This is an important part of the street code that influences the behavior of youth in areas with heavy gang activity (Anderson, 1999). This code, along with the trauma of abuse and neglect, appeared at times to exert a greater influence on youth behavior than the attempts by the authorities to engage them with community-building programs such as after-school workshops and sports leagues.

There was also a stark contrast in the behavior of officers across different roles. The officers serving in the youth outreach programs treated the youth with much greater respect than the patrol officers. This observation was consistent with practitioners' views regarding the need for law enforcement in general, whether they be on patrol or assigned to community outreach, to take on more of a guardianship role and show more understanding and empathy in light of youth experiences of social disadvantage and trauma. Furthermore, despite the efforts of police leaders to foster new organizational cultures that embrace community-oriented approaches, their well-intentioned efforts had a limited impact on the deeply rooted grievances in the community. It was also clear that community outreach initiatives, though beneficial in many ways, could not accomplish sustainable improvements in legitimacy, safety, or willingness to cooperate with the police without the resources, training, and the inter-agency partnerships that are crucial for dealing with long-standing core issues and grievances that impact troubled residents (Maguire & Katz, 2002).

Broader implications

As we consider the challenges regarding police–community relations, and the broader implications for police practice in times of crisis, it is important to acknowledge recent efforts by advocacy groups to inform criminal justice policy and police reform. Several non-profit groups have called for reforms that could potentially lead to more transparent, effective, and procedurally just policing in America. One such group is Color of Change, which has advocated for a comprehensive, public national database that tracks stops, arrests, and use-of-force incidents. Such information could be an impetus for leaders and lawmakers to identify patterns of misconduct and address policies that are soft on police brutality (Anft, 2019; Wald & Kendall-Taylor, 2019). Campaign Zero, a branch of BLM, is another group that seeks to provide broader solutions to police violence by ending broken-windows policing (the aggressive policing of minor offenses), and establishing independent prosecutions to address incidents involving the police use of force. Strategies for Youth is a group that advocates for police training in de-escalation along with youth development. Additionally, there is the American Civil Liberties Union (ACLU), an influential civil rights organization that has called for the better use of data and litigation in order to ameliorate the conflicts that exist between police and communities (Wald & Kendall-Taylor, 2019).

It should also be noted that implicit bias training, which is favored by many of the progressive groups that push for police reform, was utilized by the New York City Police Department and a growing number of agencies across the country (Baker, 2018). This training recognizes how deeply embedded and often unconscious racial bias affects judgment and decision-making, and it is believed that such training could lead to more positive interactions between the police and community members (Fridella & Lim, 2016). Some of these initiatives may seem ambitious; however, they reflect the ethos of much-needed change and they are all worthy of consideration as we contemplate a more comprehensive community-centered plan for improving police–citizen relations. These ideas provide examples of ways to reframe the conversation about police–community relations from the individual criminality of young Black men to the root causes of police abuses and the structural weaknesses in the criminal justice system (Wald & Kendall-Taylor, 2019). With these issues in mind, a path toward developing a procedural justice plan will be explored in the following sections.

Toward a comprehensive procedural justice plan

Over two decades of research on procedural justice and police legitimacy has provided reasonably strong evidence for the efficacy of procedural fairness in policing (Tyler & Fagan, 2008; Taylor & Lawton, 2012; Lee & McGovern, 2013; Meares, 2017). Based on these insights and the social conflicts that are now defining 21st-century policing, the development and implementation of a comprehensive procedural justice plan is recommended as the next logical step in police reform. A key takeaway in procedural justice research is that the fairness of the process matters and that traditional enforcement-focused policing, which emphasizes compliance, punitive outcomes, and the consequences of failing to follow the law, will be detrimental to police–community relations (Tyler, 2006; Tyler & Fagan, 2008). While efficient and purposeful law enforcement must be preserved as an important tool in policing, we suggest that hypermasculine and militaristic warrior-style policing should be properly relegated to the dustbin of history.

Alternatively, procedurally fair strategies can be utilized in all communities, and especially in communities that need to confront the demons of crime and violence and overcome a history of conflict between residents and the police. It is also imperative that such strategies be visible, transparent, inclusive, and reviewable to achieve meaningful and sustainable outcomes. In order to create a community-informed plan, neighborhood representatives should be invited to partner with police leaders to foster collaborative approaches based on shared values between police and community members, toward the maintenance of a law-abiding community. The plan should be based on the principles of procedural justice, often referred to as the four pillars, which are fairness in processes, transparency in actions, opportunities for voice, and impartiality in decision-making (Quattlebaum et al, 2018).

While the partial implementation of procedurally just principles could yield some benefit, it is recommended that comprehensive agency-wide implementation be the ultimate goal. The process for developing a comprehensive plan should prioritize cultural change within police departments prior to the rollout of procedural justice projects. This will create a space for ensuring that toxic work cultures are transitioned to ameliorative and restorative cultures within the workplace. It is also important at the planning stages, even in departments that fail to receive federal grant funding for procedural justice initiatives, to incorporate the input and oversight of academic evaluators and industry professionals who have training and experience in action research. It is crucial for the success of a comprehensive plan that evaluators be a part of the process from the outset, and that they be involved at the inputs and outputs stages of procedural justice projects. Work groups and subcommittees tasked with the development of a procedural justice model must also prescribe how procedural justice will be operationalized and evaluated, how the required police academy and in-service training for personnel will be created, how the plan will be promoted in terms of community-awareness campaigns, and how an implementation plan will be developed. It is also paramount that each step of the process is evaluated to ensure fidelity to the model.

Another recommendation to consider is that a comprehensive procedural justice plan must comprise clear performance measures for transparency and public engagement. There should be "in-house" measures for procedurally just practices within police departments as well as in officer interactions with their communities. Training programs should also be informed by the practice of procedural justice with underserved and marginalized groups such as recent immigrants and individuals with mental and behavioral health needs (Quattlebaum et al, 2018). Additionally, how patrol officers will be evaluated is a technical concern that should be addressed when developing a procedural justice plan. Furthermore, one of the challenges in evaluating officers in the field is how to assess the use of discretion. The Bayley (2018) article speaks to this issue by calling for a return to the forgotten path of police reform by re-evaluating the merits of "cop-led learning," which refers to procedures for improving the tactical choices that frontline officers make. Tactical officer-led training will encourage police agencies to make visible the discretionary decisions patrol officers make every day, by making both strategic and tactical decisions more transparent. While this may require a great deal of resources along with the restructuring of police training programs, it is believed that the returns will be worth the investment.

In concert with the development of a procedural justice plan, it is suggested that attention be paid to the organizational hierarchy of police departments and the willingness of lieutenants and mid-level managers to buy into the plan. This was expressed in a study by Worden and McLean (2017) which was conducted in two cities in the state of New York. The study raised questions regarding the utility of procedurally just policing and whether it promises more than it delivers. The analysis was based on procedural-justice-related performance measures which were incorporated into Compstat (a police performance management statistical tool used for crime reduction, information sharing, and accountability), and it was concluded that there were no significant changes in citizens' perceptions of police. Although procedural justice seemed to have a marginal effect on citizens' overall subjective experience of police, the researchers questioned the internal structure of the police organizations and their willingness to embrace the principles of procedural justice and the need for them.

The notion that perceptions of police in these jurisdictions were generally favorable to begin with, and the lack of data on potential racial and cultural differences in perceptions of police in these locations over time, provides some context for the validity of these findings. Still, an important takeaway from this study is that changes in how police organizations measure, manage, and reward procedurally just behavior is needed to secure more widespread support from line officers and supervisors. The lesson here is that if procedural justice initiatives are not coupled with organizational change then we will likely not achieve the benefits of healthy police–community relations. The concluding section addresses the issue of police violence as well as the need for community outreach and development.

Community outreach and development

Police violence could have a lasting impact on communities of color and do lasting damage to police–community relations. Therefore, despite the potential rewards of a comprehensive procedural justice plan, such strategies might not be enough to stem the decay in police–community relations. While many Americans respect and support the police, it is undeniable that within geographical pockets of disorder and neglect, police–community relations are shaped by a problematic racial history and a pervasive cognitive landscape of anger, resentment, and disillusionment (Brunson, 2007; Rothenberg, 2013; Cobbina, 2019). It is one of the greatest ironies of police professionalization that as policing in general has improved, in terms of education requirements, training, accountability, crime detection, and the use of technology, problems with police legitimacy persist and have caused a gradual decay in the effectiveness of well-intentioned strategies with minority youth in crime-prone neighborhoods. There is an ongoing bifurcation of attitudes toward police that is largely divisible by race, class, and culture and which continues to fuel the animus between the community and the police (Fingerhut, 2017).

This animus is so embedded in American life that it may seem like the most valiant attempts to ameliorate the divide will be futile. Noble efforts to "mend the fences" are often undermined by police acts of violence against residents, and such examples of institutional failure have a negative effect on Black neighborhoods. Furthermore, it is difficult to repair the damage done to communities of color when police agencies try to cover up incidents of police violence and withhold information from the public. When incidents of police violence against unarmed Black men gain public attention, they are typically described as isolated events and the officer involved may be suspended or fired if it is determined that an abuse took place. If police departments were more transparent in the aftermath of such incidents it could go a long way toward healing the divide (Lersch & Mieczkowski, 2005; Desmond et al, 2016).

As we search for a silver lining amid these daunting challenges facing police–community relations in this post-Ferguson era, it is important not to lose sight of community-based initiatives and the fact that the responsibility for positive change in times of crisis should not rest only on the shoulders of police. In order to face the contemporary challenges posed by technological advancements and globalization, projects that seek to build community efficacy are not likely to succeed without enlisting the support of a range of community partners, including local businesses and non-profit enterprises, along with local government partners that are willing to assist in the development of business improvement districts (MacDonald et al, 2010). It is recommended that local government and private sector agencies form partnerships to promote community-informed approaches, and follow through on the promise to improve the quality of life and sustain public trust. In that vein, public health partners can also help a great deal when it comes to identifying and treating at-risk individuals in crime-prone areas. In this context, a healthcare-informed response will be much more appropriate and transformational than a criminal justice response. Such partnerships are becoming even more crucial due to heightened concerns regarding viral infections, such as the coronavirus, and a range of comorbidities that disproportionately impact low-income Black residents. Responsiveness to these concerns could make a huge difference in community perceptions along with a range of indicators pertaining to the quality of life.

The impact of scarce or inconsistent public funding is yet another concern. If programs that provide support and mentorship for youths in impoverished communities were to rely solely on government funding, this could impact the ability of these projects to flourish and produce effective outcomes in the long term. The private sector must, therefore, be a part of the equation when it comes to the creation of social support networks to provide access to education and employment, and to enhance the future prospects for vulnerable families in disadvantaged neighborhoods. With the support of multi-agency networks, there can potentially be more opportunities for young residents to develop employability skills through internships and occupational-training programs that will grant them a greater stake in society and thereby help them to resist the gang lifestyle. A comprehensive procedural justice plan implemented alongside a multi-agency, community-informed improvement strategy could be the silver lining that these communities sorely need. Such an approach might not be the panacea that solves all of the complex problems that community members face on a daily basis, but it could very well be the most promising prescription for addressing police–community issues in our time.

Epilogue

As we reflect on policing in times of crisis, we acknowledge the frequent reminders of the need for difficult conversations about racial injustice. It may be a comforting notion that most officers do not intend to treat Black residents differently from their White counterparts, or to use force unjustly in neighbourhoods that lack political efficacy, yet this does not diminish the pain that many feel in the aftermath of tragic encounters with police. Given the unabated grievances that stem from the shortcomings of the justice system, it is clear that racial conflicts in America's past cannot be treated as mere historical artifacts. It is lamentable that such conflicts seem to define life in America today as law enforcement continues to face scrutiny due to the conduct of officers in Black and Brown communities. This book draws attention to the undeniable fact that within geographical pockets of disorder and neglect in urban landscapes, police–community relations are shaped by a problematic racial history and a pervasive cognitive landscape of anger, resentment, and disillusionment (Brunson, 2007; Rothenberg, 2013; Cobbina, 2019). Moreover, the unshakeable reality of police violence on the streets reminds us of the likelihood that we will experience more "Fergusons" in the near future.

Throughout the previous chapters we have suggested that noble efforts by law enforcement to "mend the fences" are often undermined by recurring incidents of perceived excessive force by police officers. The movement against racial injustice has clearly resonated with millions of people around the world and drawn an unprecedented worldwide response, and during the time of writing, this fact has become abundantly clear. On May 25, 2020, a White Minneapolis Police Department officer killed George Floyd, a 46-year-old Black man, by kneeling on Floyd's neck for seven minutes and 46 seconds, while he was handcuffed and pleading for his life with cries of "I can't breathe" (Kiang & Tsai, 2020; Nwonka, 2020). Floyd's plea seemed to echo the words uttered by Eric Garner back in 2014, whose life also ebbed away slowly and painfully while he was being restrained with a chokehold on the ground by police.

The nature of Floyd's death, occurring within the long-standing context of racial disparities in police violence against Black and Brown people, led to an emotive public response as evidenced by demonstrations all across the country (Kiang & Tsai, 2020). During this social justice battle that held the attention of the nation in the summer of 2020, many communities were also in the midst of a public health crisis that stemmed from the coronavirus global pandemic (COVID-19). At the time of writing, COVID-19 is confirmed to have infected over 17 million Americans, and over 300,000 deaths have been attributed to the virus (Dave et al, 2020). While the country struggled with an economic recession largely due to governmental responses to the public health crisis, Floyd's death led to a series of protests in cities around the US, bringing a "new wave of attention to the issue of inequality within criminal justice" and new demands for policing reform (Dave et al, 2020, p iii).

These protests were larger, fiercer, and more sustained than any demonstrations prior. McLaughlin (2020) highlights that, before Floyd's killing, the highest estimate for any American protest was 4.6 million (the 2017 Women's March), while polls indicated that as many as 21 million adults had attended a BLM or police brutality protest within a month of the Floyd killing. While many of the protests remained peaceful, some involved violence as well as instances of police coercion of protestors. In addition, people of diverse ethnic and cultural backgrounds became mobilized in protest, with solidarity marches and gatherings taking place "from Sydney to Beirut to Istanbul to London to Berlin," and with attention focusing not only on American police brutality but on entire systems of power, racism, and oppression (Daragahi, 2020). Floyd's death also resulted in the assailing officer, Derek Chauvin, being charged with second-degree murder.

Unlike previous incidents of police use of lethal force, including the shooting of Michael Brown in Ferguson, many watched the video footage of Floyd's killing, evidently feeling a combination of "shame, guilt, and anger," and decided not to go along with the status quo anymore, wakening from passivity and becoming galvanized to act together in response (Dreyer et al, 2020). Some argued that COVID-19 played a role in the protests' momentum, since the pandemic kept the public at home with more time to absorb the news about Floyd's fatal arrest and the subsequent civil unrest. As the protests continued to emerge, social media burgeoned with violent images of police tear-gassing peaceful protestors, thus sensitizing the public even more to issues of police brutality and procedural injustice (Ramsden, 2020). Social media platforms were also flooded with calls for changes in law enforcement and societal structures that worsen racism – with Ho (2020) documenting that, eight days after Floyd's death (on June 2, 2020), around 28 million people posted plain black squares to Instagram as part of #BlackoutTuesday, illustrating the way in which BLM had galvanized public attention.

Although the viral video on Floyd's death was a catalyst for the groundswell of support for the movement against anti-Black racism, it is noteworthy that there were additional incidents that contributed to the public outrage. One such incident was the death of Ahmaud Arbery, an unarmed 25-year-old Black man, who was pursued and fatally shot by two White men in February 2020 while jogging in Glynn County, Georgia. The fact that it took months for the alleged perpetrators to be arrested caused a great deal of consternation (Fausset, 2020). In addition, there was widespread anger stemming from the death of a 26-year old Black woman named Breonna Taylor in March of the same year in Louisville, Kentucky. Ms Taylor was shot several times by police officers who forced entry into her home. The police claimed that they were shot at first by Ms Taylor's boyfriend before firing multiple rounds in response. Many were suspicious of this sequence of events and argued that the alleged use of a "no-knock" search warrant, along with excessive force, had led to another unarmed Black resident dying at the hands of the police, and that months of investigation had yielded no justice (Oppel & Taylor, 2020). Video footage of yet another incident that gained national prominence in the aftermath of the Floyd protests involved the police shooting of Jacob Blake, a 29-year-old Black man, in Kenosha, Wisconsin. The video showed Blake walking away from police officers as bystanders yelled in the background. Things quickly turned deadly when an officer shot Blake several times in the back (Raice, 2020).

These high-profile, racially charged incidents fueled public outrage, increased scrutiny of the police, and impacted public perceptions of police legitimacy like never before. In this book, we have drawn attention to the shameful history in America's urban centers that has shaped the racial animus between police and residents, particularly in Black neighborhoods. We have illustrated the way in which the death of Michael Brown uncovered an apparent legitimacy crisis at the heart of American policing. Through our ethnographic research, although we have drawn attention to important illustrative examples of community-based initiatives, we have argued that such strategies may not be sufficient to stem the decay in police–community relations in the post-Ferguson era. Indeed, law enforcement must bear a seemingly impossible burden when trying to maintain order as the country endures a tragic cycle of incidents often involving young Black men and police. The demonstrations that follow, though largely peaceful, sometimes turn violent, with left-wing and right-wing actors creating an angry and sometimes lethal spectacle that seems to do greater harm to the local communities that might desperately need police reform.

In regard to recent calls for sweeping national reforms, it should be noted that professional standards, statements of core values, and codes of conduct already exist in every state and also on the federal level (McChesney, 2020). The International Association of Police Chiefs established a code of ethics in the mid-twentieth century which continues to provide guidance on officer training and professionalism. There are also policies regarding misconduct and anti-bias policing that are informed by the Community Oriented Policing Services office, which is housed in the US DOJ. There is therefore no need to reinvent the wheel. Rather, there is a need for greater awareness and compliance among law enforcement practitioners. The community should also be included in discussions about such codes of conduct, and greater transparency will lead to more fruitful conversations between police and the community. Moreover, if police are not adhering to these values and codes, then there is also a need to reinforce the mechanisms that hold police accountable. Law enforcement leaders should feel empowered to deal with disciplinary issues in collaboration with oversight boards that work with police unions and fraternities to incorporate a system of due process that can lead to remediation or dismissal of officers who are in violation of these codes of conduct. If we sustain systems in which police accountability is stymied by fraternities and external interests, then it will be extremely difficult if not impossible to rebuild public trust.

The challenge of reversing the legitimacy crisis in American policing has now become one that will most likely continue to impact the mandates of law enforcement leadership for generations to come. The recommendations presented in our concluding chapter provide a path forward as we take steps toward an uncertain future. There is clearly a need for wide-ranging conversations in which pro-police advocates find common ground with pro-community activists as they work to improve the delivery of services to the community and enhance the quality of life for residents. All voices should be included in local forums designed to bring healing and restoration, and such forums should lead to a coalition of public and private partnerships that can effectively engage in advocacy for police and community reforms.

Another reform movement that has gained traction is the call to defund police. Indeed, there may be some municipalities that could benefit from the reallocation of funding, as more resources can be directed toward community outreach and development programs as well as the establishment of public divisions that can partner with sworn officers on crisis-response teams. A carefully prescribed plan in which resources are reallocated could ensure that the calls for service that do not require a traditional law enforcement response are overseen by professionals who are trained to help residents access the care and support that they need. While national calls to abolish police might be counterproductive, conversations about reform should be localized given the variety and complexity of community needs across the more than 18,000 police agencies in the US. Now more than ever, this might be the time to encourage partnerships with police rather than the dismantling of police. There may be agencies that need more targeted funding in order to improve the quality of the services they provide and build legitimacy perceptions among community members. In this regard, blanket calls to defund police, though well-intentioned, might be tone deaf to the needs of local communities. While these might be difficult conversations, we believe this book can aid such discussions as we seek to promote workable and proactive reforms and encourage community stakeholders to collaborate in the face of generational challenges.

Notes

Introduction

[1] A fuller discussion of the Michael Brown shooting and unrest in Ferguson appears in Chapter 2.

[2] The data reported here come from the FBI's annual Uniform Crime Report. In an abundance of caution, and to protect the human subjects of this research, the data sources were not published, as a means of ensuring that the specific geographical locations of the fieldwork sites did not become apparent to the reader. More information on the locations may be available upon request on a case-by-case basis and subject to the discretion of the authors.

Chapter 1

[1] Jim Crow refers to repressive laws and customs used to restrict Black rights and sustain a system of racial segregation. This system was legally sanctioned by the US Supreme Court decision in Plessy vs Ferguson in 1896. Regarding the origin of the term "Jim Crow," the White actor Thomas Dartmouth "Daddy" Rice became popular for performing minstrel routines in blackface in the early 1830s. He introduced a fictional "Jim Crow" as a caricature of a clumsy, dimwitted Black slave. Rice's minstrel act was popular among White audiences, and as the show's popularity spread, Jim Crow became a widely used derogatory term for Black men. In the late 19th century the phrase developed into a blanket term for a wave of anti-Black laws laid down after Reconstruction (Jarrett, 2013; Andrews, 2014).

[2] The National Association for the Advancement of Colored People is a civil rights organization formed in 1909 as a biracial endeavor to advance justice for African Americans (Williams & Bond, 2013).

Chapter 3

[1] Gallagher et al (2018) reported that 2.7 percent of 868,637 post-Ferguson tweets contained #BlackLivesMatter and #AllLivesMatter. #BlackLivesMatter, however, was used most prevalently in their data (n = 767,139, 88.3 percent).

[2] Today, this technique is known as gaslighting, whereby the accused manipulates the public into questioning their own sense of the understanding of facts.

[3] To this point, the Southern Poverty Law Center publicized that the vast majority of Confederate monuments were erected nearly half a century after the American Civil War.

4   Antifa, short for Anti-fascist, is a political group that mobilized as an affront to fascism and other forms of right-wing ideologies in the US.

5   Robert E. Lee was the Commander of the Confederate States of America Army during the American Civil War.

6   A gesture used as a greeting in Nazi Germany.

7   Two Virginia state troopers also perished in a helicopter crash as they provided aerial security and public safety in Charlottesville during the Unite the Right rally.

8   This sentiment can be likened to the experiences of minorities who feel that police typecast them by their race or ethnicity.

9   The rate per 100 officers assaulted in the line of duty reached a high of 10.1 in 2017, but was at a temporal period low of 9.0 in 2014. While this may look like assaults on officers have increased since Ferguson, there were spikes as high as 9.8 and 9.9 in 2012 and 2015, respectively. Substantively, assaults on officers were uncharacteristically low during the year of the events in Ferguson.

10 Additionally, stray gunfire from one of the officers struck a civilian.

11 Prior to approaching the vehicle, the gunman shot his ex-girlfriend.

12 Two civilians were also injured in this incident.

13 To inform news and social media narratives, 80 percent of departments employ a public information officer (Chermak & Weiss, 2006). Agencies often seek to proactively bring positive attention to their agencies through social media accounts that push positive news stories of community engagement and pull citizens toward the agencies in order to share information about crime fighting strategies and achievements (Fallik et al, 2020).

14 Some scholars have even argued that police "exaggerate the extent of citizen hostility" (Wilson, 1970, p 28; see also Ridgeway et al, 2006).

15 Some researchers have even linked police brutality to the stress of policing (e.g., Kellogg & Harrison, 1991).

16 It is important to note that police occupational culture varies from one agency to another and among ranks (Reuss-Ianni, 1983; Cordner, 2017).

17 Experienced officers also often play a critical role in maintaining and socializing younger officers into the policing culture.

18 Additionally, research finds that the policing culture stigmatizes officers that look outside the group to cope with daily traumas (Kureczka, 1996).

19 Sometimes referred to as the 'blue wall of silence' or 'blue curtain of silence' in the extant literature.

20 Others, including Morgan and Pally (2016), believe that officers are withdrawing to punish politicians who have turned their back on police in difficult times. In this context, de-policing is a somewhat punitive response.

21 Officers with a strong orientation toward organizational justice and self-legitimacy were somewhat insulated from the Ferguson Effect, according to Wolfe and Nix (2016).

22 Along those lines, racial and ethnic minorities have been historically overrepresented in police search statistics, which leaves many feeling harassed (Browning et al, 1994). Unfortunately, research has yet to explore pre- and post-Ferguson search-disposition rates.

23 Use-of-force continuums and other agency policies appear to be the guiding force behind officer decision-making in many of these instances.

24 Brad is not listed in Table 3.1 because he did not participate in a formal interview. Only one informal conversation with him occurred during participant observation of police deployments in Coconut County.

[25] Police administrators have also been found to experience a loss of proactivity, motivation, job satisfaction, and to believe that crime was on the rise in the post-Ferguson era (Nix & Wolfe, 2018).

[26] Only robbery rates, which were previously declining, increased following the events in Ferguson. Cities with homicide rate increases, they found, had higher rates of violence before Ferguson (Pyrooz et al, 2016).

Chapter 5

[1] In Terry vs Ohio, 392 US 1 (1968), the US Supreme Court decided that under the Fourth Amendment of the US Constitution, a police officer may stop a suspect on the street and frisk him or her without probable cause to arrest if the police officer has a reasonable suspicion that the person has committed, is committing, or is about to commit a crime, and has a reasonable belief that the person "may be armed and presently dangerous."

[2] A "push-in" robbery commonly occurs when someone waits for a resident, usually an elderly person, to open their apartment door and then pushes that person into the apartment and robs it.

Chapter 7

[1] Unless otherwise noted.

References

Aberton, A., Sheldon, J., & Herrera, C. (2005) *Boys and Girls Club: A Synthesis of 20 Years of Research on the Boys and Girls Club*, Philadelphia, PA: Public Private Ventures.

Abt, T. (2019) *Bleeding Out*, New York: Basic Books.

Ackerman, S., & Stafford, Z. (2015) "Chicago police detained thousands of black Americans at interrogation facility," *The Guardian*, [online] August 5, Available from: www.theguardian.com/us-news/2015/aug/05/homan-square-chicago-thousands-detained [Accessed December 15, 2019].

Adams, J. (2019) "'I almost quit'": Exploring the prevalence of the Ferguson effect in two small sized law enforcement agencies in rural southcentral Virginia," *The Qualitative Report*, 24(7): 1747–64.

Adams, K. (1995) "Measuring the prevalence of police abuse-of-force," in W. Geller & H. Toch (eds), *And Justice for All*, Washington, DC: Police Executive Research Forum, pp 61–97.

Adamson, C. (2000) "Defensive localism in white and black: A comparative history of European-American and African-American youth gangs," *Ethnic & Racial Studies*, 23(2): 272–98.

Agee, C. (2017) "Crisis and redemption: The history of American police reform since World War II," *Journal of Urban History*, 44(2): 1–10.

Agnew, R. (2006) *Pressurised into Crime: An Overview of General Strain Theory*, Los Angeles: Roxbury.

Alcorn, C., Tracy, T., & Rayman, G. (2016) "Robbery suspect falls to his death while running from cops during Bronx gang raids, *Daily News*, [online] April 28, Available from: www.nydailynews.com/new-york/man-falls-death-running-cops-bronx-gang-raids-article-1.2616559 [Accessed January 2, 2020].

Alexander, M. (2010) *The New Jim Crow: Mass Incarceration in the Age of Colorblindness*, New York: The New Press.

Alonso, A. (2004) "Racialized identities and the formation of black gangs in Los Angeles," *Urban Geography*, 25(7): 658–74.

Alpert, G., MacDonald, J., & Dunham, R. (2005) "Police suspicion and discretionary decision making during citizen stops," *Criminology*, 43(2): 407–34.

Alvarez, A. (2017) "Torch-wielding white nationalists clash with counterprotesters at UVA," *Daily Beast*, [online] August 12, Available from: www.thedailybeast.com/torch-wielding-white-nationalists-clash-with-counter-protestors-at-uva [Accessed March 23, 2020].

American Civil Liberties Union (ACLU) (2014) *War Comes Home: The Excessive Militarization of American Policing*, Available from: www.aclu.org/report/war-comes-home-excessive-militarization-american-police. [Accessed January 5, 2020].

American Community Survey (2016) *Annual Estimate of the Resident Population*, Washington, DC: United States Census Bureau.

Anderson, E. (1990) *Streetwise: Race, Class, and Change in an Urban Community*, Chicago, IL: University of Chicago Press.

Anderson, E. (1999) *Code of the Street*, New York: W. W. Norton and Co.

Anderson, E. (2012) "The iconic ghetto," *The Annals of the American Academy of Political and Social Science*, 642(1): 8–24.

Anderson, M., Toor, S., Rainie, L., & Smith, A. (2018) "Activism in the social media age," *Pew Research Center*, [online] July 11, Available from: www.pewresearch.org/internet/2018/07/11/activism-in-the-social-media-age/ [Accessed February 1, 2020].

Andrews, E. (2018) "Was Jim Crow a real person?," *History*, [online] August 31, Available from: www.history.com/news/was-jim-crow-a-real-person [Accessed February 1, 2020].

Anft, M. (2019) "An activist for a young generation: Using boycotts, walkouts, protests, and media savvy, Rashad Robinson has gone up against the likes of Amazon and Facebook in the name of racial justice – and won," *The Chronicle of Philanthropy*, [online] October 1, Available from: www.philanthropy.com/article/How-Rashad-Robinson-Turned/247231 [Accessed April 2, 2020].

Atkinson, R. (2003) "Domestication by Cappuccino or a revenge on urban space? Control and empowerment in the management of public spaces," *Urban Studies*, 40(9): 1829–43

Auston, D. (2017) "Prayer, protest, and police brutality: Black Muslim spiritual resistance in the Ferguson era," *Transforming Anthropology*, 25(1): 11–22.

Baker, A. (2018) "Confronting implicit bias in the New York Police Department," *The New York Times*, [online] July 15, Available from: www.nytimes.com/2018/07/15/nyregion/bias-training-police.html [Accessed April 2, 2020].

Balko, R. (2014) *Rise of the Warrior Cop: The Militarization of America's Police Forces*, New York: Public Affairs.

Barker, T. (1986) "Peer group support for police occupational deviance," in T. Barker & D. Carter (eds), *Police Deviance*, Cincinnati: OH: Pilgrimage, pp 9–21.

Bayley, D. (2018) "The forgotten path to police reform in the United States: An essay," *Policing and Society*, 28(2): 125–36.

Beck, G. (1972) "Los Angeles Police Department – SWAT (Special Weapons and Tactics Teams)," *FBI Law Enforcement Bulletin*, 41(4): 8–10.

Bell, J. (2017a) "Dead canaries in the coal mines: The symbolic assailant revisited," *Georgia State University Law Review*, 34(3): 513–79.

Bell, J. (2017b) "The symbolic assailant revisited," *Indiana Legal Studies Research Paper*, 371: 1–57.

Bergbahn, V. (1982) *Militarism: The History of an International Debate, 1861–1979*, New York: Cambridge University Press.

Blake, D. (2016) "Guardian vs. warrior: The many roles of a police officer," *Police One*, [online] July 12, Available from: www.policeone. com/community-policing/articles/197064006-Guardian-vs-warrior-Themany-roles-of-a-police-officer/ [Accessed January 7, 2020].

Blake, J. (2017) "MS-13 as a terrorist organization: Risks for Central American asylum seekers," *Michigan Law Review Online*, 116(39): 39–49.

Bollinger, B. (2018) *An Examination of the Ferguson Effect on Law Enforcement's On-the-Job Behavior*, Thesis, Southeast Missouri State University.

Bonilla, Y. & Rosa, J. (2015) "#Ferguson: Digital protest, hashtag ethnography, and the racial politics of social media in the United States," *American Ethnologist*, 42(1): 4–17.

Bonner, M. (2009) "Media as social accountability: The case of police violence in Argentina," *The International Journal of Press/Politics*, 14(3): 296–312.

Bourdieu, P. (1990) *In Other Words: Essay towards a Reflexive Sociology*, Cambridge: Polity Press.

Boyer, T. (2019) "New York activists, academics urge end to gang database," *Juvenile Justice Information Exchange*, [online] December 13, Available from: https://jjie.org/2019/12/13/new-york-activists-academics-urge-end-to-gang-database/ [Accessed January 8, 2020].

Braga, A. & Weisburd, D. (2015) "Focused deterrence and the prevention of violent gun injuries: Practice, theoretical principles, and scientific evidence," *Annual Review of Public Health*, 36(1): 55–68.

Braga, A., Kennedy, D., Waring, E., & Piehl, A. (2001) "Problem-oriented policing, deterrence, and youth violence: An evaluation of Boston's Operation Ceasefire," *Journal of Research in Crime and Delinquency*, 38(3): 195–225.

Braga, A., Papachristos, A., & Hureau, D. (2014) "The effects of hot spots policing on crime: An updated systematic review and meta-analysis," *Justice Quarterly*, 31(4): 633–63.

Bratton, W. & Murad, J. (2018) "Precision policing: A strategy for the challenges of 21st century law enforcement," *Manhattan Institute*, [online] October 1, Available from: www.manhattan-institute.org/html/urban-policy-2018-precision-policing-strategy-21st-century-law-enforcement-11508.html [Accessed January 8, 2020].

Brotherton, D. (2015) *Youth Street Gangs*, London: Routledge.

Browning, S., Cullen, F., Cao, L., Kopache, R., & Stevenson, T. (1994) "Race and getting hassled by the police: A research note," *Police Studies*, 17(1): 1–11.

Brunson, R. (2007) "'Police don't like Black people:' African-American young men's accumulated police experiences," *Criminology & Public Policy*, 6(1): 71–101.

Brunson, R. & Miller, J. (2006) "Young black men and urban policing in the United States," *British Journal of Criminology*, 46(4): 613–40.

Brunson, R. & Weitzer, R. (2009) "Police relations with Black and white youths in different urban neighborhoods," *Urban Affairs Review*, 44(6): 858–85.

Brunson, R., Braga, A., Hureau, D., & Pegram, K. (2015) "We trust you, but not that much: Examining police–black clergy partnerships to reduce youth violence," *Justice Quarterly*, 32(6): 1006–36.

Buehler, J. (2017) "Racial/ethnic disparities in the use of lethal force by US police, 2010–2014," *American Journal of Public Health*, 107(2): 295–7.

Bureau of Justice Statistics (n.d. a) *National Crime Victimization Survey (NCVS)*, [online], Available from: www.bjs.gov/index.cfm?ty=dcdetail&iid=245 [Accessed March 23, 2020].

Bureau of Justice Statistics (n.d. b) *Contacts between Police and the Public*, [online], Available from: www.bjs.gov/index.cfm?ty=pbse&sid=18 [Accessed January 20, 2020].

Burnett, J. (2017) "'Show me your papers' law temporarily blocked by Federal judge," *NPR*, [online] August 31, Available from: www.npr.org/2017/08/31/547510929/show-me-your-papers-law-temporarily-blocked-by-federal-judge [Accessed February 19, 2020].

Butler, P. (2017) *Chokehold Policing Black Men*, New York: The New Press.

Campbell, B., Nix, J., & Maguire, E. (2018) "Is the number of citizens fatally shot by police increasing the post-Ferguson era?" *Crime & Delinquency*, 64(3): 398–420.

Campbell, D. & Campbell, K. (2010) "Soldiers as police officers/police officers as soldiers: Role evolution and revolution in the United States," *Armed Forces and Society*, 36(2): 327–50.

Caparini, M. & Hwang, J. (2019) "Police reform in Northern Ireland: Achievements and future challenges," *Stockholm International Peace Research Institute*, [online] October 28, Available from: www.sipri.org/commentary/topical-backgrounder/2019/police-reform-northern-ireland-achievements-and-future-challenges [Accessed April 1, 2020].

Capellan, J., Lautenschlager, R., & Silva, J. (2019) "Deconstructing the Ferguson effect: A multilevel mediation analysis of public scrutiny, de-policing, and crime," *Journal of Crime and Justice*. DOI: org/10.1080/0735648X.2019.1652921

Carlson, J. (2019) "Police warriors and police guardians: Race, masculinity, and the construction of gun violence," *Social Problems*. DOI: org/10.1093/socpro/spz020

Carney, N. (2016) "All lives matter, but so does race: Black lives matter and the evolving role of social media," *Humanity & Society*, 40(2): 180–99.

Carr, P., Napolitano, L., & Keating, J. (2007) " 'We never call the cops and here is why': A qualitative examination of legal cynicism in three Philadelphia neighborhoods," *Criminology*, 45(2): 445–80.

Carriere, K. & Encinosa, W. (2017) "The risk of operational militarization: Increased conflict against militarized police," *Peace Science and Public Policy*, 23(3): 1–13.

Carter, D. (1985) "Police brutality: A model for definition, perspective, and control," in T. Barker & D. Carter (eds), *Police Deviance* (3rd edn), Cincinnati, OH: Pilgrimage, pp 9–21.

Centers for Disease Control and Prevention (2018) *Injury Prevention and Control: Adverse Childhood Experiences (ACE) Study*, [online], Available from: www.cdc.gov/violenceprevention/acestudy/ [Accessed March 4, 2020].

Chaffetz, J. & Cummings, E. (2016) *Law Enforcement Use of Cell-Site Simulation Technologies: Privacy Concerns and Recommendations*, [online], Available from: https://info.publicintelligence.net/US-CellSiteSimulatorsPrivacy.pdf. [Accessed January 7, 2020].

Chan, J. (1997) *Changing Police Culture: Policing in a Multicultural Society*, Cambridge: Cambridge University Press.

Chermak, S. & Weiss, A. (2006) "Community policing in the news media," *Police Quarterly*, 9(2): 135–60.

Chin, W. (2016) "Racial cumulative disadvantage: The cumulative effects of racial bias at multiple decision points in the criminal justice system," *Wake Forest Journal of Law and Policy*, 6(2): 441–58.

Clampet-Lundquist, S., Carr, P., & Kefalas, M. (2015) "The sliding scale of snitching: A qualitative examination of snitching in three Philadelphia communities," *Sociological Forum*, 30(2): 265–85.

Clark, J. (1965) "Isolation of the police: A comparison of the British and American situations," *Journal of Criminal Law, Criminology, and Police Science*, 56: 307–19.

Cloward, R. & Ohlin, L. (1960) *Delinquency and Opportunity: A Theory of Delinquent Gangs*, New York: The Free Press.

Cobbina, J. (2019) *Hands Up, Don't Shoot*, New York: New York University Press.

Cobbina, J., Miller, J., & Brunson, R. (2008) "Gender, neighborhood danger, and risk-avoidance strategies among urban African-American youths," *Criminology*, 46(3): 673–709.

Cohen, A. (1955) *Delinquent Boys: The Culture of the Gang*, New York: The Free Press.

Collins, P. (2004) *Black Sexual Politics*, New York: Routledge.

Connell, N., Miggans, K., & McGloin, J. (2008) "Can a community policing initiative reduce serious crime? A local evaluation," *Police Quarterly*, 11(2): 127–50.

Connell, R. (2005) *Masculinities*, Cambridge: Polity Press.

Cooper, F. (2008) "Who's the man?," *Columbia Journal of Gender & Law*, 18(1): 671–742.

Cordner, G. (2017) "Police culture: Individual and organizational differences in police officer perspectives," *Police: An International Journal of Police Strategies and Management*, 40(1): 11–25.

Correll, J., Park, B., Judd, C., & Wittenbrink, B. (2002) "The police officer's dilemma: Using ethnicity to disambiguous potentially threatening individuals," *Journal of Personality and Social Psychology*, 83(6): 1029–314.

Crichlow, V. & McGarrell, E. (2016) "Merchants in the Motor City: An assessment of Arab and Chaldean business owners' perceptions toward public officials and law enforcement," *Criminology, Criminal Justice, Law and Society*, 16(1): 1–19.

Culhane, S., Boman, J., & Schweitzer, K. (2016) "Public perceptions of the justifiability of police shootings: The role of body cameras in a pre- and post-Ferguson experiment," *Police Quarterly*, 19(3): 251–74.

Cullum, J. (2016) "When serving meets surviving – Officer mindset matters," *Community Policing Dispatch: The e-newsletter of the COPS Office*, 9, [online] July, Available from: https://cops.usdoj.gov/html/dispatch/07-2016/serving_meets_surving.asp [Accessed January 20, 2020].

Curry, G., Decker, S., & Egley, A. (2002) "Gang involvement and delinquency in a middle school population," *Justice Quarterly*, 19(2): 275–92.

Dahlgren, P. (1995) *Television and the Public Sphere*, Thousand Oaks, CA: Sage.

Daragahi, B. (2020) "Why the George Floyd protests went global," *Atlantic Council*, [online] June 10, Available from: www.atlanticcouncil.org/blogs/new-atlanticist/george-floyd-protests-world-racism/ [Accessed August 25, 2020].

Dave, D., Friedson, A., Matsuzawa, K., Sabia, J., & Safford, S. (2020) "Black Lives Matters protests, social distancing and COVID-19," *Center for Health, Economics and Policy Studies: Working Paper Series*, San Diego, CA: San Diego University.

Davey, J., Obst, P., & Sheehan, M. (2000) "Developing a profile of alcohol consumption patterns of police officers in a large scale sample of an Australian Police service," *European Addition Studies*, 6(4): 205–12.

Davis, A. (2015) "'YouTube effect' has left police officers under siege, law enforcement leaders say," *The Washington Post*, [online] October 8, Available from: www.washingtonpost.com/news/post-nation/wp/2015/10/08/youtube-effect-has-left-police-officers-under-siege-law-enforcement-leaders-say/ [Accessed March 28, 2020].

Davis, D. & Silver, B. (2004) "Civil liberties vs. security: Public opinion in the context of the terrorist attacks on America," *American Journal of Political Science*, 48(1): 28–46.

Decker, S. (2007) "Expand the use of police gang units," *Criminology and Public Policy*, 6(4): 729–34.

Decker, S. & Pyrooz, D. (2010) "On the validity and reliability of gang homicide: A comparison of disparate sources," *Homicide Studies*, 14: 359–76.

Decker, S., van Gemert, F., & Pyrooz, D. (2009) "Gangs, migration, and crime: The changing landscape in Europe and the USA," *Journal of International Migration and Integration*, 10(4): 393–408.

Decker, S., Melde, C., & Pyrooz, D. (2013) "What do we know about gangs and gang members and where do we go from here?" *Justice Quarterly*, 30(3): 369–402.

Defense Logistics Agency (2018) 1033 *Program FAQs, Defense Logistics Agency*, [online], Available from: www.dla.mil.ezproxy.fau.edu/DispositionServices/Offers/Reutilization/LawEnforcement/ProgramFAQs.aspx [Accessed April 8, 2018].

Dejong, C., Mastrofski, S., & Parks, R. (2001) "Patrol officers and problem solving: An application of expectancy theory," *Justice Quarterly*, 18(1): 31–61.

Delehanty, C., Mewhirter, J., Welch, R., & Wilks, J. (2017) "Militarization and police violence: The case of the 1033 program," *Research & Politics*, 4(2): 28–46.

Della Porta, D. & Diani, M. (2005) *Social Movements: An Introduction* (2nd edn), Oxford: Wiley-Blackwell.

Densley, J. & Pyrooz, D. (2020) "The Matrix in context: Taking stock of police gang databases in London and beyond," *Youth Justice*, 20(1–2): 11–30.

Department of Health and Human Services (2007) *Results from the 2007 National Survey on Drug Use and Health: National Findings*, Washington, DC: Department of Health and Human Services.

Department of Justice (2015) *Department of Justice Report Regarding the Criminal Investigation into the Shooting Death of Michael Brown by Ferguson, Missouri Police Officer Darren Wilson*, [online] March 4, Available from: www.justice.gov/sites/default/files/opa/press-releases/attachments/2015/03/04/doj_report_on_shooting_of_michael_brown_1.pdf [Accessed April 8, 2020].

Desmond, M., Papachristos, A., & Kirk, D. (2016) "Police violence and citizen crime reporting in the black community," *American Sociological Review*, 81(5): 857–76.

Deuchar, R. (2013) *Policing Youth Violence: Transatlantic Connections*, London: IOE Press.

Deuchar, R. (2018) *Gangs and Spirituality: Global Perspectives*, Cham: Palgrave MacMillan.

Deuchar, R. & Bhopal, K. (2017) *Young People and Social Control: Problems and Prospects from the Margins*, Basingstoke: Palgrave MacMillan.

Deuchar, R., Miller, J., & Barrow, M. (2015) "Breaking down barriers with the usual suspects: Findings from a research-informed intervention with police, young people and residents in the West of Scotland," *Youth Justice*, 15(1): 57–75.

Deuchar, R., Fallik, S., & Crichlow, V. (2018a) "Despondent officer narratives and the 'post-Ferguson' effect: Exploring law enforcement perspectives and strategies in a Southern American State," *Policing & Society*, 29(9): 1042–57.

Deuchar, R., Søgaard, T., Holligan, C., Miller, K., Bone, A., & Borchardt, L. (2018b) "Social capital in Scottish and Danish neighbourhoods: Paradoxes of a police-community nexus at the front line," *Journal of Scandinavian Studies in Criminology and Crime Prevention*, 19(2): 187–203.

Deuchar, R., Crichlow, V., & Fallik, S. (2019) "Cops in crisis?: Ethnographic insights on a new era of politicization, activism, accountability and change in transatlantic policing," *Policing and Society*, 30(1): 47–64.

Ditton, J. & Farrall, S. (2017) *The Fear of Crime*, New York: Routledge.

Dobrin, A., Fallik, S., & Mello, B. (2018) "SWAT unit proactive search warrant deployments: A mixed effects model exploration," *Policing*, DOI: 10.1093/police/pay100

Dodge, M. (2006) "Friendship, persuasion, and pretense," *Youth Violence & Juvenile Justice*, 4(3): 234–46.

Dolan, M., Shallwani, P., & Kesling, B. (2014) "Ferguson: Violence flares again as police confront protesters," *Wall Street Journal*, [online] August 19, Available from: www.wsj.com/amp/articles/ferguson-violence-flares-again-as-police-confront-protesters-1408407117?tesla=y

Domanick, J. (2015) *Blue: The LAPD and the Battle to Redeem American Policing*, New York: Simon and Schuster.

Doyle, M. (1980) "Police culture: Open or closed," in: V. Leonard (ed), *Fundamentals of Law Enforcement: Problems and Issues*, St Paul, MN: West, pp 61–83.

Dreier, H. (2018) "I've been reporting on MS-13 for a year. Here are the 5 things Trump gets most wrong," *ProPublica*, [online] June 25, Available from: www.propublica.org/article/ms-13-immigration-facts-what-trump-administration-gets-wrong [Accessed November 11, 2019].

Dreyer, B., Trent, M., Anderson, A., Askew, G., Boyd, R., Coker, T., ... & Montoya-Williams, D. (2020) "The death of George Floyd: Bending the arc of history towards justice for generations of children," *Pediatrics*, 146(3): e2020009639.

Du Bois, W. (1953) *The Souls of Black Folk*, New York: The Modern Library.

Ebert, J. (2017) "Jeff Sessions in Nashville outlines plan to send surplus military weapons, equipment to local police," *The Tennessean*, [online] August 28, Available from: www.tennessean.com/story/news/politics/2017/08/28/jeff-sessions-nashvilleoutlines-plan-send-surplus-military-weapons-equipment-local-police/603661001/ [Accessed January 5, 2020].

Edwards, G. & Rushin, S. (2018) "The effect of President Trump's election on hate crimes," *SSRN*, [online] January 18, Available from: https://papers.ssrn.com/sol3/papers.cfm?abstract_id=3102652 [Accessed January 20, 2020].

Eide, A. & Thee, M. (1980) *Problems of Contemporary Militarism*, New York: St Martin's Press.

Ekins, E. (2016) "Policing in America: Understanding public attitudes toward the police. Results from a national survey," *Cato Institute*, [online] December 7, Available from: www.cato.org/survey-reports/policing-america [Accessed February 1, 2020].

Engel, R. (2008) "A critique of the 'outcome test' in racial profiling," *Justice Quarterly*, 25(1): 1–35.

Epp, C., Maynard-Moody, S., & Haider-Markel, D. (2014) *Pulled Over: How Police Stops Define Race and Citizenship*, Chicago, IL: University of Chicago Press.

Esbensen, F., Peterson, D., Taylor, T., & Freng, A. (2009) "Similarities and differences in risk factors for violent offending and gang membership," *The Australian and New Zealand Journal of Criminology*, 42: 310–35.

Fader, J. (2016) "Criminal family networks: Criminal capital and cost avoidance among urban drug sellers," *Deviant Behavior*, 37(11): 1325–40.

Fallik, S. & Novak, K. (2013) "Police Discretion and Control: Biased-Based Policing," in G. Bruinsma & D. Weisburd (eds), *Encyclopedia of Criminology and Criminal Justice*, New York: Springer Verlag, pp 154–62.

Fallik, S., Deuchar, R., & Crichlow, V. (2019) "Body-worn cameras in the post-Ferguson era: An exploration of law enforcement perspectives," *Journal of Police and Criminal Psychology*. DOI: 10.1007/s11896-018-9300-2.

Fallik, S., Deuchar, R., Crichlow, V., & Hodges, H. (2020) "Policing through social media: A qualitative exploration," *International Journal of Police Science and Management*. DOI: 0rd/10.1177/1461355720911948

Farrington, D. & Loeber, R. (2000) "Epidemiology of juvenile violence," *Child and Adolescent Psychiatric Clinics of North America*, 9(4): 733–48.

Fausset, R. (2020) "What we know about the shooting death of Ahmaud Arbery," *The New York Times*, [online], Available from: www.nytimes.com/article/ahmaud-arbery-shooting-georgia.html. [Accessed December 1, 2020].

Federal Bureau of Investigation (2017) "Crime in the United States: Expanded Homicide Data Table 13," [online], Available from: https://ucr.fbi.gov/crime-in-the-u.s/2017/crime-in-the-u.s.-2017/tables/expanded-homicide-data-table-13.xls [Accessed August 28, 2019].

Federal Bureau of Investigation (n.d. a) "Uniform Crime Reporting (UCR) Program," [online], Washington, DC: Department of Justice, Available from: www.fbi.gov/services/cjis/ucr [Accessed March 20, 2020].

Federal Bureau of Investigation (n.d. b) "Law Enforcement Officers Killed and Assaulted (LEOKA) Program," [online], Washington, DC: Department of Justice, Available from: www.fbi.gov/services/cjis/ucr/leoka [Accessed March 20, 2020].

Feiberg, A., Branton, R., & Martinez-Ebers, V. (2019) "Counties that hosted a 2016 Trump rally saw a 226 percent increase in hate crimes," *Washington Post*, [online] March 22, Available from: www.washingtonpost.com/politics/2019/03/22/trumps-rhetoric-does-inspire-more-hate-crimes/ [Accessed March 20, 2020].

Felker-Kantor, M. (2019) *Policing Los Angeles*, California: UNC Press.

Fields, R. (2019) "The Ferguson effect on police officers' culture and perceptions in local police departments," Dissertation, Walden University.

Fine, M., Freudenberg, N., Payne, Y., Perkins, T., Smith, K., & Wanzer, K. (2003) " 'Anything can happen with police around': Urban youth evaluate strategies of surveillance in public places," *Journal of Social Issues*, 59(1): 141–58.

Fingerhut, H. (2017) "Deep Racial, Partisan Divisions in Americans' Views of Police Officers," [online], Available from: www.pewresearch.org/fact-tank/2017/09/15/deep-racial-partisan-divisions-in-americans-views-of-police-officers/ [Accessed February 1, 2020].

Forman, J. (2004) "Community policing and youth as assets," *Journal of Criminal Law & Criminology*, 95(1): 1.

Forman, J. (2017) *Locking Up Our Own*, New York: Farrar, Straus and Giroux.

Fradella, H. & White, M. (2017) "Reforming stop-and-frisk," *Criminology, Criminal Justice, Law & Society*, 18(3): 45–65.

Fridell, L. & Lim, H. (2016) "Assessing the racial aspects of police force using the implicit- and counter-bias perspectives," *Journal of Criminal Justice*, 44(1): 36–48.

Fredricks, J., Hackett, K., & Bregman, A. (2010) "Participation in boys and girls clubs: Motivation and stage environment fit," *Journal of Community Psychology*, 38(3): 369–85.

Freire, P. (1972) *Pedagogy of the Oppressed*, London: Sheed and Ward.

Fritsch, J. (2000) "The Diallo Verdict: The Overview; 4 Officers in Diallo Shooting are Acquitted of all Charges," [online], Available from: www.nytimes.com/2000/02/26/nyregion/diallo-verdict-overview-4-officers-diallo-shooting-are-acquitted-all-charges.html [Accessed December 20, 2019].

Fritsch, E., Caeti, T., & Taylor, R. (1999) "Gang suppression through saturation patrol, aggressive curfew, and truancy enforcement: A quasi-experimental test of the Dallas anti-gang initiative," *Crime & Delinquency*, 45(1): 122–39.

Fyfe, J. (1988) "Police use of deadly force: Research and reform," *Justice Quarterly*, 5(2): 165–205.

Gallagher, R., Reagan, A., Danforth, C., & Dodds, P. (2018) "Divergent discourse between protests and counter-protests: #BlackLivesMatter and #AllLivesMatter," *PLOS ONE*, 13(4).

Gau, J. (2011) "The convergent and discriminant validity of procedural justice and police legitimacy: An empirical test of core theoretical propositions," *Journal of Criminal Justice*, 39(6): 489–98.

Gau, J. & Brunson, R. (2010) "Procedural justice and order maintenance policing: A study of inner-city young men's perceptions of police legitimacy," *Justice Quarterly*, 27(2): 255–79.

Gau, J., Corsaro, N., Steward, E., & Brunson, R. (2012) "Examining macro-level impacts on procedural justice and police legitimacy," *Journal of Criminal Justice*, 40(4): 333–43.

Geller, W. & Scott, M. (1992) *Deadly Force: What Do We Know*, Washington, DC: Police Executive Research Forum.

Gill, C., Weisburd, D., Telep, C., Vitter, Z., & Bennett, T. (2014) "Community-oriented policing to reduce crime, disorder and fear and increase satisfaction and legitimacy among citizens: A systematic review," *Journal of Experimental Criminology*, 10(4): 399–428.

Giroux, H. (2005) *Border Crossings*, Abingdon: Routledge.

Giwa, S., James, C., Anucha, U., & Schwartz, K. (2014) "Community policing – a shared responsibility: A voice-centered relational method analysis of a police/youth-of-color dialogue," *Journal of Ethnicity in Criminal Justice*, 12(3): 218–45.

Gold, R. (1958) "Roles in sociological field observations," *Social Forces*, 36(3): 217–23.

Goldman, A. (2017) "Trump reverses restrictions on military hardware for police," *New York Times*, [online] August 28, Available from: www.nytimes.com/2017/08/28/us/politics/trump-police-military-surplus-equipment.html [Accessed December 20, 2019].

Goldsmith, A. (2005) "Police reform and the problem of trust," *Theoretical Criminology*, 9(4): 443–70.

Goldsmith, A. (2015) "Disgracebook policing: Social media and the rise of police indiscretion," *Policing and Society*, 25(3): 249–67.

Goldstein, H. (1967) "Administrative problems in controlling the exercise of police authority," *Journal of Criminal Law and Criminology*, 58(2): 160–72.

Goodman, J. (2014) "Dozens of gang suspects held in raids in Manhattan," *New York Times*, [online] June 4, Available from: www.nytimes.com/2014/06/05/nyregion/dozens-of-suspected-gang-members-arrested-in-raid-of-2-harlem-housing-projects.html [Accessed December 20, 2019].

Goolkasian, G., Geddes, R., & DeJong, W. (1985) *Coping with Police Stress*, Washington, DC: United States Department of Justice.

Gottfredson, M. & Gottfredson, D. (1988) *Decision Making in Criminal Justice: Toward the Rational Exercise of Discretion* (Vol. 3), New York: Springer Science & Business Media.

Gramlich, J. (2019) "5 facts about crime in the U.S.," *FactTank, News in the Numbers: Pew Research Center*, [online] October 17, Available from: www.pewresearch.org/fact-tank/2019/10/17/facts-about-crime-in-the-u-s/ [Accessed March 20, 2020].

Graziano, L., Rosenbaum, D., & Schuck, A. (2014) "Building group capacity for problem solving and police–community partnerships through survey feedback and training: A randomized control trial within Chicago's community policing program," *Journal of Experimental Criminology*, 10(1): 79–103.

Green, J. & Pranis, K. (2007) "Gang wars: The failure of enforcement tactics and the need for effective public safety strategies," *Justice Policy Institute*, [online] July, Available from: www.justicepolicy.org/research/1961 [Accessed January 6, 2020].

Groger, J. (1997) *Memory and Remembering: Everyday Memory in Context*, New York: Longman.

Habermas, J. (1991) "The public sphere," in C. Mukerji & M. Schudson (eds), *Rethinking Popular Culture: Contemporary Perspectives in Cultural Studies*, Berkeley, CA: University of California Press, pp 398–404.

Hagedorn, J. (2008) *A World of Gangs: Armed Young Men and Gansta Culture*, Minneapolis, MN: University of Minnesota.

Hammersley, M. (2006) "Ethnography: Problems and prospects," *Ethnography and Education*, 1(1): 3–14.

Hare, B. (2016) "How did we get here from Ferguson?" *CNN*, [online] August 9, Available from: www.cnn.com/2016/08/09/us/ferguson-michael-brown-timeline/index.html [Accessed February 1, 2020].

Harper, G., Davidson, J., & Hosek, S. (2008) "Influence of gang membership on negative affect, substance use, and antisocial behavior among homeless African American male youth," *American Journal of Men's Health*, 2(3): 229–43.

Hasan, M. (2019) "After El Paso, we can longer ignore Trump's role in inspiring mass shootings," *The Intercept*, [online] August 4, Available from: https://theintercept.com/2019/08/04/el-paso-dayton-mass-shootings-donald-trump/ [Accessed March 28, 2020].

Hattem, B. (2016) "How massive gang sweeps make growing up in the projects a crime," *The Gothamist*, [online] October 24, Available from: https://gothamist.com/news/how-massive-gang-sweeps-make-growing-up-in-the-projects-a-crime [Accessed January 6, 2020].

Herbert, S. (2001) " 'Hard Charger' or 'Station Queen'? Policing and the masculinist state," *Gender, Place & Culture*, 8(1): 55–71.

Herbert, S. (2006) "Tangled up in blue: Conflicting paths to police legitimacy," *Theoretical Criminology*, 10: 481–504.

Hill, K. (2016) *Beyond the Rope: The Impact of Lynching on Black Culture and Memory*, Cambridge: Cambridge University Press.

Ho, S. (2020) "A social media 'blackout' enthralled Instagram. But did it do anything?" *NBC News*, [online] June 13, Available from: www.nbcnews.com/tech/social-media/social-media-blackout-enthralled-instagram-did-it-do-anything-n1230181 [Accessed August 25, 2020].

Hoggett, J., Redford, P., Toher, D., & White, P. (2019) "Challenges for police leadership: Identity, experience, legitimacy and direct entry," *Journal of Police and Criminal Psychology*, 34(1): 145–55.

Holmes, M. & Smith, B. (2008) *Race and Police Brutality: Roots of an Urban Dilemma*, Albany, NY: State University of New York Press.

Howell, B. & Bustamante, P. (2019) *Report on the Bronx 120 Mass Gang Prosecution*, [online], Available from: www.bronx120.report [Accessed January 6, 2020].

Howell, J. & Egley, A. (2005) "Moving risk factors into developmental theories of gang membership," *Youth Violence and Juvenile Justice*, 3(4): 334–54.

Howell, J. & Griffiths, E. (2019) *Gangs in America's Communities* (3rd edn), Thousand Oaks, CA: Sage.

Howell, J., Braun, M., & Bellatty, P. (2017) "The practical utility of a life-course gang theory for intervention," *Journal of Crime and Justice*, 40: 358–75.

Huebner, B., Martin, K., Moule, R., Pyrooz, D., & Decker, S. (2016) "Dangerous places: Gang members and neighborhood levels of gun assault," *Justice Quarterly*, 33(5): 836–62.

Hughes, T. (2001) "Police officers and civil liability: 'The ties that bind?'," *Policing: An International Journal of Police Strategies and Management*, 24(2): 240–62.

Hunt, J. (1984) "The development of rapport through the negotiation of gender in field work among police," *Human Organization*, 43(4): 283–96.

Husain, N. (2019) "Laquan McDonald timeline: The shooting, the video, the verdict and the sentencing," *Chicago Tribune*, [online] January 18, Available from: www.chicagotribune.com/news/laquan-mcdonald/ct-graphics-laquan-mcdonald-officers-fired-timeline-htmlstory.html [Accessed January 30, 2020].

Hylton, W. (2016) "Baltimore vs. Marilyn Mosby," *New York Times*, [online] September 28, Available from: www.nytimes.com/2016/10/02/magazine/marilyn-mosby-freddie-gray-baltimore.html [Accessed March 28, 2020].

Immigration & Customs Enforcement (2016) *Significant Prospective Event Activity Report*, [online], Available from: www.documentcloud.org/documents/3475709-ICE-Officials-Discussing-Bronx-Gang-Raid.html#document/p3 [Accessed January 6, 2020].

Intravia, J., Wolff, K., & Piquero, A. (2018) "Investigating the effects of media consumption on attitudes toward police legitimacy," *Deviant Behavior*, 39(8): 963–80.

Jackson, J., Bradford, B., Hough, M., Myhill, A., Quinton, P., & Tyler, T. (2012) "Why do people comply with the law? Legitimacy and the influence of legal institutions," *British Journal of Criminology*, 52(6): 1051–71.

James, N. (2018) *Recent Violent Crime Trends in the United States. Congressional Research Service*, [online], Available from: https://fas.org/sgp/crs/misc/R45236.pdf [Accessed August 28, 2019].

Jarrett, G. (2013) "What is Jim Crow?" *PMLA (Publications of the Modern Language Association*, 128(2): 388–90.

Juris, J. (2008) "Performing politics: Image, embodiment, and affective solidarity during anti-corporate globalization protests," *Ethnography*, 9(1): 61–97.

Kadleck, C. (2003) "Police employee organizations," *Policing: An International Journal*, 26(2): 341–50.

Kane, R. & White, M. (2009) "Bad cops: A study of career-ending misconduct among New York City Police Officers," *Criminology and Public Policy*, 8(4): 751–69.

Katz, C. & Maguire, E. (eds) (2020) *Transforming The Police: Thirteen Key Reforms*, Long Grove, IL: Waveland Press.

Kellogg, T. & Harrison, M. (1991) "Post-traumatic stress plays a part in police brutality," *Law Enforcement News*, 12: 16.

Kennedy, D. (2012) *Deterrence and Crime Prevention: Reconsidering the Prospect of Sanction*, New York: Routledge.

Kerner, O. (1988) *Kerner Report: Report of the National Advisory Commission on Civil Disorders*, New York: Pantheon.

Kesling, B. & Pervaiz, S. (2014) "Ferguson police tactics challenged as conflict evolved," *The Wall Street Journal*, [online] August 21, Available from: www.wsj.com/articles/ferguson-police-tactics-challenged-as-conflict-evolved-1408675855 [Accessed January 6, 2020].

Kiang, M. & Tsai, A. (2020) "Statements issued by academic medical institutions after George Floyd's killing by police and subsequent unrest in the United States: Cross-sectional study," *MedRxiv*. https://doi.org/10.1101/2020.06.22.20137844.

King, M. & Washington, J. (2003) *A Testament of Hope: The Essential Writings and Speeches*, New York: HarperCollins.

Klein, M. (1993) "Attempting gang control by suppression: The misuse of deterrence principles," *Studies on Crime & Crime Prevention*, 2(1): 88–111.

Klein, M. (2004) *Gang Cop*, Lanham, MD: AltaMira Press.

Klein, R. (2018) "Trump said 'blame on both sides' in Charlottesville, now the anniversary puts on the spot," *ABC News*, [online] August 12, Available from: https://abcnews.go.com/Politics/trump-blame-sides-charlottesville-now-anniversary-puts-spot/story?id=57141612 [Accessed March 12, 2020].

Kochel, T., Park, R., & Mastrofski, S. (2013) "Examining police effectiveness as a precursor to legitimacy and cooperation with police," *Justice Quarterly*, 30(5): 895–925.

Korte, G. (2015) "Obama bans some military equipment sales to police," *USA Today*, [online] May 18, Available from: www.usatoday.com/story/news/politics/2015/05/18/ obama-police-military-equipment-sales-new-jersey/27521793/ [Accessed January 6, 2020].

Kraska, P. (2007) "Militarization and policing: Its relevance to 21st century police," *Policing: A Journal of Policy and Practice*, 1(4): 501–13.

Kraska, P. & Cubellis, L. (1997) "Militarizing Mayberry and beyond: Making sense of American paramilitary policing," *Justice Quarterly*, 14(4): 607–29.

Kraska, P. & Kappeler, V. (1997) "Militarizing American police: The rise and normalization of paramilitary units," *Social Problems*, 44(1): 1–18.

Kraska, P. & Paulsen, D. (1997) "Grounded research into US paramilitary policing: Forging the iron fist inside the velvet glove," *Policing and Society*, 7(4): 253–70.

Kunelman, M. & Galvan, A. (2019) "Trump words linked to more hate crime? Some experts think so," *Associated Press*, [online] August 7, Available from: www.apnews.com/7d0949974b1648a2bb592cab 1f85aa16 [Accessed March 10, 2020].

Kureczka, A. (1996) "Critical incident stress in law enforcement," *FBI Law Enforcement Bulletin*, 65: 10–6.

La Vigne, N., Jannetta, J., Fontaine, J., Lawrence L., & Esthappan, S. (2019) *The National Initiative for Building Community Trust and Justice: Key Process and Outcome Evaluation Findings*, [online], Available from: www.urban.org/research/publication/national-initiative-building-community-trust-and-justice [Accessed January 25, 2020].

Lamberth, J. (1994) *Revised Statistical Analysis of the Incidence of Police Stops and Arrests of Black Drivers/Travellers on the New Jersey Turnpike between Exits or Interchanges 1 And 3 From Years 1988 Through 1991*, [online], Available from: www.lamberthconsulting.com/downloads/ new_jersey_study_report.doc [Accessed March 20, 2020].

Lauger, T. & Densley, J. (2018) "Broadcasting badness: Violence, identity, and performance in the online gang rap scene," *Justice Quarterly*, 35(5): 816–41.

Lee, M. & McGovern, A. (2013) "Force to sell: Policing the image and manufacturing public confidence," *Policing and Society*, 23(2): 103–24.

Lersch, K. & Mieczkowski, T. (2005) "Violent police behavior: Past, present, and future research directions," *Aggression and Violent Behavior*, 10(5): 552–68.

Levitt, S. (2002) "Using electoral cycles in police hiring to estimate the effects of police on crime: Reply," *The American Economic Review*, 92(4): 1244–50.

Lieblich, E. & Shinar, A. (2018) "The case against police militarization," *Michigan Journal of Race and Law*, 23(1): 105–53.

Littlejohn, E. (1981) "Civil liability and the police officer: The need for new deterrents to police misconduct," *University of Detroit Journal of Law*, 58: 365–431.

Loader, I. & Sparks, R. (2016) "Ideologies and crime: Political ideas and the dynamics of crime control," *Global Crime*, 17(3–4): 314–30.

Loo, R. (2003) "A meta-analysis of police suicide rates: Findings and issues," *Suicide and Life-Threatening Behavior*, 33(3): 313–25.

Lopez, G. (2016) "Why was Michael Brown shot?" *Vox*, [online] January 27, Available from: www.vox.com/2015/5/31/17937818/ michael-brown-police-shooting-darren-wilson [Accessed January 5, 2020].

Lucas, L. (2015) "Functionally suspect: Reconceptualizing 'race' as a suspect classification," *Michigan Journal of Race and Law*, 20(2): 255–85.

Lynch, T. (2014) "Ferguson, a war zone or a US city?" *CNN*, [online] August 14, Available from: www.cnn.com/ 2014/08/14/opinion/ lynch-ferguson-police/index.html [Accessed January 7, 2020].

MacDonald, H. (2016a) "'Ferguson Effect' detractors are wrong," *Quillette*, [online] March 21, Available from: www.quillette.com/ 2016/03/21/ferguson-effect-detractors-are-wrong [Accessed December 13, 2019].

MacDonald, H. (2016b) *The War on Cops: How the New Attack on Law and Order Makes Everyone Less Safe*, New York: Encounter Books.

MacDonald, J., Golinelli, D., Stokes, R., & Bluthenthal, R. (2010) "The effect of business improvement districts on the incidence of violent crimes," *Injury Prevention*, 16(1): 327–32.

Madhani, A. (2014) "St. Louis County chief defends militarization of police," *USA Today*, [online] September 16, Available from: www. usatoday.com/story/news/nation/2014/09/16/ferguson-st-louis-county-michael-brown-militarization/15736907/ [Accessed January 6, 2020].

Maguire, E. & Katz, C. (2002) "Community policing, loose coupling, and sensemaking in American police agencies," *Justice Quarterly*, 19(3): 503–36.

Maguire, E. & King, W. (2004) "Trends in the policing industry," *Annals of the American Academy of Political and Social Science*, 593(1): 15–41.

Maguire, E., Nix, J., & Campbell, B. (2017) "A war on cops? The effects of Ferguson on the number of U.S. police officers murdered in the line of duty," *Justice Quarterly*, 35(4): 739–58.

Maitra, D., Mclean, R., & Deuchar, R. (2018) "'If you want to get paid, you've got to do it': A qualitative study on the morality of crime," *Deviant Behavior*, 39(7): 949–61.

Manning, P. (1977) *Police Work: The Social Organization of Policing* (2nd edn), Cambridge, MA: MIT Press.

Manning, P. (1984) "Community policing," *American Journal of Police*, 3(1): 205–27.

Martin, C., McKean, H., & Veltkamp, L. (1986) "Post-traumatic stress disorder in police and working with victims: A pilot study," *Journal of Police Science and Administration*, 14: 98–101.

Maslow, A. (1966) *The Psychology of Science: A Reconnaissance*, New York: Gateway Editions.

Mastrofski, S. & Ritti, R. (2000) "Making sense of community policing: A theory-based analysis," *Police Practice and Research*, 1(2): 183–210.

Mastrofski, S., Worden, R., & Snipes, J. (1995) "Law enforcement in a time of community policing, *Criminology*, 33(4): 539–63.

Mastrofski, S., Reisig, M., & McCluskey, J. (2002) "Police disrespect toward the public: An encounter-based analysis," *Criminology*, 40(3): 519–52.

Matt, D. (2014) "The Ferguson effect: A cop's-eye view," *The New York Post*, [online] October 14, Available from: http://nypost.com/2014/10/14/the-ferguson-effect-a-cops-eye-view/ [Accessed January 30, 2020].

Matthews, R. (2002) *Armed Robbery*, Cullompton: Willan Publishing.

Mazerolle, L. (2013) "Procedural justice and police legitimacy: A systematic review of the research evidence," *Journal of Experimental Criminology*, 9(3): 245–74.

Mazerolle, L. & Wickes, R. (2015) "Police legitimacy in community context," *Journal of Contemporary Justice*, 31(2): 128–31.

Mazerolle, L., Bennett, S., Davis, J., Sargeant, E., & Manning, M. (2013) "Legitimacy in policing: A systematic review," *Campbell Systematic Reviews*, 9(1): 1–146.

McChesney, K. (2020) "What will it take for police reform to work? The church's abuse scandal offers some lessons," *American Magazine*, [online] September 20, Available from: www.americamagazine.org/faith/2020/09/04/what-will-it-take-police-reform-work-churchs-abuse-scandal-offers-some-lessons [Accessed December 1, 2020].

McKenna, J., Martinez-Prather, K., & Bowman, S. (2016) "The roles of school-based law enforcement officers and how these roles are established: A qualitative study," *Criminal Justice Policy Review*, 27(4): 420–43.

McLaughlin, E. (2020) "How George Floyd's death ignited a racial reckoning that shows no signs of slowing down," *CNN*, [online] August 9, Available from: https://edition.cnn.com/2020/08/09/us/george-floyd-protests-different-why/index.html [Accessed August 25, 2020].

McLean, K., Wolfe, S., Rojek, J., Alpert, G., & Smith, M. (2019) "Police officers as warriors or guardians: Empirical reality or intriguing rhetoric?" *Justice Quarterly*. DOI: org/10.1080/07418825.2018.1533031.

McNamara, J. (1967) "Uncertainties in police work: The relevance of police recruits backgrounds and training," in D. Bordua (ed), *The Police, Six Sociological Essays*, New York: Wiley, pp 163–252.

Meares, T. (2017) "The path forward: Improving the dynamics of community–police relationships to achieve effective law enforcement policies," *Columbia Law Review*, 117(5): 1355–68.

Meisner, J., Gorner, J., & Heinzmann, D. (2018) "Chicago cops stripped of powers as FBI probes ripoffs of drug dealers," *The Chicago Tribune*, [online] February 1, Available from: www.chicagotribune.com/news/breaking/ct-met-chicago-cops-stripped-fbi-sting-20180131-story.html [Accessed January 4, 2020].

Melde, C. & Esbensen, F. (2011) "Gang membership as a turning point in the life course," *Criminology*, 49(2): 413–552.

Melde, C., Taylor, T., & Esbensen, F. (2009a) " 'I got your back': An examination of the protective function of gang membership in adolescence," *Criminology*, 47(2): 565–94.

Melde, C., Esbensen, F., & Taylor, T. (2009b) " 'May piece be with you': A typological examination of the fear and victimization hypothesis of adolescent weapon carrying," *Justice Quarterly*, 26(2): 348–76.

Melucci, A. (1995) "The Process of collective identity," in H. Johnston & B. Klandermans (eds), *Social Movements and Culture*, London: UCL Press, pp 41–63.

Melucci, A. (1996) *The Process of Collective Identity*, Cambridge: Cambridge University Press.

Meminger, D. (2019) "20 years ago: Amadou Diallo killed by police in a hail of 41 bullets," *Spectrum News, NY*, [online] February 3, Available from: www.ny1.com/nyc/all-boroughs/news/2019/02/03/20-years-ago--amadou-diallo-was-killed-by-police-in-a-hail-of-41-bullets [Accessed January 6, 2020].

Mock, B. (2017a) "How police are using stop-and-frisk four years after a seminal court ruling," *City Lab*, [online] August 18, Available from: www.citylab.com/equity/2017/08/stop-and-frisk-four-years-after-ruled-unconstitutional/537264/ [Accessed January 20, 2020].

Mock, B. (2017b) "What police and poor communities really think of each other," *City Lab*, [online] February 23, Available from: www.citylab.com/equity/2017/02/how-poor-communities-view-the-police/517485/ [Accessed December 19, 2019].

Molina, B. (2018) "Cashing checks, napping, more activities leading to police calls on black people in 2018," *USA Today*, [online] December 17, Available from: www.usatoday.com/story/news/nation/2018/12/20/black-people-doing-normal-things-who-had-police-called-them-2018/2374750002/ [Accessed March 21, 2020).

Morgan, S. & Pally, J. (2016) *Ferguson, Gray, and Davis: An Analysis of Recorded Crime Incidents and Arrests in Baltimore City, March 2010 through December 2015*, [online], Available from: http://socweb.soc.jhu.edu/faculty/morgan/papers/MorganPally2016.pdf [Accessed December 13, 2017].

Moule, R., Parry, M., Burruss, G., & Fox, B. (2019) "Assessing the direct and indirect effects of legitimacy on public empowerment of police: A study of public support for police militarization in America," *Law & Society Review; Amherst*, 53(1): 77–107.

Mourtgos, S. & Adams, I. (2019) "The rhetoric of de-policing: Evaluating open-ended survey responses from police officers with machine learning-based structural topic modelling," *Journal of Criminal Justice*, 64: 61–73.

Muhammad, K. (2011) *The Condemnation of Blackness: Race, Crime, and the Making of Modern Urban America*, Cambridge, MA: Harvard University Press.

National Gang Center (2012) "Estimated Number of Gangs, 1996–2012," *National Gang Center*, [online], Available from: www.nationalgangcenter.gov/Survey-Analysis/Measuring-the-Extent-of-Gang-Problems#estimatednumbergangs [Accessed August 28, 2019].

Newburn, T. (2016) *Criminology* (3rd edn), Abingdon: Routledge.

Newell, C., Pollock, J., & Tweedy, J. (1992) "Financial aspects of police liability," *ICMA Baseline Data Report*, 24: 1–8.

Nguyen, T. (2005) *We Are All Suspects Now: Untold Stories from Immigrant Communities after 9/11*, Boston, MA: Beacon.

Nix. J. & Wolfe, S. (2016) "Sensitivity to the Ferguson Effect: The role of managerial organizational justice," *Journal of Criminal Justice*, 47: 12–20.

Nix, J. & Wolfe, S. (2017) "The impact of negative publicity on police self-legitimacy," *Justice Quarterly*, 34(1): 84–108.

Nix, J. & Wolfe, S. (2018) "Management-level officers' experience with the Ferguson effect," *Policing: An International Journal*, 41(2): 262–75.

Nix, J., Wolfe, S., & Campbell, B. (2018) "Command-level police officers' perceptions of the 'war on cops' and de-policing," *Justice Quarterly*, 35(1): 33–54.

Novak, K., Smith, B., & Frank, J. (2003) "Strange bedfellows: Civil liability and aggressive policing," *Policing: An International Journal of Police Strategies and Management*, 26(2): 352–68.

Novak, K., Cordner, G., Smith, B., & Roberg, R. (2017) *Police & Society* (7th edn), New York: Oxford University Press.

Nwonka, C. (2020) "The protests over George Floyd's death show how film and culture can be tools of anti-racism, but we must continue to value them beyond this moment," *LSE US Centre*, [online], Available from: https://blogs.lse.ac.uk/usappblog/2020/06/08/the-protests-over-george-floyds-death-show-how-film-and-culture-can-be-tools-of-anti-racism-but-we-must-continue-to-value-them-beyond-this-moment/ [Accessed August 25, 2020].

Office of Independent Review (2003) *Second Annual Report*, Los Angeles: Los Angeles Sheriff's Department.

Oh, I. (2018) "This is why republicans won't condemn Trump's 'Go Back' home tweets," *Mother Jones*, [online] July 15, Available from: www.motherjones .com/politics/2019/07/trump-racist-go-back-home-tweets/ [Accessed March 20, 2020].

Oppel, R. & Taylor, D. (2020) "What you need to know about Breonna Taylor's death," *The New York Times*, [online] October 30, Available from: www.nytimes.com/article/breonna-taylor-police.html [Accessed December 1, 2020].

Ortega, D. (2018) "The challenge of improving police behavior in Latin America," *Brookings*, [online] March 20, Available from: www.brookings.edu/research/the- challenge-of-improving-police-behavior-in-latin-america/ [Accessed April 1, 2020].

Owen, S. (2017) "Monitoring social media and protest movements: Ensuring political order through surveillance and surveillance discourse," *Social Identities: Journal of the Study of Race, Nation and Culture*, 23(6): 688–700.

Owusu-Bempah, A. (2017) "Race and policing in historical context," *Theoretical Criminology*, 21: 23–34.

Paoline, E. (2003) "Taking stock: Toward a richer understanding of police culture," *Journal of Criminal Justice*, 31(3): 199–214.

Papachristos, A. (2009) "Murder by structure: Dominance Relations and the Social Structure of Gang Homicide," *American Journal of Sociology*, 115(1): 74–128.

Park, Y., Jang, S., Lee, H., & Yang, G. (2018) "Divide in Ferguson: Social media, social context, and division," *Social Media and Society*, 18(1): 1–13.

Parker, K. & Reckdenwald, A. (2008) "Concentrated disadvantage, traditional male role models, and African-American juvenile violence," *Criminology*, 46(3): 711–35.

Pate, A. & Fridell, L. (1993) *Police Use-of-force* (Vol. 1), Washington, DC: The Police Foundation.

Patterson, G. (2003) "Examining the effects of coping and social support on work and life stress among police officers," *Journal of Criminal Justice*, 31(3): 215–26.

Paul, R. (2014) "Rand Paul: We must demilitarize the police," *Time*, [online] August 13, Available from: http://time.com/3111474/rand-paul-ferguson-police/ [Accessed January 20, 2020].

Payne, B. (2001) "Prejudice and perceptions: The role of automatic and controlled processes in misperceiving a weapon," *Journal of Personality and Social Psychology*, 81: 181–92.

Pennella, J. & Nacci, P. (1997) *Department of Justice and Department of Defense Joint Technology Program: Second Anniversary Report*, US Department of Justice, [online], Available from: www.ncjrs.gov/pdffiles/164268.pdf [Accessed December 1, 2020].

Perry, B. (2009) "Impacts of disparate policing in Indian country," *Policing and Society*, 19(3): 263–81.

Philadelphia Integrity and Accountability Office (2003) *Disciplinary System*, Philadelphia, PA: Philadelphia Police Department.

Pinkney, C. & Robinson-Edwards, S. (2018) "Gangs, music and the mediatisation of crime: Expressions, violations and validations," *Safer Communities*, 17(2): 103–18.

Police Executive Research Forum (2019) *The Workforce Crisis, and What Police Agencies Are Doing about It*, [online], Available from: www.policeforum.org/assets/WorkforceCrisis.pdf [Accessed February 2, 2020].

Polletta, F. & Jasper, J. (2001) "Collective identity and social movements," *Annual Review of Sociology*, 27(1): 283–305.

Portland City Auditor (2017) "Gang enforcement patrol," *Portland City Auditor, Audit Services Division*, [online] March, Available from: www.portlandoregon.gov/auditservices/article/677598 [Accessed January 20, 2020].

Potter, G. (2013) "The history of policing in the United States," *EKU Online*, [online], Available from: https://plsonline.eku.edu/sites/plsonline.eku.edu/files/the-history-of-policing-in-us.pdf [Accessed April 6, 2020].

President's Task Force on 21st Century Policing (2015) *Final Report of the President's Task Force on 21st Century Policing*, Washington, DC: Office of Community Oriented Policing Services.

Pyrooz, D. (2014) "From your first cigarette to your last dyin' day," *Journal of Quantitative Criminology*, 30: 349–72.

Pyrooz, D. & Densley, J. (2018a) "Is gang activity on the rise? A movement to abolish gang databases makes it hard to tell," *The Conversation*, [online] July 5, Available from: https://theconversation.com/is-gang-activity-on-the-rise-a-movement-to-abolish-gang-databases-makes-it-hard-to-tell-99252 [Accessed August 28, 2019].

Pyrooz, D. & Densley, J. (2018b) "On public protest, violence, and street gangs," *Society*, 55(3): 229–36.

Pyrooz, D., Sweeten, G., & Piquero, A. (2013) "Continuity and change in gang membership and gang embeddedness," *Journal of Research in Crime and Delinquency*, 50: 239–71.

Pyrooz, D., Decker, S. & Moule, R. (2015) "Criminal and routine activities in online settings: gangs, offenders, and the internet," *Justice Quarterly*, 32(3): 471–99.

Pyrooz, D., Turanovic, J., Decker, S., & Wu, J. (2016a) "Taking stock of the relationship between gang membership and offending: A meta-analysis," *Criminal Justice & Behavior*, 43(3): 365–97.

Pyrooz, D., Decker, S., Wolfe, S., & Shjarback, J. (2016b) "Was there a Ferguson Effect on crime rates in large U.S. cities?" *Journal of Criminal Justice*, 46: 1–8.

Quattlebaum, M., Meares, T., & Tyler, T. (2018) *Principles of procedurally just policing. Technical Report*, The Justice Collaboratory at Yale Law School, [online] January, Available from: https://law.yale.edu/sites/default/files/area/center/justice/principles_of_procedurally_just_policing_report.pdf [Accessed April 9, 2020].

Queally, J. & Ormseth, M. (2019) "An ultra-violent MS-13 gang entered the U.S., then stalked LA with blades and bats," *Los Angeles Times*, [online] July 16, Available from: www.latimes.com/california/story/2019-07-16/ms-13-murders-los-angeles-gang [Accessed June 20, 2020].

Radil, S., Dezzani, R., & McAden, L. (2017) "Geographies of US Police Militarization and the Role of the 1033 Program," *The Professional Geographer*, 69(2): 203–13.

Rahr, S. & Rice, S. (2015) "From warriors to guardians: Recommitting American police culture to democratic ideals," in *New Perspectives in Policing Bulletin*, Washington, DC: U.S. Department of Justice, National Institute of Justice.

Raice, S. (2020) "Jacob Blake Shooting: What Happened in Kenosha, Wis.?" *The Wall Street Journal*, [online] August 28, Available from: www.wsj.com/articles/jacob-blake-shooting-what-happened-in-kenosha-wisconsin-11598368824 [Accessed September 6, 2020].

Ramsden, P. (2020) "How the pandemic changed social media and George Floyd's death created a collective conscience," *The Conversation*, [online] June 15, Available from: https://theconversation.com/how-the-pandemic-changed-social-media-and-george-floyds-death-created-a-collective-conscience-140104 [Accessed August 25, 2020].

Ransby, B. (2017) "Black Lives Matter is democracy in action," *The New York Times*, [online] October 12, Available from: www.nytimes.com/2017/10/21/opinion/sunday/Black-lives-matter-leadership.html [Accessed February 1, 2020].

Reed, E., Silverman, J., Ickovics, J., Gupta, J., Welles, S., Santana, M., & Raj, A. (2010) "Experiences of racial discrimination & relation to violence perpetration and gang involvement among a sample of urban African American men," *Journal of Immigrant and Minority Health*, 12(3): 319–26.

Reisig, M. (2007) "Procedural justice and community policing – what shapes residents' willingness to participate in crime prevention programs?" *Policing: A Journal of Policy & Practice*, 1(3): 356–69.

Reisig, M., Bratton, J., & Gertz, M. (2007) "The construct validity and refinement of process-based policing measures," *Criminal Justice and Behavior*, 34(8): 1005–28.

Reisig, M., Wolfe, S., & Holtfreter, K. (2011) "Legal cynicism, legitimacy, and criminal offending: The nonconfounding effect of low self-control," *Criminal Justice and Behavior*, 38(1): 1265–79.

Reisig, M., Tankebe, J., & Meško, G. (2012) "Procedural justice, police legitimacy, and public cooperation with the police among young Slovene adults," *Varstvoslovje; Maribor*, 14(2): 147–64.

Reiss, A. (1971) *The Police and the Public*, New Haven, CT: Yale University Press.

Reuss-Ianni, E. (1983) *Two Cultures of Policing: Street Cops and Management Cops*, New Brunswick, CT: Transaction Books.

Rice, S. & Parkin, W. (2010) "New avenues for profiling and bias research: The question of Muslim Americans," in S. Rice and M. White (eds), *Race, Ethnicity, and Policing: New and Essential Readings*, New York: New York University Press, pp 450–67.

Richardson, J. (2009) "Men do matter: Ethnographic insights on the socially supportive role of the African American uncle in the lives of inner-city African American male youth," *Journal of Family Issues*, 30(8): 1041–69.

Richmond, R., Wodak, A., Kehoe, L., & Heather, N. (1998) "How healthy are the police? A survey of life-style factors," *Addiction*, 93: 1729–37.

Ridgeway, G. (2007) *Analysis of Racial Disparities in New York Police Department's Stop, Question, and Frisk Practices*, New York: Rand Corporation.

Ridgeway, G., Schell, T., Riley, K., Turner, S., & Dixon, T. (2006) *Police–Community Relations in Cincinnati: Year Two Evaluation Report*, Santa Monica, CA: Rand Corporation.

Riley, K., Turner, S., Mac Donald, J., Ridgeway, G., Schell, T., Wilson, J., Dixon, T., Fain, T., Barnes-Proby, D., & Fulton, B. (2006) *Police–Community Relations in Cincinnati*, Santa Monica, CA: Rand Corporation.

Rodgers, D. (2019) "What gangs tell us about the world we live in," *The Conversation*, [online] April 2, Available from: https://theconversation.com/what-gangs-tell-us-about-the-world-we-live-in-114221 [Accessed August 28, 2019].

Roelofse, C. (2010) "A critical assessment of the constitutional mandate of the South African police service in accordance with criminological perspectives on crime prevention," *Acta Criminologica: African Journal of Criminology & Victimology*, 23(2): 42–60.

Rosenfeld, R. (2015) "Was there a 'Ferguson effect' on crime in St Louis?" *The Sentencing Project*, [online], Available from: www.sentencingproject.org/wp-content/uploads/2015/09/Ferguson-Effect.pdf [Accessed December 1, 2020].

Rosenfeld, R. & Wallman, J. (2019) "Did de-policing cause the increase in homicide rates?" *Criminology & Public Policy*, 18(1): 51–75.

Rosenfeld, R., Jacobs, B., & Wright, R. (2003) "Snitching and the code of the street," *British Journal of Criminology*, 43: 291–310.

Rothenberg, P. (2013) *Race, Class, and Gender in the United States: An Integrated Study* (9th edn), New York: Worth Publishing.

Russell-Brown, K. (2009) *The Color of Crime*, New York: New York University Press.

Schneider, D. & Schneider, C.(2000) *Slavery in America: From Colonial Times to the Civil War*, New York: Facts on Files.

Schwartz, C. (2015) "Close to home: Warrior or guardian? A good officer is both," *The Press Democrat*, [online] August 29, Available from: www.pressdemocrat.com/opinion/4402654-181/close-to-home-why-officers?artslide¼0 [Accessed December 1, 2020].

Shaw, C. & McKay, H. (1942) *Juvenile Delinquency and Urban Areas*, Chicago, IL: University of Chicago Press.

Sherman, L. & Rogan, D. (1995) "Effects of gun seizures on gun violence: 'Hot spots' patrol in Kansas City," *Justice Quarterly*, 12(4): 673–93.

Shjarback J., Pyrooz, D., Wolfe, S., & Decker, S. (2017) "De-policing and crime in the wake of Ferguson: Racialized changes in the quality and quality of policing among Missouri police departments," *Journal of Criminal Justice*, 50: 42–52.

Simon, A. (2018) "People are angry President Trump used this word to describe undocumented immigrants," *Time*, [online] June 18, Available from: https://time.com/5316087/donald-trump-immigration-infest/ [Accessed March 1, 2020).

Simon, C. (2018) "How social media has shaped Black Lives Matter, five years later," *USA Today*, [online] December 16, Available from: www.usatoday.com/story/news/2018/07/12/Black-lives-matter-movement-and-social-media-after-five-years/778779002/ [Accessed December 20, 2019].

Simpson, I. (2015) "Prosecutions of U.S. police killings surges to highest in decade," *Huffington Post*, [online] October 26, Available from: www.huffpost.com/entry/prosecution-police-killings_n_562e26aee4b0ec0a3894eb23

Skogan, W. (2006) *Police and Community in Chicago: A Tale of Three Cities*, New York: Oxford University Press.

Skolnick, J. (1968) *The Police and the Urban Ghetto*, Chicago, IL: American Bar Association.

Skolnick, J. (2011) *Justice without Trial: Law Enforcement in Democratic Societies* (4th edn), New Orleans, LA: Quid Pro Books.

Slocum, L., Greene, C., Huebner, B., & Rosenfeld, R. (2019) "Changes in enforcement of low-level and felony offenses post-Ferguson: An analysis of arrests in St Louis, Missouri," *Criminology, Criminal Justice, Law & Society*, 20(2): 25–45.

Solis, C., Portillos, E., & Brunson, R. (2009) "Latino youths' experiences with and perceptions of involuntary police encounters," *The Annals of the American Academy of Political and Social Science*, 623(1): 39–51.

Sommers, S. & Ellsworth, P. (2003) "How much do we really know about race and juries – A review of social science theory and research," *Chicago-Kent Law Review*, 78(3), 997–1031.

St Pierre, T., Kaltreider, D., Mark, M., & Aikin, K. (1992) "Drug prevention in a community setting: A longitudinal study of the relative effectiveness of a three-year primary prevention program in Boys & Girls Clubs across the nation," *American Journal of Community Psychology*, 20(6): 673–706.

Statista (2019) *Violent Crime in the US – Statistics and Facts.* Statista Research Department, [online] November 9, Available from: www. statista.com/topics/1750/violent-crime-in-the-us/ [Accessed August 28, 2019].

Stoughton, S. (2015) "Law enforcement's 'warrior' problem," *Harvard Law Review Forum,* 128: 225–34

Stoughton, S. (2016) "Principled policing: Warrior cops and guardian officers," *Wake Forest Law Review,* 51: 611–23.

Strauss, A. & Corbin, J. (1998) *Basics of Qualitative Research: Techniques and Procedures for Developing Grounded Theory,* Thousand Oaks, CA: Sage.

Sullivan, M. (2005) "Maybe we shouldn't study 'gangs': Does reification obscure youth violence?" *Journal of Contemporary Criminal Justice,* 21(2): 170–90.

Sunshine, J. & Tyler, T. (2003) "The role of procedural justice and legitimacy in shaping public support for policing," *Law and Society Review,* 37(3): 513–48.

Sutherland, E. H. (1947) *Principles of Criminology* (4th edn), Philadelphia, PA: J. B. Lippincott.

Swanson, K. (2017) "Trump tells cops they should rough people up more during arrests," *Vox,* [online] July 28, Available from: www.vox. com/policy-and-politics/2017/7/28/16059536/trump-cops-speech-gang-violence-long-island [Accessed January 20, 2020].

Swatt, M., Gibson, C., & Piquero, N. (2007) "Exploring the utility of general strain theory in explaining problematic alcohol consumption by police officers," *Journal of Criminal Justice,* 35(6): 596–611.

Taylor, C., Lerner, R., von Eye, A., Bobek, D., Balsano, A., Dowling, E., & Anderson, P. (2004) "Internal and external developmental assets among African American male gang members," *Journal of Adolescent Research,* 19(3): 303–22.

Taylor, R. & Lawton, B. (2012) "An integrated contextual model of confidence in local police," *Police Quarterly,* 15(14): 414–45.

Thrasher, F. (1927) *The Gang: A Study of 1313 Gangs in Chicago,* Chicago, IL: University of Chicago Press.

Tise, L. (1987) *Proslavery: A History of the Defense of Slavery in America, 1701–1840,* Athens, GA: University of Georgia Press.

Todak, N. (2017) "The decision to become a police officer in a legitimacy crisis," *Women and Criminal Justice,* 27(4): 250–70.

Tonry, M. (1995) *Malign Neglect,* Oxford: Oxford University Press.

Torres, J., Reling, T., & Hawdon, J. (2018) "Role conflict and psychological impacts of the post-Ferguson period on law enforcement motivation, cynicism, and apprehensiveness," *Journal of Police and Criminal Psychology*, 33(4): 358–74.

Trammell, K. (2019)" Barack Obama pays tribute to Nipsey Hussle," *CNN Entertainment*, [online] April 1, Available from: www.cnn.com/2019/04/11/entertainment/obama-letter-nipsey-hussle-trnd/index.html [Accessed April 10, 2020].

Trujillo, J. & Vitale, A. (2019) "Gang takedowns in the De Blasio era. The dangers of 'precision policing,'" Policing and Social Justice Project at Brooklyn College, [online], Available from: https://static1.squarespace.com/static/5de981188ae1bf14a94410f5/t/5df14904887d561d6cc9455e/1576093963895/2019+New+York+City+Gang+Policing+Report+-+FINAL%29.pdf [Accessed December 1, 2020].

Turner, F. & Fox, B. (2017) "Public servants or police soldiers? An analysis of opinions on the militarization of policing from police executives, law enforcement, and members of the 114th congress US house of representatives," *Police Practice and Research*, 20(2): 122–38.

Tyler, T. (2002) "A national survey for monitoring police legitimacy," *Justice Research and Policy*, 4(1): 71–86.

Tyler, T. (2004) "Enhancing police legitimacy," *Annals of the American Academy of Political and Social Science*, 593: 84–99.

Tyler, T. (2006) *Why People Obey the Law.* Princeton, NJ: Princeton University Press.

Tyler, T. & Fagan, J. (2008) "Legitimacy and cooperation: Why do people help the police fight crime in their communities?" *Ohio State Journal of Criminal Law*, 6(1): 231–75.

Tyler, T. & Huo, Y. (2002) *Trust in the Law: Encouraging Public Cooperation with the Police and Courts*, New York: Russell Sage Foundation.

Tyler, T. & Wakslak, C. (2004) "Profiling and police legitimacy: Procedural justice, attributions of motive, and acceptance of police authority," *Criminology*, 42(2): 253–81.

Tyler, T., Fagan, J., & Geller, A. (2014) "Street stops and police legitimacy: Teachable moments in young urban men's legal socialization," *Journal of Empirical Legal Studies*, 11(1): 751–85.

US Department of Justice (2015) "Justice Department announces findings of two Civil Rights Investigations in Ferguson, Missouri: Justice Department finds a pattern of Civil Rights violations by the Ferguson Police Department," *Department of Justice, Office of Public Affairs*, [online] March 4, Available from: www.justice.gov/opa/pr/justice-department-announces-findings-two-civil-rights-investigations-ferguson-missouri [Accessed November 20, 2019].

US Department of Justice (2016) *Investigation of the Baltimore City Police Department*, US DOJ Civil Rights Division, [online] August 10, Available from: www.justice.gov/crt/file/883296/download [Accessed January 20, 2020].

US House Committee on Armed Services, Subcommittee on Oversight and Investigations (2014) *Department of Defense Excess Property Program in Support of U.S. Law Enforcement Agencies: An overview of DoD authorities, roles, responsibilities, and implementation of Section 1033 of the 1997 National Defense Authorization Act*, US House of Representatives Committee Repository, [online] November 13, Available from: https://docs.house.gov/Committee/Calendar/ByEvent.aspx?EventID=102730 [Accessed April 8, 2020].

USA Census Bureau (2017) *Quick Facts Data*, [online], Available from: www.census.gov/quickfacts/fact/table/US/PST045216 [Accessed April 14, 2018]

Van Maanen, J. (1974) "Working in the street: A developmental view of police behavior," in H. Jacob (ed), *The Potential for Reform of Criminal Justice*, Beverly Hills, CA: Sage, pp 83–130.

Van Maanen, J. (1978) "The asshole," in P. Manning & J. Van Maanen (eds), *Policing: A View from the Street*, Los Angeles, CA: Goodyear Press, pp 221–38.

Vigil, J. (1988) *Barrio Gangs: Street Life and Identity in Southern California*, Austin, TX: University of Texas Press.

Violanti, J. (1995) "Trends in police suicide," *Psychological Reports*, 77(2): 688–90.

Violanti, J. & Aron, F. (1995) "Police stressors: Variations in perception among police personnel," *Journal of Criminal Justice*, 23: 287–94.

Vollmer, A. (1936) *The Police in Modern Society*, Mattituck, NY: McGrath Publishing.

Vorenberg, M. (2004) *Final Freedom: The Civil War, the Abolition of Slavery, and the Thirteenth Amendment*, Cambridge: Cambridge University Press.

Wacquant, L. (2008) *Urban Outcasts: A Comparative Sociology of Advanced Marginality*, Cambridge: Polity.

Wald, J. & Kendall-Taylor, N. (2019) "Have Americans lost interest in real police reform?" *The Crime Report*, [online] July 30, Available from: https://thecrimereport.org/2019/07/30/have-americans-lost-interest-in-real-police-reform/ [Accessed April 1, 2020].

Waldrep, C. (2006) *Lynching in America: A History in Documents*, New York: New York University Press.

Walker, S. (2001) *Police Accountability: The Role of Citizen Oversight*, Belmont: Wadsworth.

Walker, S. & Katz, C. (2017) *Policing in America: An Introduction* (9th edn), New York: McGraw-Hill.

Wallace, D., White, M., Gaub, J., & Todak, N. (2018) "Body-worn cameras as a potential source of depolicing: Testing for camera-induced passivity," *Criminology*, 56(3): 481–509.

Washington Post (2015, 2016) "People shot dead by police," *The Washington Post*, [online], Available from: www.washingtonpost.com/graphics/national/police-shootings/ [Accessed February 1, 2020].

Weisburd, D. & Eck, J. (2004) "What can police do to reduce crime, disorder, and fear?" *Annals of the American Academy of Political and Social Science*, 593(1): 42–65.

Weisburd, D., Greenspan, R., Hamilton, E., Williams, H., & Bryant, K. (2000) *Police Attitudes toward Abuse of Authority: Findings from a National Study*, Washington, DC: National Institute of Justice.

Weisburd, D., Telep, C., Hinkle, J., & Eck, J. (2010) "Is problem-oriented policing effective in reducing crime and disorder? Findings from a Campbell systematic review," *Criminology & Public Policy*, 9(1): 139–72.

Weisburd, D., Telep, C., & Lawton, B. (2014) "Could innovations in policing have contributed to the New York City crime drop even in a period of declining police strength?: The case of stop, question and frisk as a hot spots policing strategy," *Justice Quarterly*, 31(1): 129–53.

Weitzer, R. (2000) "White, black, or blue cops? Race and citizen assessments of police officers," *Journal of Criminal Justice*, 28(4): 313–24.

Weitzer, R. & Tuch, S. (2002) "Perceptions of racial profiling: Race, class, and personal experience," *Criminology*, 40(2): 435–56.

Welch, K. (2007) "Black criminal stereotypes and racial profiling," *Journal of Contemporary Criminal Justice*, 23(3): 276–88.

Westley, W. (1970). *Violence and the Police: A Sociological Study of Law, Custom, and Morality*, Cambridge, MA: MIT Press.

White, M. & Malm, A. (2020) *Cops, Cameras & Crisis: The Potential & The Perils of Body-Worn Cameras*, New York: New York University Press.

White, M., Dario, L., & Shjarback, J. (2019) "Assessing dangerousness in policing: An analysis of officer deaths in the United States," *Criminology and Public Policy*, 18(1): 11–35.

White House (2017) "Remarks by President Trump to Law Enforcement Officials on MS-13, Van Nostrand Theatre, Ronkonkoma, New York," WhiteHouse.gov, [online] July 28, Available from: www.whitehouse.gov/briefings-statements/remarks-president-trump-law-enforcement-officials-ms-13/ [Accessed February 20, 2020].

White House (2019) "Remarks by President Trump at the International Association of Chiefs of Police Annual Conference and Exposition, McCormick Place Convention Center Chicago, Illinois," WhiteHouse. gov, [online] October 28, Available from: www.whitehouse.gov/briefings-statements/remarks-president-trump-international-association-chiefs-police-annual-conference-exposition-chicago-il/ [Accessed February 14, 2020].

Whyte, W. (1943) *Street Corner Society*, Chicago, IL: University of Chicago Press.

Williams, J. & Bond, J. (2013) *Eyes on the Prize: America's Civil Rights Years, 1954–1965*, London: Penguin Books.

Wilson, J. (1970) *Varieties of Police Behavior: The Management of Law Enforcement in Eight Communities*, New York: Harvard University Press.

Wilson, J. & Kelling, G. (1982) "Broken windows," *Atlantic Monthly*, 249(3): 29–38.

Wilson, W. (1996) *When Work Disappears*, New York: Vintage Books.

Winton, R. & Puente, M. (2020) "Officers falsely portrayed people as gang members, falsified records, LAPD says," *LA Times*, [online] January 6, Available from: www.latimes.com/california/story/2020-01-06/dozens-of-lapd-officers-accused-of-portrayed-innocent-people-as-gang-members-falsifying-records [Accessed March 15, 2020].

Withrow, B. (2006) *Racial Profiling: From Rhetoric to Reason*, Upper Saddle River, NJ: Pearson Education.

Wolfe, S. & Nix, J. (2016) "The alleged 'Ferguson Effect' and police willingness to engage in community partnership," *Law and Human Behavior*, 40(1): 1–10.

Wolfe, S., Nix, J., Kaminski, R., & Rojek, J. (2016) "Is the effect of procedural justice on police legitimacy invariant? Testing the generality of procedural justice and competing antecedents of legitimacy," *Journal of Quantitative Criminology*, 32(2): 253–82.

Wolff, K., Baglivio, M., Klein, H., Piquero, A., DeLisi, M., & Howell, J. (2020) "Adverse childhood experiences (ACEs) and gang involvement among juvenile offenders: Assessing the mediation effects of substance use and temperament deficits," *Youth Violence and Juvenile Justice*, 18(1): 24–53.

Wooff, A. (2016) " 'Soft' policing in rural Scotland," *Policing*, 11(2): 123–31.

Worden, R. & McLean, S. (2017) *Mirage of Police Reform: Procedural Justice and Police Legitimacy*, Berkeley, CA: University of California Press.

World Population Review (2020) *Crime Rate by State 2019*, [online], Available from: http://worldpopulationreview.com/states/crime-rate-by-state/ [Accessed December 1, 2020].

Yablonsky, L. (2000) *Juvenile Delinquency into the 21st Century*, Belmont, CA: Wadsworth and Thomson Learning.

Index

Note: References to tables are in *italics*; references to endnotes are the page number followed by the note number (231n3).

CPSIA information can be obtained
at www.ICGtesting.com
Printed in the USA
JSHW042245290622
27684JS00003B/97